ENDORSEMENTS

I've known Rob since he was in high school. One phrase I'd use to describe him is consistent. In a world where everyone is trying to build their platform Rob has consistently lived out what he preaches. In his new book, You Misspelled Christian, Rob uses humor, application, and life lessons to get back to the basics of Jesus' message...love God and love people.

> —**Clayton King,** Teaching Pastor, New Spring Church,
> Founder and President, Crossroads Summer Camps
> and Crossroads Missions

Rob Shepherd is an outstanding leader, trusted friend and a modern voice to believers everywhere. In his latest book, You Misspelled Christian, Rob explores the life of Jesus and his mission of bringing heaven to earth. He gives practical insight that when applied will renew your heart and spirit to the God-given purposes for your life. I highly recommend you read it and most importantly apply it to your life. You'll be glad you did.

> —**Chris Sonksen,** Lead Pastor at South Hills Church,
> Helping churches get unstuck through ChurchBOOM.org,
> Author of When Your Church Feels Stuck and Quit Church

If you have ever been frustrated with the church, then You Misspelled Christian is for you. Rob has written an encouraging book to help inspire Christians to be the Church. If you are tired of doing church consider this book your caffeine boost.

—**Tyler Reagin**, President of Catalyst
Author of *The Life-Giving Leader*

From the heart and hand of a man who lives this. Rob doesn't want to play church or create a façade that confuses a watching world. This book will help you shrug off the gravitational pull to create a world that makes you the center of the universe and keep Jesus on display.

—**Chad Childress**, Senior Director, Planter Discovery
Send Network, North American Mission Board

In a culture where our own story has become the focal point of our identity and existence, Rob's book is a refreshing reminder of the truth of why Jesus came to earth to redeem and restore us back to Him. You will be stirred throughout this book to re-root yourself back into the significance of the life we live through the eyes of Jesus.

—**Chad Johnson,** Chief of Staff
at The John Maxwell Company

I love the local Church! It's not perfect by any means, but I love seeing what God can do in this world through His Church. It's because of this love for the Church that I think we need to continue to work on it. In You Misspelled

Christian, my friend Rob Shepherd inspires us to be the Church Jesus has called us to be. Rob is an authentic voice who will inspire you and spur you on.

—**Susan Wanderer**, Minister to Families, Mount Ararat Church
Co-Host, *She Speaks Stories* Podcast

For those who would dare to bring heaven to earth,
this book is for you.

For those looking to destroy a book in an Amazon review, this book is not for you. This book contains hand-drawn pictures by the author, has frequent pop culture references, tells lots of stories, and is written by an imperfect pastor. If that doesn't appeal to you, then this book is not for you…and that is okay. There are lots of other books out there. Find one that will help you grow and inspire you to love Jesus and love others.

To Monica, Reese, and Hayden:
Thank you for bringing heaven to my world!
I love you with my whole heart.

To Next Level Church: We are better together.
The world isn't changed by a lone preacher. It's changed by a
community. I'm honored to lead you and inspired to serve you. Let's
keep loving Jesus, loving people, and making a difference!

YOU
MISSPELLED
CHRISTIAN

YOU
MISSPELLED
CHRISTIAN

How To Bring Heaven To Your Current Circumstances

ROB SHEPHERD

EQUIP PRESS

A division of Outreach Media Group
Colorado Springs

YOU
MISSPELLED
CHRISTIAN

Published by Equip Press, Colorado Springs, CO

Scripture quotations marked (ESV) are taken from The ESV® Bible (The Holy Bible, English Standard Version®) copyright © 2001 by Crossway, a publishing minis-try of Good News Publishers. ESV® Text Edition: 2011. The ESV® text has been reproduced in cooperation with and by permission of Good News Publishers. Unauthorized reproduction of this publication is prohibited. Used by permission. All rights reserved.

Scripture quotations marked (KJV) are taken from the King James Bible. Accessed on Bible Gateway at www.BibleGateway.com.

Scripture quotations marked (NASB) are taken from the New American Standard Bible® (NASB), copyright © 1960, 1962, 1963, 1968, 1971, 1972, 1973, 1975, 1977, 1995 by The Lockman Foundation, www.Lockman.org. Used by permission.

Scripture quotations marked (NIV) are taken from the Holy Bible, New International Version. Copyright © 1973, 1978, 1984, 2011 by Biblica, Inc.® Used by permission. All rights reserved worldwide.

Scripture quotations marked (NKJV) are taken from the New King James Version®. Copyright © 1982 by Thomas Nelson, Inc. Used by permission. All rights reserved.

Scripture quotations marked (NLT) are taken from the Holy Bible, New Living Translation, copyright © 1996, 2004, 2015 by Tyndale House Foundation. Used by permission of Tyndale House Publishers, Inc., Carol Stream, Illinois 60188. All rights reserved.

Scripture quotations marked (NRSV) are taken from the New Revised Standard Version Bible, copyright © 1989 the Division of Christian Education of the National Council of the Churches of Christ in the United States of America. Used by permission. All rights reserved.

First Edition: 2018
You Misspelled Christian / Rob Shepherd
Paperback ISBN: 978-1-946453-37-2
eBook ISBN: 978-1-946453-38-9

CONTENTS

INTRODUCTION

DON'T SKIP THIS!

My name is Robert Christopher Shepherd. Since middle school, I've gone by Rob. My middle name, as far as I know, has always been Christopher. It's on my birth certificate. The name Christopher was given to me by my parents. Both of my parents are alive and in good health. All of that is important in order to understand the humor in the following story.

My wife and I went through ten years of infertility. Okay, that's not funny. The funny is coming. Keep reading. We were told we were pregnant with twin boys. I write "we" loosely. My wife did all the hard work. It was an amazing answer to lots of prayers. The names were going to be Hayden Christian Shepherd and Reese Clayton Shepherd.

At a lunch with my wife, one of my parents (who will remain nameless) was talking to my wife about our future kids' names. The conversation took an unintentional humorous turn when said parent of mine remarked, "I didn't know Rob liked his middle name so much."

After a few seconds of processing, my wife asked in confusion, "What do you mean?" Said parent replied, "I've never heard Rob talk about liking his middle name. I didn't know he wanted to pass Christian on to his son."

Um…

In case you are skimming this intro and missed a very important detail…*my middle name is not Christian.*

It's Christopher.

It's a story we still laugh at today. It ended up not mattering because the week of our baby shower, we found out that the original ultrasound was wrong. We were having a boy and a girl.

We ended up going with the names Hayden Clayton Shepherd and Reese Parker Shepherd. I can't help but think of that story whenever I hear the name Christian.

When you hear the name Christian, what do you think of?

If you grew up having a positive experience with church, you may think about a loving person who influenced your life for Jesus. Or, maybe you instantly think about Jesus.

Not everyone has positive opinions about the name Christian. For many, "Christian" means anti-science, bigoted, old-fashioned, or angry.

Being a Christian comes with weight. We are to carry the message of Jesus with us. Everywhere we go, we represent Jesus. The type of work we produce, the way we treat our family, the type of neighbor we are, and how we handle conflict all represent Jesus.

Someone is always watching.

That has led many Christians to go into hiding to escape the world. It's just too much pressure. But as I read about Jesus' life, I don't see him escaping the world. I see him living and bringing life along the way.

I'm far from perfect. You would see that even more in my writing if I didn't have an editor proofreading this. You would also see it if you hung out with me for an hour. That is way too optimistic. You would discover I was imperfect if you hung out with me for three minutes.

My hope with this book is to show we don't have to be perfect to follow Jesus. We have to be intentional. If you want to live like Jesus, you cannot live for yourself.

Even in failure, we can model to others what it looks like to follow Jesus. You see, somewhere along the way, the term Christian started meaning something different than its original intent. Originally, followers of Jesus were called "The Way." If that doesn't sound cultish, I don't know what does. Add to that the fact that the early Christians called each other "brother and sister." Add to that the fact that they often greeted one another with a holy kiss. Add to that they would drink wine together for communion and say it was the blood of Jesus. From an outsider looking in, the Way looks cray cray. That's short for crazy.

At some point, the Way were called Christians. We read about this in the book of Acts. The Way were called Christians because they were radically following Jesus. It was a name given to them because of their actions, by outsiders. That is, the unchurched, non-Jesus following people watched the way Christians lived and as a result gave them the name Christian.

Back then, there weren't denominations. There weren't different theological camps of Christianity. It was a small group of people willing to give up everything to follow Jesus. They weren't perfect. They were changed.

They were changed because Jesus said he was going to rise from the dead...and he did. That changed a small group of people so much that the way they lived changed the entire world. Because that's what following Jesus does. It changes us for the better. It takes our mess and turns it into a masterpiece. It takes brokenness and makes it whole.

You simply cannot follow Jesus and remain the same. Following Jesus leads to life change. You can believe in Jesus and not change. You can go to church and not change. You cannot, however, follow Jesus and stay the same. Scripture is clear.

Whoever claims to live in him must live as Jesus did. (1 John 2:6)

If Christian means anything other than "living for Jesus by doing what he said," then we've misspelled Christian. It may be a religion, but it's not Christian.

Often when I see someone post something online that I disagree with, I joke with them that they misspelled something. For example, I'm a huge Lakers fan. When I see one of my friends say, "LeBron James is the greatest of all time," I'll reply with "You misspelled Kobe." It's a joke with a point. So is the title of this book.

For many, Christian means something that Jesus never intended it to mean. When anyone thinks of anything other than loving God and loving people, they've misspelled Christian.

What if everyone who read this book took the message of Jesus seriously? What if everyone who read this book would follow Jesus more closely, become more authentic, and love the unlovable like Jesus did? Who knows, maybe together we would change the world.

For many, it is a temptation to skip the intro. I'm glad you didn't. I'm incredibly honored that you are reading this book. I'm honored you are reading this, but I want more for you than to just finish this book. I want you to experience God and be inspired to bring heaven to your world.

Would you take a second to pray and ask God to speak to your heart? Even if you end up hating this book, God can use it to change your life. He is big like that. In Scripture we read how God once used a donkey to communicate a powerful truth to a knucklehead. I'm praying that even if you view me as a donkey, God can still use the words in this book to bring life change to you. If you are going to go through the trouble of reading a book, then it's my prayer you'd be open to allowing God to change your life. You don't have to pray the following, but if you are open to it, here is a prayer to pray before reading chapter one.

Prayer: God, what do you want me to get out of this book? I ask that you would soften my heart, speak to me, and give me the courage to do whatever you tell me to do. Help me to be sensitive to what you say and bold enough to do it. In Jesus' name, amen.

CHAPTER 1

DOING CHURCH IS TIRING

I'm tired of doing church. Now you need to hear that I love the church. I love the fact that I grew up in the church. I didn't just grow up in church. In middle school, I fully embraced the church culture. It was the 1990s and early 2000s, so I kissed dating goodbye, was a bona fide Jesus Freak, asked for a Bible for graduation with my name engraved on it, read the first nine books in the Left Behind series (there ended up being like twenty and I couldn't keep up), and spent a whole month praying the Prayer of Jabez. I realize, for a big portion of the people reading this, those references make no sense. That's okay. What you need to know is that I loved Jesus, and I had a T-shirt to prove it. I was all in to the Christian culture... and I loved every second of it.

As an adult, I still love the church. I love the church, and when I write *church* I don't just mean my church, Next Level. I mean the Big C Church as a whole.

I love the church, but I'm tired of doing church.

When I read about Jesus' mission and what he did, I get excited. I read about how this poor man's teachings literally turned the world upside down. I read about how Jesus healed people. Really healed people. I read about how people were set free. I read about how people were forgiven. I read about people who were hurting and found hope. I read about a radical movement. And then I go to church. The early church was radical. The modern church is recreational. We go to church like we go to a restaurant. If we like what's served, we will feel good about our choice to go that day. If it's really good, we might even put a tip in the offering plate. If we don't like what is served, we will complain about it.

We serve a God who forgives sinners, yet Christians often don't think twice about holding grudges, fighting for what we want, living with bitterness, or giving those who have wronged us exactly what they deserve.

Often the most outspoken Christians are the ones who show the least amount of grace or end up in a scandal.

In the early days of the church, the message of Jesus shook entire governments. It was so powerful that the Roman government felt it was a threat and tried to snuff it out. The problem was the more they persecuted the church, the more the message of Jesus spread.

In Andronicus's "History" we read the Emperor Trajan ruled for nineteen years. His vicegerent for Palestine wrote to him saying, "The more Christians I kill, the more they love their religion." Trajan therefore ordered him to stop using the sword against them.

What? The more they were killed, the more they loved?

The early church was known for doing an amazing job of caring for people. The message of Jesus was so radical people were forced to accept it or violently reject it.

How did we go from being a part of a movement that shook the world to an irrelevant social club?

Today, most people don't think about the church. Even for those who go to church it's often an afterthought. With increasingly busy schedules, it's easy to think that church is expendable.

Then, when our culture does think about Christians, it's often because one of us is ticked off at someone and ranting about them on a news channel.

Today, "49% of unchurched Americans cannot identify a single way Christianity has positively impacted the United States," says the Barna Research Group.

That's heartbreaking.

Not a single way? A Christian invented Chick-fil-A. Christian chicken should count as something! Maybe the 49 percent of unchurched Americans don't like pickles on their chicken sandwiches? I digress.

Most people today aren't anti-God. Spirituality is important to a lot of people. In fact, in some circles, spirituality is at an all-time high. It's just the way that Christians treat outsiders and each other has left very little to attract anyone to.

This is interesting because Jesus left his followers to be his hands and feet to the world. When someone meets a Christian, their interaction with them impacts their opinion of Jesus.

Way too often, Christians form their camps and then dig their feet in. We are typically known more for what we are against than what we are for.

I was reminded of this not too long ago. I was out of town and a few of our staff went to a meeting about hosting the homeless during the cold winter months at a local church. It takes multiple churches to pull this off. A host church provides the building and then various churches come together to provide the meals and the volunteers.

Add to that the local government has reached out to the church to help with this ministry. People are always screaming separation of church and state, but this is one time where the lines are blurred and it's a great thing. The church helps meet a need in the city!

This is a good thing. Christians actually caring about the poor is a great thing! But at this meeting it was presented that the cost for hosting would be seventy dollars, which was a thirty-dollar increase from the year before. The host church's representative who presented this was verbally crucified. Instantly it became a big deal. Now, I wasn't there but my staff said that it got ugly. People were fussing and fuming and throwing this poor guy under the bus. Finally, one of our church members stood up and said, "Next Level will pay the whole thing. We are talking about a few hundred bucks here." That instantly shut everyone up!

Now the crazy thing is the same kind of thing happened the year before. We got together with a group of churches to figure out how we were going to transform this building into a homeless shelter and people were ugly toward one another. The littlest task becomes impossibly difficult when you gather a group of Christians in the room.

How many Christians does it take to change a light bulb? Well, that depends on what denomination of Christian you are talking about.

Maybe you can relate to this humorous take on the light bulb question?

How many Christians does it take to change a light bulb (broken down by denominations)?

Charismatic: Two – One to change the light bulb and the other one to interpret what God said through it.

Pentecostal: Ten – One to change the bulb and nine to pray against the spirit of darkness.

Presbyterians: None – Lights will go on and off at predestined times.

Roman Catholic: None – Candles only.

Baptists: At least fifteen – One to change the light bulb and three committees to approve the change and decide who brings the potato salad and fried chicken.

Episcopalians: Three – One to call the electrician, one to mix the drinks, and one to talk about how much better the old one was.

Nazarene: Six – One woman to replace the bulb wshile five men review church lighting policy.

Lutherans: None – Lutherans don't believe in change.

Amish: What's a light bulb?[1]

Imagine getting all of these groups in a room. Each one has a different take on everything.

The following Monday, when I got to the office the volunteer told me about the meeting at the church. After retelling how ugly people were to each other, he mentioned how he offered for us to pay for it all. He then said, "I hope it's okay that I did that?" Heck to the yeah it's okay! I didn't have a fat clue where that money was

---

1   Author Unknown.

going to come from, but I believed that God would provide for his people to do what he has called us to do. And guess what? He did. The following week, multiple people at our church gave above and beyond so that we could host the homeless. That's what I'm talking about!

It's not just church meetings. It's Christians as a whole fighting. I see it happen online all the time. Christians are constantly calling out other Christians or unchurched people who do not hold to the same standards of morality. Contrary to popular belief, one of the fruits of the Spirit is not complaining.

We have different denominations, different theologies, and different opinions, and when someone from within our camp doesn't agree, we unleash hell on them. That'll teach them the love of God! Sense the sarcasm. I wish there were a sarcasm font. It would make written communication so much more effective.

I once read a blog post that said,

> "My fear is that no one in the history of mankind has ever said, 'I saw two Christians on twitter attacking each other and that made me want a lifelong relationship with their Christ.'"[2]
>
> —Jon Acuff

It's not supposed to be this way.

---

2   Jon Acuff, "Why It's Hard to Be a Christian Online," *Stuff Christians Like,* February 19, 2014, http://stuffchristianslike.net/2014/02/19/hard-christian-online/.

The mandate for Christians is they (the world) will know that we are Christians by our love. But today, Christians are known for everything but love. In fact, I don't know if you've felt this, but it's becoming harder and harder to tell people I'm a Christian without feeling instantly judged. It's like as soon as I say, "I'm a Christian," it's assumed I'm close-minded, anti-science, homophobic, and judgmental. How did a movement that started with people imitating what they saw Jesus do end up becoming what we have today?

A quote that I heard for the first time in high school haunts me. Maybe you have heard it before…

"I like your Christ, I do not like your Christians. Your Christians are so unlike your Christ."[3]

—Gandhi

That quote is heartbreaking. That quote is a reflection of the church not representing Jesus. That quote is a reflection of the church forgetting its calling.

How in the world did we get so far away from what Jesus wanted us to be?

BUT AREN'T WE SUPPOSED TO BE PERSECUTED?

If you grew up in the church you may be thinking, "But aren't we supposed to be hated because we love Jesus?" After all Jesus did say,

---

3   This quote is famously attributed to Gandhi, but there is debate on when and where he said it.

You will be hated by everyone because of me, but the one who stands firm to the end will be saved. (Matthew 10:22)

That settles it. Jesus said it. I believe it. Everyone will always hate us.

Hold up, wait a minute.

Context is crucial.

Jesus did say that, but it was to his disciples. Jesus was sending them out to witness for him. Jesus specifically says to go to the "lost sheep of Israel" and not to those that are not Jewish. This is important because in this instance…everyone does not mean every one. Jesus is making the point that the disciples will be persecuted by the religious elite. And they were.

In the same chapter Jesus tells his disciples, "When you are persecuted in one place, flee to another" (Matthew 10:23). His point is that people will disagree with his message. Some will even hate it. But not all. When you are persecuted, flee and move on to a place that is receptive to the message. Because some will be receptive.

History teaches us that the love of the early church impacted the world. Some hated them, but many were won over because of how much Christians loved people. Whenever you read Scripture, it's important to read it as a whole and not as a sound bite. When something in Scripture is confusing, use Scripture to help clear things up.

Peter was one of Jesus' twelve disciples. He was there when Jesus said, "You will be hated on by everyone." When Peter has a chance to write to the early church about the persecution they are experiencing, look at what he says…

Be careful how you behave among your unsaved neighbors; for then, even if they are suspicious of you and talk against you, they will end up praising God for your good works when Christ returns. (1 Peter 2:12 TLB)

It's important how we live because people are watching. Live such an amazing life that even when people hate you they will be won over and praise God.

People will criticize Christians, but not every criticism is persecution. Way too many Christians live as martyrs. Our culture is changing. It is becoming less "Christian." That doesn't change our calling. We are called to impact culture by loving God and loving people.

PERSECUTION COMPLEX

Be careful of the persecution complex that comes along with a lot of Christianity. Our world is changing, but not everyone hates all things Christianity. It's often said that we need to get back to America's Christian roots. It's a nice thought, but it's not based on history.

In American history, 1776 is a very important year. The interesting thing about this year is only 17 percent of the population attended church on a regular basis. That's less than today. Today, some research shows that 40 percent of Americans go to church weekly.

If less than 17 percent of the population attended church, then why do we look back and think they had something right that we have wrong now?

We want to believe it was different than it is now. It wasn't that different. Describing the spiritual climate of America in the 1800s...

"Over the wider American landscape, however, colonists were notably 'unchurched' and 'un-Christian.' Scattered around in separate households (unlike the Puritans who concentrated in villages), most Americans had no church to go to and little connection to what we would call organized religion. Even where there were churches to attend, many went either irregularly or simply because the church was one of the rare places—along with the tavern—to see people in a sparsely-developed society."[4]

Pastors think they have it rough today, but the early days of America were not better. One American minister in the 1800s wrote...

"[T]here are American families in this part of the country who never saw a bible, nor heard of Jesus Christ [. . .] the whole country, from Lake Erie to the Gulf of Mexico, is as the valley of the shadow of death."

Every time anyone makes a move in America that doesn't support Christian beliefs, the faithful freak out. The truth is that Christianity thrives in persecution. When following Jesus costs you something, the result is monumental.

I don't believe we need to return to the good old days of America's past. Every generation presents its unique challenges. Instead of complaining about how we think things are, Christians should seek to love the unlovable no matter the spiritual climate.

Jesus' message was radical because it presented love in the midst of hate. As long as we view it as *Us* versus *Them* we will never make an impact. In order to change the world, you have to interact with people who do not believe like you do. Some will not

---

4   Claude S. Fischer, "A Christian America? What History Shows," *Made in America* (blog), March 26, 2010, https://madeinamericathebook. wordpress.com/2010/03/26/a-christian-america-what-history-shows/.

like that, but some will be won over because of the love of God shown in you.

Somehow as Christians we have made everything about us. It's all about us versus them. It should be everything is about Jesus.

A PERSONAL EXAMPLE OF WHAT WE'VE DONE

There is a pastor in Atlanta, Georgia, who is incredibly well respected.

He is my favorite preacher today. Maybe you've heard him preach or even read one of his books. He is one of the most practical and best teachers of God's truths. His name is Andy Stanley.

The picture was taken after I heard him speak at a conference. I saw him in the lobby but was too scared to talk to him. I told my friend to snap a picture as soon as I stood behind him and to make it look like we were talking together. Andy had no idea I was there. Now, I tell you all of that to say that a few years after this I had a crazy opportunity. A friend of mine, Chad, helped run a huge conference and Andy was speaking at it. The conference was in California, not too far from LA. I flew out to hang out with my friend and enjoy the conference. One afternoon my friend said, "I'm going to pick Andy up from the airport, would you like to go with me?" In the Christian conference world, when you say "Andy," there is only one. I instantly peed my pants. Okay, not literally, but I figuratively wet myself. This was a really big deal for me. I was out of my mind excited. Besides getting married, having kids, becoming a Christian, planting a church, skydiving, writing a book, seeing U2 in concert, signing autographs because a group of Needtobreathe fans thought I was in the band, writing a second book (you are reading it), and inviting TobyMac (Christian music artist) to my wedding, this was the greatest moment of my life.

We drove to the airport and pulled up to the curb right outside the exit doors. We were sitting there for about five minutes when a cop pulled up and said, "Can you give me one good reason why I shouldn't give you a ticket?" He then told us that it's illegal to park in front of the airport. My friend explained that he was picking up one of the speakers for a large conference and that he was from Atlanta. Thankfully, the cop showed us mercy. We got out of the ticket but couldn't stay parked there.

It was time for Andy's flight to land, it was on time, and Chad said, "He never checks a bag." Chad knew because he knows Andy. So, we had to circle around the airport, but Chad was afraid that Andy would come out, not see us, and have to wait. Chad's plan was to go into the airport and have me circle.

Chad said, "I need you to circle around as I go inside to meet Andy. It's only a few turns to circle around. What could go wrong?" Now, I knew that something could go wrong. You see, I don't have a sense of direction. That's worse than a bad sense of direction. In fact, a bad sense of direction would be a step up from what I have. I get lost in my own home and it's not that big of a home. I don't know which direction is north, south, east, or west. What's that thing called that Catholics do before and after a prayer? You know, the thing with their fingers where they touch their head, heart, and finish it with a touch to the shoulder, shoulder. Well, whatever it's called, I couldn't do it because I don't know my north from my south or my east from my west.

And to make this even more stressful, I am not from California. So, Chad got out of the car and I got into the driver's seat. The car was a *huge* SUV. Back home I drive a Honda Civic. This had all the makings of a sitcom.

I circled around the airport and saw that it was a little tricky. First, I had to merge into traffic on the right and then I had to take a left and merge to traffic on the left. It was a little confusing, but I made it through with no big deal. Well, I circled and circled and circled and there was no sign of my friend or Andy. It was around the dozenth time circling when my brain started drifting. I think I got cocky. I started thinking about what I was going to say to Andy. This was a once-in-a-lifetime opportunity and, in my excitement, I had not thought through a single question for him.

Should I lead with a joke? I was thinking about "Hi, I'm Rob. Nice to meet you, Rick Warren." That's a joke pastors will get. Or should I lead with a question about him? Should I ask him a leadership question? Should I ask him to be the godfather to my children? As they say, "Go big or go home."

I started playing out potential questions and pretending to be cool. Well, somehow in my zone out I missed that I naturally merged to the right. When it came to the next merge, I thought that I hadn't already merged to the right, so I got in the right lane. The lane that was supposed to be the left lane that took me back to the airport. Are you tracking with me? This was the makings of a disaster.

I instantly knew that I made a mistake when the first sign I saw read "You are now leaving John Wayne Airport." I was freaked! Really freaked! I don't know if I've ever felt as much stress as I felt in that moment, and I was in the hospital room as my wife gave birth to twins without an epidural.

Now, I knew I wasn't that far from the airport, so I just needed to figure out how to circle back around. Thankfully, I had a smartphone and pulled out the map app. No problem...right? Or so I thought. When I turned on the GPS, it said I had nine miles until I could get back to the airport and close to twenty minutes. *That's impossible!*

How could one turn get me that far away?

Now to make matters worse, traffic was awful. It was jammed! I'm talking about a parking lot. I'm talking about everyone and their mother was sitting in that traffic. It's true. You were there. In a car. Your mom was there too. Everybody was sitting in that traffic. Every. Body! At this point my stress level is at DEFCON 1.

It was right at this point that my friend Chad texted me and said, "He's here."

Are you joking me?

I quickly had a panic attack, screamed out, "Dear God no!" and then took the first exit I saw. At this point I was sweating so bad it was spewing off my face. I turned the AC up as high as it could go and started looking for a gas station to ask for directions. Stereotypically men don't ask for directions. I'm not too proud to ask for directions. I was about to mess up this once-in-a-lifetime opportunity.

I pulled the SUV into the gas station, put it in park, left it running, jumped out, and left my door wide open. I didn't have time to close it. I ran into the gas station and made a Kramer-like (from *Seinfeld*) entrance. I declared in a loud and panicked voice, "How do I get to the airport?" Every person in the gas station stopped moving. The cashier didn't say a word. He simply pointed to his left. I declared, "Thank you!" and then ran out the door.

After whipping into the gas station and asking for help, I found out that I was on the road that the airport was on. After a few minutes I got back to the airport and pulled in front of the door. I knew at this point they had to have been waiting. It'd been too long. I was now an embarrassment to my friend Chad. Chad would probably get fired. I'd no longer be able to pastor because if Jesus couldn't trust me with the small things, then why is he going to trust me with the big things? Andy Stanley would inevitably hate me, and he would use this in a sermon about not having foolish friends entitled "Your friends will determine the quality and direction of your life." The sermon would be epic, but my life would be over.

After I pulled in front of the airport, I looked at my cell phone to see another text from Chad. It read "He checked a bag. It's going to be a while."

Praise God from whom all blessings flow! Andy never checks a bag, but this time he did.

I ended up freaking out about nothing. I ended up stressed and worried. I *freaked out* and it ended up not being anything to freak out over. I ended up getting to pick Andy up. I got to talk to him. I even got to cool down enough that the sweat stopped pouring out from my head from all the stress. My hand wasn't even sweating when I shook his. It was glorious.

Now, I know why I freaked out so badly. I freaked out because I messed up who the main character of the story was. Let me ask you, who do you think the main character of the story was?

It's not me.

The main character should be Andy. I was there for him. I was there to greet him. I was there to pick him up. I was playing a really small part of his story. And the truth of the matter is that even if I was late because of a dumb mistake, it wouldn't have made that big of a difference to Andy. At the end of the day I cared way more about myself than I did Andy. I freaked because I didn't want to look bad to Andy. I made it all about me.

Stick with me on this.

It's the same thing with God. You see, you and I live each day like we are the main characters of the story. We freak out over stuff that isn't worth freaking out over. We get stressed over our to-do lists. We panic because we don't think we look good. We freak when we don't know what to do. We allow our mistakes to define us. All of our worry, stress, anxiety, and fear come from placing ourselves as the main character of the story. The truth of the matter is we play a small part in the much larger story of life. You see, this world is not about you and it's not about me. Ultimately, the main character is Jesus. When we focus on him our story changes.

BACK TO THE POINT

So now getting back to the church. I believe the church has transitioned from a radical movement into a social club that tags on the name of Jesus. It's easy for us to panic when things don't go our way.

The church is filled with imperfect people, so there will always be issues. But, you know, a lot of the hurt that has come out of the church has come from arguments where someone didn't get their way.

If we don't like the music anymore at church, if the sermons aren't deep enough for us, if someone doesn't include us like we think they should, if the church grows and we no longer have access to the pastor, if someone doesn't agree with our opinion, we talk behind their back, spread gossip, vent to the wrong people, and then eventually either cause the person we disagree with to leave or we leave feeling broken.

When we focus on our needs, wants, and desires, we end up freaking out when things don't go the way we think they should. I'm talking *freak out*. Le freak, c'est chic. Freak out!

THE BASIS OF THIS BOOK

There are two verses that will point out what this book is all about. Let's start with the first one...

Once, on being asked by the Pharisees when the kingdom of God would come... (Luke 17:20a)

Let's stop there for just a second. So, a Pharisee is a master of the Jewish religion. And this Pharisee asks Jesus when the kingdom of God would come.

Now this is an interesting question. Jesus lived in a day and age of kings. Kings have kingdoms. In his day, the king was called

Caesar and his kingdom was Rome. Now Caesar's kingdom was something that everyone was familiar with. Caesar built an empire around himself. Caesar made decrees that you would worship him as god or you would die.

Now that seems extreme, but that's not that different than how we live today. We live as if we are the king and everyone is here to meet our needs. We may not make a decree that commands people to worship us or they will die or agree with us or we will crucify them, but we sure do make this world all about us. We act like we are the star of the movie and everyone else is a supporting character. Including God.

We fight for our right to party, except the party is based off what we feel we are entitled to. Feel free to push back on what I just wrote, but I want you to think about it for a second.

Specifically, think about who you call an idiot. Maybe you don't call them that to their face, but there are times where someone does something and it causes you to dismiss their worth. Christians often come off as dismissive to those who do not agree with us. One of the lowest levels of thinking is to label people idiots for simply believing something different. It is common but it's childlike. To hate something because you do not get your way is a childlike response.

I'm convinced that adults are simply older versions of toddlers. We may freak out a little differently, but the same things we react to as toddlers tend to be what we freak out about as adults.

When I don't get my way, I freak. When someone takes something that is mine, I freak. When someone doesn't agree with me, I freak.

As adults we tend to freak out about being left out, not getting what is fair, or not getting our way. It's easy to view others as idiots when they don't do what you want them to do. The problem is the people who are idiots in our lives are the very people Jesus wants us to love.

I'm not immune to calling someone an idiot. I can get so fiery passionate about my point that I quickly think, "If you disagree with me you are a card-carrying idiot." Id. Iot. Id to the iot. Idiot. Our way of thinking is a part of the kingdom we've built. And when someone disagrees it is easy to pull out the idiot card.

You see, it's not a matter of if we are building our kingdom. It's a matter of if we realize in what ways we are building a kingdom of "me."

I SAW THE SIGN

So how do you know if you are building your kingdom and asking God to be a part of it? It's not an easy thing to see. I believe there are a few questions we need to ask to see whose kingdom we are building.

Signs That Point to Whose Kingdom You Are Building…
1. **Are you easily offended by those who disagree with you?** If you take disagreements personally, it's a sign you view your opinions as a part of who you are. It's your world and everyone else just lives in it.
2. **Do you have any friends who do not think/look just like you?** People who do not look like you can make you feel uncomfortable. Your kingdom is about what makes you feel comfortable. It's about what is easy. It's about who will serve you. If people who disagree with you don't have a seat at your table, then all signs point to building a kingdom about you.

3. **Do you hold grudges?** It's impossible to overcome a grudge when all you are thinking about is yourself. When we think about ourselves, offenses become magnified and the thought of forgiving seems like an impossible task. When building Jesus' kingdom, forgiveness is a way of life. That doesn't mean you don't get hurt or that it's easy. It's just easier.

4. **Do you have relationships with others who do not benefit you directly?** When it is your kingdom, people are to be used. If someone doesn't benefit you then you do not have time for them. Think about that friend/family member/church member who has wandered from God. When someone leaves the faith, it should break our hearts. Jesus, the great Shepherd, leaves the ninety-nine to go after the one. When it's about your kingdom, the offense is paid if anyone leaves. It's a personal rejection instead of a heartbreak. Or think about the person who doesn't directly benefit you. Can you make time for someone who doesn't directly benefit you? Often we treat people like they are expendable. In the kingdom of God, people matter because God says they matter and not just because they can benefit you.

5. **Is it easy to become prideful when you succeed?** As humans it's easy to magnify our successes and minimize our failures. In God's kingdom we understand that success and failure look different. If I fail, it's simply a lesson to learn and not the end of the world. If I succeed, it is because of the grace

of God. I play a part in the story, but I am not the story.

6. **Can you move past your failures?** You are in charge of the kingdom, so your mistakes are magnified. When you mess up it's a gigantor deal. It's of epic proportions. When the kingdom is all about you, God's grace seems like a fairy tale. It's too hard to grasp because we magnify our mistakes.

7. **Do you spend lots of time worrying about temporary things?** When it's your kingdom you do whatever you can to hold on to your stuff. It's yours. When something breaks it's a big deal. When you lose something it's monumental. Temporary things should be thought about but not obsessed about. There is nothing wrong with having stuff, unless your stuff has you.

8. **Is it difficult to ask for help?** The king or queen of the kingdom doesn't seek help. That would be too humiliating. You can overcome any situation. Even though you haven't, you will. One day. It would just be too embarrassing to seek help.

9. **What are you addicted to?** The average American has $7,000 in credit card debt. Why? Because we have to have what we want now. We deserve it. Addictions are simply obsessions with ourselves. Whether it's porn, food, alcohol, or some other addiction, at the end of the day it screams we are more concerned with our temporary happiness than an eternal reward.

10. **Do you primarily pray when you need something?** The main time that you think about God is when you

need something. When your world falls apart. When you need him to come through. When life is good God takes a back seat. Why? Because you are in charge. This is your kingdom.

In the case of this Pharisee, he was hoping to hear about the kingdom of God. They were wanting the same things that Caesar had but with God in charge. Why? Because this would benefit them greatly. They wanted Israel to once again rule and reign. They wanted God to come in and wipe out all of their enemies. They wanted to become a world power again. They wanted the kingdom of God because it would greatly benefit them. Now Jesus hears that question and responds in a way that must have been frustrating. Look at what he said…

> Jesus replied, "The coming of the kingdom of God is not something that can be observed, nor will people say, 'Here it is,' or 'There it is,' because the kingdom of God is in your midst." (Luke 17:20b–21)

Now this phrase "the kingdom of God is in your midst" has been debated by lots of people. No one knows the exact meaning of this phrase. I think the context supports Jesus meant his kingdom is not going to look like other kingdoms. The kingdom that Jesus ushered in said things like "the first shall be last and the last shall be first." It said things like "love your enemies and pray for those that persecute you." It said things like "I do not condemn you." Jesus' kingdom wouldn't look like other kingdoms. It isn't a kingdom built with stone. It's a movement that cannot be contained by walls. It's not something that is just for one type of person. It's for anyone. And here's the crazy thing about Jesus' kingdom. You don't go to it. It comes to you. And you can take it everywhere you go.

The Second Verse That Points Out What This Book Is All About...

"The kingdom is the society in which God's will is lived out by ordinary folk."[5]

—Scot McKnight

There is a famous story in the gospel of John where a Pharisee named Nicodemus sneaks out at night to meet Jesus. This is the second verse that helps shape what this book is all about. Let's look at what went down.

He came to Jesus at night and said, "Rabbi, we know that you are a teacher who has come from God. For no one could perform the signs you are doing if God were not with him."
Jesus replied, "Very truly I tell you, no one can see the kingdom of God unless they are born again."
"How can someone be born when they are old?" Nicodemus asked. "Surely they cannot enter a second time into their mother's womb to be born!"
(John 3:2–4)

---

5   Scot McKnight, *One.Life: Jesus Calls, We Follow* (Grand Rapids: Zondervan, 2010).

Now this story is interesting because Jesus says no one can see the kingdom of God unless they are born again. I have always thought that when Jesus referred to no one can see the kingdom unless they are born again it was talking about heaven. But the authors of each of the gospels have a point when they were writing. In John's gospel it's clear that Nicodemus can't see Jesus' kingdom. Why? Because he can't get out of his own way. Nicodemus is spiritually blind and can't see what Jesus is all about. Translation: he is not willing to accept that Jesus is king and therefore he can't see his kingdom. His kingdom on earth. Now John has a point in writing this and he follows it up with a guy who does see Jesus' kingdom. His name is First Baptist John. Well, that's not technically his name. He is known as a guy who baptized. Let's look at what happens…

> After this, Jesus and his disciples went out into the Judean countryside, where he spent some time with them, and baptized. Now John also was baptizing at Aenon near Salim, because there was plenty of water, and people were coming and being baptized. (This was before John was put in prison.) An argument developed between some of John's disciples and a certain Jew over the matter of ceremonial washing. They came to John and said to him, "Rabbi, that man who was with you on the other side of the Jordan—the one you testified about—look, he is baptizing, and everyone is going to him." (John 3:22–26)

Did you catch what happened? John the Baptist was here first. Way before Mark the Methodist or Pete the Pentecostal. John was even there before Jesus started his ministry. And John had an awesome ministry. John was the hot ticket. John was nicely building a kingdom. He had followers. He had crowds. He had people who cared about him. And one of his followers comes to John and says, "Yo dog, that guy that you testified about, he is baptizing people now. That's your gig, John. You are called John the Baptist for crying out loud! John, you are losing your entourage. John, start to freak out. John, this isn't how we planned it. John, more people are paying attention to Jesus than you." That's from the ROB translation of the Bible. It's a paraphrase. I digress.

But look how John responds.

> To this John replied, "A person can receive only what is given them from heaven. You yourselves can testify that I said, 'I am not the Messiah but am sent ahead of him.' The bride belongs to the bridegroom. The friend who attends the bridegroom waits and listens for him, and is full of joy when he hears the bridegroom's voice. That joy is mine, and it is now complete. He must become greater; I must become less." (John 3:27–30)

Now, I don't think it's a coincidence that Nicodemus couldn't see Jesus' kingdom because he was spiritually blind and the author of this verse follows that up with someone who does see his kingdom. John the Baptist responds with

> "He must become greater; I must become less."

And that, my friends, is what Christians are called to do. Christianity isn't about us. It's not about our kingdom. It's not about our preferences. It's about getting out of the way. Why? Because it's not about us. It's about Jesus. We have to intentionally make our mission all about Jesus and less about ourselves.

What's amazing is we accomplish more when we aren't so focused on ourselves. We ultimately end up living a fuller life, having a better story, and experience a story worth telling when we get out of the way and put Jesus first.

Are You Still With Me?

Not one of us is perfect. I'm not perfect. But that does not excuse us from making this world all about us.

Jesus came to establish a kingdom. He died to establish a kingdom. He rose again to establish a kingdom.

Does your life reflect the type of kingdom Jesus died for?

Does the way that you spend your money reflect the kind of kingdom Jesus died for? Does the way that you talk to others reflect the kind of kingdom Jesus died for? Does the way that you treat others reflect the type of kingdom Jesus died for? Does your thought life reflect the type of kingdom Jesus died for? Does your life reflect the type of kingdom Jesus died for?

If not, why?

None of us are perfect. We are all in progress, but some of us are not progressing. We are stuck. We are stuck on ourselves. Until we kick ourselves off the throne and establish Jesus, we will continually live like it's all about us, and our lives will reflect problems that are all about us.

There are times and areas of every Christian's life that do not reflect the type of kingdom Jesus died for. We are all works in progress. When you feel convicted of an area that doesn't match the kingdom Jesus died for, don't resist conviction. Don't run from it. Don't let it turn to shame. As a great coach would do, Jesus points out areas we need to work on and loves us to become better.

We all struggle, doubt, and wander. Struggling should be a vacation home, and not permanent residence. We all fall...get back up. When we fall let's fall into the arms of grace, and then get back to living for Jesus.

I don't know about you, but as a Christian I want to live for Jesus. After all, it's called Christian not Rob-ian. It's also not called You-ian. It's not called a _____(insert your name here)ian.

Way too many of us are misspelling Christianity. We are spelling it with our name first.

My prayer is that together, with the help of God, we will be able to dethrone ourselves and truly say, "He must increase, and I must decrease."

A CHALLENGE FOR CHURCH

In America, having so many options for church is a blessing and a curse. The blessing is we truly need all types of churches to reach all types of people. The other side of that blessing is, with so many options, Christians have the luxury of consuming church and leaving for another church whenever something doesn't sit right with them.

How can we change this? How can we change being consumers more than participators?

I believe it starts with each individual. We all have a part to play. We cannot control other people. We can only work on controlling ourselves for the glory of God.

What if we committed to a church? What would happen if we simply declared to not get easily offended at church? What would happen if we made a decision to go all in to the church we are planted at? What would happen if we committed to forgive the people we are at church with? What if we committed to not go anywhere?

Maybe I'm wrong, but I feel that a lot of churched people have one foot already out the door and are ready to jump ship to another church. It seems like we are waiting for something to go wrong.

Of course, there are plenty of unhealthy churches out there. There are lots of horror stories of pastors who abuse power, bad leadership, and toxic environments. That's not what I'm writing about and this is not who I'm writing to.

I've been on staff at four very different churches. One thing they all had in common was people who got easily offended and jumped ship to another church.

After almost three years at a church I was a part of, I got a call from a kind person who was leaving. I respected the call because many don't call. They just leave. What stuck with me about this call was the opening line. The first words I heard were "We knew this church wasn't our church home when we started coming." That's fair. I don't believe there is a one-size-fits-all church. What felt unfair is that I didn't view them as "not my people." I went all in. We invested in the best way we knew how to. We cared about them. And still do. To hear that they knew it was a matter of time before they left was hard. I want every person to find a church home and thrive there. I would have encouraged them to find a church a lot sooner if I had known they didn't feel at home at our church. After three years they walked away. I was left picking up the pieces.

Please hear me. I am not competitive when it comes to church. I truly do want everyone to find the best church home for themselves.

But something has to change. People change churches like they do underwear. Often.

Find a church that is your home church. Not a perfect church. Those don't exist. Find a church and support the vision and mission. Find a church and commit to be there. Go all in.

Start with one year.

Now, if you've been at a church for more than a year, ask yourself if you've truly gone all in. If not, start by going all in for one year. Join a group, volunteer, give, encourage the pastor and staff, commit to keep unity. Say to yourself this is "my church."

You are not going all in for a pastor, program, or denomination. You are going all in for Jesus. The church is the bride of Jesus. Go all in for him.

The church doesn't belong to a pastor. The church doesn't belong to a denomination. The church doesn't belong to a committee or board. The church is Jesus'.

The common reasons I hear people leaving a church have very little to do with sin or some type of abuse.

The big reasons people leave are...
- The church is getting too big.
- I'm no longer being fed.
- I don't agree with the new direction of the church.

Very rarely do I hear "God is calling me to another church." The vast majority of the time, the reason someone starts to think about leaving a church is because of an offense. It often takes a little digging to find the offense, but most of the time there is an offense somewhere at the root of their decision to leave.

Because confrontation is difficult, we often find it easier to simply leave.

What I've found in the church world is that when someone does tell a pastor the reason they are leaving, it is rarely the real reason.

I'm convinced that we often present a portion of the truth. It's the truth we find will be the least hurtful. This makes sense because as good Christians we aren't looking to hurt others. The problem is it's not fully honest.

We present the tip of the iceberg when the real reason is under the water. It's not a lie. It's just not the real reason.

It can be difficult to put the real reason into words, so it's easier to either just leave or give a partial reason. That's not helpful to you and it's not helpful to the church.

I'm not implying that you should blast a church. I think we need honest conversation that comes with love.

A pastor friend of mine told me what one exiting member of his church said. A well-meaning person said, "I am called to be a missionary and I don't think I can be a goer in a sending church." Um...what?

Literally the church he pastors is set up to send missionaries. The reason he was given was this person didn't think she could go to the mission field out of a church that sends people to the mission field. I'm convinced that there is more to that story.

Often when someone leaves they say the reason is because they are not being fed, don't agree with the vision, or something has just changed. Often when I dig in a little more I find that they were cut from the worship team, had a need that they didn't see being met, or were offended because their expectations were not met.

Years ago, a person left the church I was on staff at because the pastor didn't know his name. There were almost four thousand people at the church. What offended him is they had met the pastor before and a few months later he didn't remember their encounter. That's an unrealistic expectation.

It stinks to not be remembered but show some grace.

Here's a challenge for you. For one year go all in at your church. Just commit to believe the best about the church, people, and staff. Find ways to make the church better. Contribute. When there is a problem seek to bring a possible solution. Strive to have everything you are a part of turn to gold.

It will be hard work.

It will be frustrating.

People are difficult.

But it's so worth it.

Church comes to life when you are all in.

Strive to make church more about Jesus and less about you. He must increase…we must decrease.

The church has become recreational because we view it through a selfish lens. For one year, fight past bias, preference, and the need to fight for your rights…and look for ways to make it all about Jesus.

For one year, commit to help be the type of church you wish church was. Go all in. And then…do it again. Commit to be the church until God calls you somewhere else.

Application: Reflect on one area of your life where God is not on the throne. Is it with finances, physical, or relational? What is one step you can take this week to put Jesus on the throne of that area?

Questions:

1. Is your current church experience reflecting the radical movement that Jesus started? If not, what can you do about it? And no, firing your pastor is not an acceptable answer.

2. Which of the "Signs That Point to Whose Kingdom You Are Building" do you relate to the most? Why?

3. What are some practical ways that we can dethrone ourselves and live for Jesus?

4. Does "he must become greater, I must become less" mean that we can never talk about ourselves? Why or why not?

5. What are some ways that a Christian's life could reflect the type of movement that Jesus died for?

CHAPTER 2

HEAVEN ON EARTH

If I were to ask you what Jesus' main teaching was, I wonder what you would say. Some would say that it was love. I think that Jesus did teach love, but I think that he taught something more specific than love. Some would say that his message was to seek and save the lost. I think that is a great message and it is one of the ones Jesus taught, but I don't think that was Jesus' main teaching. Jesus taught a lot of great things. He taught new commands on how to truly love God and to love people. Jesus was an incredible teacher! Jesus taught on money and possessions and how they can rule us if we let them. Jesus taught a lot about helping the poor. In fact, Jesus' ministry was primarily to the poor. And yet that wasn't the number one thing Jesus taught on. Jesus' main teaching, believe it or not, can be summed up incredibly well by a pop singer from the greatest decade in the history of decades: the 1980s. In the late eighties Belinda Carlisle summed up Jesus' main teaching, and I don't think she had a fat clue what she was doing. Maybe you've heard it: "Heaven Is a Place on Earth."[1]

And yes, I do like Belinda Carlisle. You can go ahead and take my man card if you want to, but unlike most guys I don't have imaginary man cards. I was given real man cards and I was given seven, so take it and I'll still feel secure in my manhood.

I digress. I don't have a fat clue what inspired Belinda Carlisle to write this song, but it is without a doubt Jesus' main message, heaven is a place on earth. When Jesus first started his ministry he declared his message. Look at what Jesus said:

---

1   "Heaven Is a Place on Earth" by Belinda Carlisle, MCA, 1987.

"The time has come," he said. "The kingdom of God has come near. Repent and believe the good news!" (Mark 1:15)

Now to us this doesn't seem like that big of a deal, but Jesus was echoing some of Israel's most famous prophets. Israel was at one time a world leader. Because of their poor life choices, they ended up being ruled by others. So, for years Israel had prophets who would talk about the day when God would one day reestablish his reign and Israel would become a power again. Look at what the prophet Zephaniah said years before Jesus:

Sing, Daughter Zion;
shout aloud, Israel!
Be glad and rejoice with all your heart, Daughter Jerusalem!
The Lord has taken away your punishment,
he has turned back your enemy.
The Lord, the King of Israel, is with you;
never again will you fear any harm.
On that day
they will say to Jerusalem,
"Do not fear, Zion;
do not let your hands hang limp.
The Lord your God is with you,
the Mighty Warrior who saves.
He will take great delight in you;
in his love he will no longer rebuke you,
but will rejoice over you with singing."
"I will remove from you

all who mourn over the loss of your appointed festivals,
which is a burden and reproach for you.
At that time I will deal
with all who oppressed you.
I will rescue the lame;
I will gather the exiles.
I will give them praise and honor
in every land where they have suffered shame.
At that time I will gather you;
at that time I will bring you home.
I will give you honor and praise
among all the peoples of the earth
when I restore your fortunes
before your very eyes,"
says the Lord. (Zephaniah 3:14–20)

Zephaniah is predicting a time where God will be the king of Israel. They will no longer need a physical king because God will reign. Zephaniah calls God a mighty warrior. He's painting this picture of what is to come one day.

So, Jesus then comes on the scene, and let's look at what he says one more time.

"The time has come," he said. "The kingdom of God has come near. Repent and believe the good news!" (Mark 1:15)

What time has come? The time of God's reign as king. They no longer have to look for a future event. The event is here in Jesus. The similarities are evident. But there are differences too. Whereas the prophets looked ahead to an undetermined time in the future when God would return to rule over his people, Jesus says, "The time is now. The reign of God has now come near!"

Jesus' main message was that the kingdom of God was at hand. Heaven has come to earth! So the response is to repent. Stop living for yourself and start living for Jesus. Now!

The phrase "kingdom of God" appears *fifty-three* times in the New Testament. The synonymous phrase "kingdom of heaven" appears *thirty-two* times in the book of Matthew. Now that you know this, it will change the way you read the Gospels. It's like when you buy a new car and then notice just how many other people drive the same kind of car. It's like that. Now, you'll see just how often Jesus talks about the kingdom.

The kingdom of God or the kingdom of heaven is here. It's not just something that we wait for one day. This is really important!

New Testament scholar Gordon Fee once said,

"You cannot know anything about Jesus, anything, if you miss the kingdom of God."[2]

Somehow Christianity has focused on heaven being a place that we will one day go to and missed that Jesus said heaven came to earth, ooh baby do you know what that's worth? Now, I believe that heaven is real. I believe that heaven is a place that those who have followed Jesus go to. In fact, I hope that all of you reading this with me will be in heaven. I hear it's a big house where we can play football. And all the nineties youth group kids just had a flood of memories pour back into their minds thanks to that song

---

2 From a lecture by Gordon Fee, professor of New Testament studies at Regent College.

from Audio Adrenaline. Everyone else who didn't go to youth group in the nineties doesn't have a fat clue what just happened. Google it.

I believe there is a big, big house with lots and lots of room, but Jesus' message was not just that heaven is one day coming. His message was both/and. Heaven is here now and it's a place that you can one day go to.

Jesus came to give us the gospel, which means good news. But the good news is not just that God will one day save your soul from hell. The good news is that the kingdom of heaven is here. It's in our midst. You are not called to sit around and wait for heaven. Until we get to heaven it's our calling to make heaven on earth. If you have been changed by Jesus' good news, then it's your calling to bring heaven on earth.

ON EARTH AS IT IS IN HEAVEN

"How is someone going to truly want Heaven if they've never truly experienced a glimpse of it on earth?"[3]
                                                    —Rob Shepherd

Did I just quote myself? Yes, yes I did. Quotes stand out so much more, and even though I don't believe that I'm anyone special to quote, I do believe that statement is worth pondering. Why would someone want heaven if they've truly never experienced it on earth?

I think that Jesus' most compelling argument for making heaven on earth comes from one of the most famous things he

---

3   If you are reading the footnotes you are a special person and I love you.

ever said. In Jesus' most famous sermon he teaches the crowd that had gathered how to pray. He gives them a template and I want to spend some time looking at what Jesus said.

> "This, then, is how you should pray:
> "'Our Father in heaven,
> hallowed be your name,
> your kingdom come,
> your will be done,
> on earth as it is in heaven.
> Give us today our daily bread.
> And forgive us our debts,
> as we also have forgiven our debtors.
> And lead us not into temptation,
> but deliver us from the evil one.'"
> (Matthew 6:9–13)

Did you catch what Jesus said? When you pray, you pray to God, and what is one of the first things that you should pray? "Your kingdom come, your will be done, on earth as it is in heaven." Well, how is God's will done in heaven? It's done because every heavenly being is living to serve God. There is no question about what God's will is. In heaven they live God's will. Heaven is a place of perfection. Now it's fascinating to discover how much this prayer of Jesus is similar to the prayers offered up by faithful Jews in the first century. Consider, for example, the following prayer that many scholars believe to have been offered daily in the time of Jesus:

> "May God establish his kingdom in your lifetime
> and in your days and in the lifetime of all the

house of Israel, even speedily and at a near time."
(Kaddish prayer)[4]

You see, the people in Jesus' day were desperate for God's kingdom to come. They understood that the way that they were living was not the best kingdom. They prayed and looked forward to a day when they could experience the best kingdom.

When Jesus declared that the kingdom of heaven was near, he was saying that prayers like this are being answered now! Christians are to be so radically changed by Jesus' good news that we live our lives in a way that shows people how God's kingdom is greater than all other kingdoms. The question for you to answer is, have you been changed by Jesus' good news? If you've experienced Jesus, if you believe in him, then it is now up to you and other Christians to show the world that God's kingdom is here.

HELL ON EARTH

So far this has been just an idea, but let's talk about this practically. How is receiving Jesus' message making heaven here on earth? Maybe it's hard to picture heaven on earth, but it's not hard to picture hell. Humans are great at bringing hell on earth. If you've ever seen the movie *Hotel Rwanda*, then you know what hell on earth looks like. Whenever a husband abuses his wife, that's hell on earth. When people are selfish in marriage, it is hell on earth. Where there are lonely and hurting people, it is hell on earth. Being

---

4   Mark Roberts, "Where is the Kingdom of God?" *Patheos*, May 12, 2011, http://www.patheos.com/blogs/markdroberts/2011/05/12/where-is-the-kingdom-of-god/.

trapped in an addiction is hell on earth. Living with guilt is hell on earth. Living in apathy is hell on earth. The fact that every food that tastes amazing is bad for me is hell on earth. We don't have to look far to see hell on earth. It's everywhere we look. As of this writing there is a fashion trend known as the men's romper. Hell is real and has come to earth.

Not all that long ago, I stumbled upon a news story that completely messed with me. There was a man from Australia who was out jogging in Oklahoma and three teens decided to kill him because they were bored. That same week there was a World War II vet waiting for friends to go into a bowling alley and he was beaten to death. Hell is all over this earth. People don't have to wait to die to experience hell. This is why Jesus' message is so profound. He has come to bring the kingdom of heaven to us. In Jesus we can experience heaven on earth. We've got to get this because hell is everywhere.

Some people don't choose their hell. A neglected child didn't choose his hell. Sometimes, because people are broken, we experience hell. We didn't choose it. Hell found us.

As a pastor I get asked a lot why God would allow bad things to happen. There was one time I was asked by someone who had good reason to ask. I was then told about how this person had a neighbor who lost a child because of an abusive boyfriend. That is horrible. I was at a loss for words. This person was shook because he was so upset that God would allow this to happen. As difficult as it is to wrestle with, I'm not sure God is to blame for that hell.

God's plan is for Christians to be his hands and feet. There is no plan B. So when we allow hell to exist on earth, it feels as if God is absent. People want to know where a good God is during difficult circumstances, but I want to know where good Christians are when others hurt. Hell is real. You don't have to die to get there. You don't have to look far to find it. Sometimes hell is thrown on people. What would our world look like if Christians brought heaven to people's hell? What would our world look like if Christians took serious God's command to love others like we have been loved by him?

So often we are consumed with living for our own kingdom that we ignore the hell others are experiencing. There is so much hell on earth it can be overwhelming, but if each Christian did their part there would be a lot more heaven.

Sometimes we don't choose hell, it chooses us. Other times people choose the hell they live in. Addiction is hell. Feeling the stress of debt can feel like hell. Being codependent and continually choosing to be around people who hurt you is a living hell. We are so broken we self-destruct. Sometimes, in our hurt, we choose a way out that becomes a living hell.

CHOOSING HELL

But why do people choose hell?

1. It's easier. It takes no discipline or work to find hell. Zig Ziglar, a wordsmith genius, once said, "If you aim at nothing, you will hit it every time." Yup. Hell is like shooting fish in a barrel. It's that easy. Do what you want, when you want, and how you want. Jesus said, "Enter through the narrow gate. For wide is the gate and broad is the road that leads to destruction, and many enter through it. But small is the gate and narrow the road that leads to life, and only a few find it" (Matthew 7:13–14). It's easy to

find destruction. It starts with a feeling that we enjoy and before we know, it's an addiction. For the vast majority of us reading this, what made us choose to start following God or go back to God was that easy living led to rock bottom. It was rock-bottom hell that led us to realize our way was destructive. Easy, but destructive.

2. They've never experienced heaven. I'm amazed at how quickly people will change their lifelong stances on something. But we have all heard and love those stories of atheists who became Christians. What finally convinced them? Most likely it was a taste of heaven. What they had might not have even tasted like hell. Especially in America, you can live a comfy life and mistake it for heaven. As long as the bills are paid, nobody is trying to kill me, and I have my health, I'll think life is pretty good. I love the title of Jim Collins's book *Good to Great*. We often settle for good when we could experience great. And far too many people, even good churchgoers, have never experienced heaven, so we settled for far less.

Jim Collins's full quote is powerful.

"Good is the enemy of great. And that is one of the key reasons why we have so little that becomes great. We don't have great schools, principally because we have good schools. We don't have great government, principally because we have good government. Few

people attain great lives, in large part because it is just so easy to settle for a good life."[5]

Living a good life where we've settled for less than is hell.

The devil is a liar. He disguises hell by giving it a makeover and promising that it will make our lives better. Hell is the churchgoer who feels judged by God based off their works. Hell is enjoying the comforts of earth but never accomplishing what God created you to do. Hell is enjoying the spoils of earth so much that God becomes a second, third, or an afterthought. Satan is wily and smart. He has to know that hitting rock-bottom hell will spur many on to radically living for Jesus. So instead of rock bottom he will give us comfort. A comfort that becomes all about our kingdom.

When this happens even going to church can become about us and our kingdom. Church so often isn't about falling madly in love with Jesus and learning to love other people. We make it about having our needs met. We make it about enjoying ourselves for an hour on Sunday. We can become so comfortable with this that we actually don't want others to join the church. We like knowing everyone in the church. We like having everyone know us. We like the music a certain way. We like what we like. We've created kingdoms that masquerade as the bride of Christ.

As Christians it's our job to bring heaven to earth in such a way that it leads people to think twice about their comfy kingdom of hell.

A few years ago my wife and I went to Cozumel, Mexico. While sitting on the beach, we noticed large groups of people were paying money for a banana boat ride. It was this long raft shaped

---

5   Jim Collins, *Good to Great: Why Some Companies Make the Leap…And Others Don't* (New York: Harper Business, 2001). Quote accessed online.

like a banana. As people came and went everyone was smiling, laughing, and having an amazing time. So, we decided to give it a shot.

It was not an amazing ride. First off, it was hard as sitting bareback on a diamond. Second of all, the driver should have been certified blind. He drove this thing like a maniac. I am convinced his goal was to knock every passenger off of the banana boat. He would take sharp turns and people would go flying. There I was trying to hold on to this thing as hard as I can while bouncing up and down on an incredibly hard banana boat. Not to mention worrying about my wife. She flew off the banana boat at some point. I'm not sure when because I was holding on for dear life. It was awful. At one point I thought about just diving off and swimming back to the beach.

When we finally did get back to the beach, I wanted to buy a T-shirt that said, "I survived the banana boat ride in Cozumel, Mexico." They didn't have one for sale. They didn't have one because everyone else thought this was fun.

We were so beat up from our banana boat experience that when a nice elderly Cozumel woman told us in broken English that she gave massages for ten dollars on the beach, we jumped at it. Next thing we knew we were lying under a tent on a beach in Cozumel getting a massage from...gorilla hands. That's not her official title, but her hands were incredibly rough feeling, and I am convinced that if I was blind I would think a gorilla was giving me that massage. To make up for her sandpaper hands, she dumped a gallon of baby oil on my back and legs. The best way to describe the massage is the words *mild form of torture*. I was trying really hard not to laugh while the whole ordeal was going on. How come nobody else warned us?

All of a sudden, I heard my wife belt out, "Ow, ow, OW, OWWWW!" I looked over and the masseuse, and I use that term lightly, was pulling on her toes one by one and giving them a good yank. It was kind of like a game I play with my kids called "this little piggy," but it looked like she was trying to pull my wife's toes out of socket. I'm not sure what technique this was, but it made me laugh out loud.

We ended up spending money on a torture device called a banana boat ride and its cousin the torturous massage. I'm pretty sure they were in cahoots together.

It was hell on earth and we paid for it.

Now, my theory as to why we know it was bad and everyone else seemed to be having a great time was that they had never experienced anything better. To them that was fun. Or maybe it was the alcohol that everyone else was drinking. Either way, it was awful and they enjoyed it. I joked that I wanted to move down to Cozumel and start a business that shows people what real fun is.

What does this have to do with hell on earth? I'm glad you asked.

If people only have hell to experience, they'll get used to it and pay good money for it because that's all they know. As Christians we should be able to quickly offer a better experience. How many people are spending their time getting beat up on the banana boat of life only to follow it up with a massage from hell and leave feeling like it was paradise? It's only paradise if you've never experienced something better.

Christians should set the example for everyone. Christians should throw the best parties because it's what God did when we repented of our sin and came home to him. Christians should have the most fun because we know how to enjoy this world the most. Even when going through our own personal hell, we should set an example. Sure, we will get this wrong. That's where grace comes in. But even when we get it wrong we should be the example of what humanity is supposed to look like.

Today, many people are experiencing hell on earth and they are paying for it. They are choosing to follow a kingdom that is wasting away. The world is broken and it's up to us to shine a light for Jesus in order to show there is a better way. Ooh baby, do you know what that's worth? Heaven is a place on earth.

The kingdom of God is neither solely up in heaven nor limited to human hearts but is something we strive to experience in all aspects of our earthly life.

For those who have experienced the kingdom of God now, our calling is to bring heaven on earth for as many people as we can.

I think that's what Jesus wants us to do. In fact, I think that's what he did. Have you ever thought about why Jesus did miracles? It wasn't to prove that he was God. In fact, he got upset at people when they wanted him to do miracles to prove that he was God. Jesus did miracles because people were experiencing hell. Jesus was bringing the kingdom of God to the people. He was allowing people to experience just a taste of heaven. As a Christian you are called to do what Jesus did. You are called to bring miracles to the sick, life to the dead, blessings to the poor, and comfort for the needy. You are called to bring heaven on earth, ooh baby, do you know what that's worth?

LEAVE THE WORLD BETTER THAN YOU FOUND IT

In my area of Virginia, public schools are not real fond of churches renting their space. I'm not sure the official reason, but the reason that has been given to me multiple times is that churches did not take care of the space. With the additional wear and tear, it became a nuisance to deal with the churches.

Right out of seminary I started working for a church plant that rented space from the YMCA. Every week we did setup and teardown in order to pull off services. One of the things that stuck with me greatly was my pastor's commitment to leave the Y better than we found it. The Y was newer and in good condition. The phrase, though, was a commitment to excellence.

After setting up early in the morning, and then doing two services, everyone was tired. It would be easy to not take out the trash, sweep, or clean up behind ourselves. It would be easy to rush teardown so we could all get home. But our goal was to always leave the Y better than we found it.

What if that's God's desire for our time on earth?

Until Jesus comes back there will always be problems in the world.

Christians should be so committed to bringing heaven to earth that we push to make everything we touch better.

I think all of us have the desire to change the world. It may be buried deep down, but it's there. The issue is life is so hectic. If we are not intentional with trying to change the world, it won't happen. We can hope to change the world, but unless we are intentional, we will get wrapped up in our own schedules and to-do lists and we will be left wondering where all the time went.

Hope is a beautiful feeling, but it's a terrible strategy.

In order to change the world, we have to commit to do something.

We cannot be passionate about every cause. We cannot give to every need. Change happens when we consistently give over time. So, what is it that you can do to bring heaven to earth consistently?

68

PRACTICAL IDEAS

There are a few practical ways I've tried to consistently bring heaven to earth. You are welcome to borrow mine or reject them. If you are serious about bringing heaven to earth, you will intentionally pick something.

Here are some ideas to get you started.

1. When you think something nice, say it.

One of the most practical things that has changed the way I live is simply doing something nice whenever I think about it. If I don't act immediately, I often forget. If I cannot act immediately, I put it in my calendar to remember it later. Whenever I think something nice about someone, I send them a text, email, or note. Whenever I think about doing something nice, I do it. Way too often nice thoughts leave me, and in this case the thought doesn't count. What counts is bringing heaven to earth.

2. When you can do something, do it.

I'm not always in a place to do something life changing. I have limited funds. I have limited energy. But here is something that can make a huge difference over time. When there is something you can do…do it.

Often people walk over problems because we think, "That's not my job."

It frustrates me at church when I see people walk over a piece of trash. Anyone can pick that up. Trash picking up isn't a spiritual gift. It's not on a job description.

Often, we are so busy running to something that we ignore little things. Over time, doing the little things can make a massive difference.

To make things better, we have to take initiative.

If you see the dishwasher needs to be unloaded, you can wait for someone else to do it or you can take initiative and do it. This goes for other household chores.

If everyone reading this committed to make the world better than the way they found it, the world would be better. It may be a smaller section of the world, but you never know how your kindness and intentionality can make a difference.

It doesn't have to be your job for you to do something about it.

I make a pretty mean homemade chocolate chip cookie. In fact, they have become locally famous by the people who know me. There are a lot of problems in the world and I do not have all the answers. Often when I see someone is down or having a tough day, I'll make cookies. My wife and I often do cookie drops to friends, family, or church members. Every human has a struggle. I can't fix everything, but everyone wants to know they are important. Making cookies is a small way I try to show others they matter.

A major difference in my life is having a few key people check in on me regularly. A lot of times we only communicate with someone when we need something. Receiving a just-because text means a lot to me. I greatly appreciate those who make the time to check in. I once shared how most pastors are lonely. Most pastors are needed by people but poured into by few. That's a problem. That's a problem that someone can do something about. If you listen to those around you, then you'll find ways to make a difference. After I mentioned the loneliness of pastors, a friend of mine, Jimmy, made a commitment to check in on me. On a regular basis he texts me just because. That is full of awesome!

If there is a problem and you can do something about it, then do it. Even if it's using the talents and gifts you have. Even if it's picking up trash. Even if it's something that seems small...do it. Over time, a lot of consistent little differences matter.

3. If you love someone, show them.

We often wait until someone is dead or moving to tell them how we feel. Why?

I think it is because feelings make us feel weird. It's awkward to tell someone how you feel. It's vulnerable.

The day and time someone dies are only known by God. We live like we have eternity to love those God has given us, but we don't.

If you love someone, tell them...often.

Tell them specifically what you love about them. Tell them why you love them. Show them you love them.

You do not have to adopt my ideas. You can make your own. The point is to be intentional about bringing heaven to earth. Ohh baby do you know what that's worth?

Application: Find one person this week that you can bring heaven to earth for and make a difference.

Questions:

1. What is your favorite song from the eighties?
2. Let's spend some time brainstorming. What are some ways that we can bring heaven to earth in our community? In your family? In your church? In this group? To the nations?
3. What are some areas in which you've experienced hell on earth?

4. Who do you know that needs to experience heaven this week? How can we pray for them?

5. What is God saying to you from this chapter?

CHAPTER 3

JESUS ISN'T A PURSE

We often treat Jesus like he's an accessory to our lives. We like to walk our own way, do our own thing, and then add Jesus to our lives. Like a purse, belt, or hat, we add Jesus to who we are.

Our identity is so wrapped in what we do that we've tried to force Jesus into a verb. When I lived in Texas I saw there were Cowboy Christians. It was a church that reached out to those who found their identity in the Wild West. They were cowboys who loved horses, chaps, boots...and Jesus.

We have groups for athletes who love Jesus. They love sports, train hard to become great at athletics, spend lots of money on equipment...and love Jesus.

We have Christian books, clubs, and even food. When I worked at a Christian bookstore, I bought and took a bite of the Bible Bar. It tasted gag nasty. I guess for some religion is all about penance for sins and the Bible Bar is a way to pay. I took one bite of that thing and instantly thanked God for Snickers.

Jesus isn't a verb. He's a noun.

Jesus is a person who is building a kingdom.

We often live like Jesus owes us something. The thought is "Make what I am doing better." Like an accessory. Jesus isn't a purse.

Jesus isn't an addition. He is in place of. To truly get the benefits of Jesus' kingdom, you have to allow him to replace your entire operating system.

To some of the first Christians, the apostle Paul coached them by writing...

> **You were taught, with regard to your former way of life, to put off your old self, which is being corrupted by its deceitful desires; to be made new in the attitude of your minds; and to put on the new self, created to be like God in true righteousness and holiness. (Ephesians 4:22–24)**

Imagine having a computer that becomes corrupted. There is a file that is so corrupted the entire computer will not work properly. Naturally you buy a new computer. Now imagine you copy the corrupted file and intentionally place it on your computer.

Why would you do that?

Maybe it's because you were used to the old operating system? Maybe it was because you didn't understand just how serious the virus was?

Who knows the reason. The truth is if you were to do that it would be incredibly difficult to explain.

That's Paul's point.

When a person becomes a Christian, they get a new operating system. The new system reveals just how corrupt the old system was.

The problem is the old system is comfortable. It's easy. It's what everyone else is doing. In order to go back to the old system, you have to be intentional. You don't accidentally go back. At the same time, in order to move forward you have to be intentional. You don't accidentally move forward.

The pull to our old self is strong. I feel it. I desire comfort. I want life to be easy.

I often hear people offer judgmental statements about those who receive government handouts. I'm not in a place to judge. The truth is, when it comes to my struggles, I often just want God to give me a handout and quickly fix it.

A few years ago, I was deeply hurt by some people that I cared about. In every relationship it takes two, so I never want to paint a picture that I always handle things perfectly. There was lots of drama. Lots of hurt feelings. Lots of sleepless nights. The end of it was the most personal to me. In one heated conversation it was said to me, "I disagree with you, but I view our relationship like my marriage. I don't always agree with my wife, but I'm not going anywhere." Two weeks later this friend walked away.

I did not take that well.

At this time, I had recently been diagnosed with sleep apnea. I bought a CPAP that worked wonders. I had no idea how tired I was all the time until I started using the CPAP. After using the CPAP, I no longer felt like falling asleep all throughout the day. One night after the conversation I mentioned above, I woke up feeling like I couldn't breathe. I have done enough counseling to know about panic attacks. I sat quietly for a few minutes feeling like I wasn't getting any air. I moved to jump up when I realized I hadn't turned on my CPAP that night. Oops. I thought, "I'm not having a panic attack! Yay!"

I wish that was the case.

The next night the same thing happened, but this time the CPAP machine was on. I jumped out of bed and my wife asked, "What's wrong?" I declared, "I can't breathe." It took a few minutes, but I eventually was able to get my breath back.

Sometimes people view things like worry, panic, or depression as weakness. I don't. The human body is complex. It is often difficult to understand what is going on inside. Emotions are especially difficult to decipher. During this season I was reading my Bible daily. I believed in God! I was plugged into the church. Being a Christian doesn't mean we are immune from issues. Seeking help is not weak. It's incredibly strong. Seeking help and then applying what we learn is often how God grows our faith.

I ended up seeing a counselor because of this situation. Through some time, seeing a counselor, and having a great support system, I thought I moved on. I no longer had panic attacks. My demeanor went back to the happy optimism that I typically experience.

I thought I had moved on, but one thing made it clear that I had not.

From April to September of that year, I put on sixty pounds. I'm a stress eater. I also have yet to experience the joy of seeing abs. Sometimes I think I want a six-pack, but then pizza. Pizza is glorious. Pizza makes me feel happy. It also makes me gain weight.

In September of that year, I was faced with the reality of what I had done. I ate my feelings and got myself to the heaviest I'd ever been in my life. I immediately started dieting, working out more, and making changes. It's amazing to me how easy it is to gain weight and how difficult it is to lose. After one week I felt exhausted. I asked God to just take the weight off me. He didn't listen. I was looking for a handout.

It may not be with weight, but in some area of your life you've wanted God to instantly fix something. When life gets hard humans have to resist getting soft.

Life isn't easy. It's challenging.

Often the problems that we spend years getting ourselves into we want God to instantly fix.

I'm not saying that God won't instantly heal someone. It's been my experience that quick fixes and handouts do not solve the real problem. When we endure the hard work of life change, we receive the reward. The reward is life change.

The apostle Paul wrote…

> [C]ontinue to work out your salvation with fear and trembling, for it is God who works in you to will and to act in order to fulfill his good purpose. (Philippians 2:12b–13)

As humans we tend to be people of extremes. A lot of people fall into one of two camps. One camp is about being a self-made human. Working hard will fix everything. The other camp is all about having no power. I'm not sure either camp is healthy. On the one side, being a self-made person leads to pride and disastrous pitfalls. On the other hand, living a powerless life leads to a victim mentality. It's the thought that life is difficult because it's someone else's fault.

I love what Paul wrote in the verse you just read. Paul paints a picture of a tension.

The tension is we are powerless over sin. We are weak. If we had the power to defeat sin, we wouldn't stumble so often. Paul writes, "It is God who works in you." At the same time Paul says, "Continue to work out your salvation."

Translation: Do your part and trust God to do his.

To be "saved" is a gift from God. It's not something that I can do on my own. Once a person is saved it takes a relationship to experience growth. Doing nothing and asking God to do all the work is lazy. Doing everything and not trusting God is prideful. There is a tension that we have to face.

I love what author Mark Batterson says,

"PRAY like it depends on God. WORK like it depends on you."[1]

There are days I don't feel like going to the gym. That's where I ask God to give me the strength to go against what I want to do. There are lots of times where I don't want to read the Bible. But if I wait until I feel like doing what I should do, I'll never arrive. I like comfort. You do too.

It's in the times where I feel like my spirit is resisting that I know just how desperately I need God. My natural pull is to go back to the old operating system and rebel. In those moments I need God to do what only he can do.

Followers of Jesus aren't perfect, but they also aren't resisting. I am far from perfect. Thank God for grace. But when you feel you are being resistant to Jesus' following, you are allowing your old self to come out.

---

1   Mark Batterson (@MarkBatterson), Twitter, January 1, 2013, 8:29 a.m.

Whenever I feel resistance to doing something good, I know my heart is trying to go backward. The heart is so deceptive.

A prayer I often pray is "God, soften my heart." I don't want to resist God. I want to be ready to say yes to anything he asks me to do. If he asks me to give financially, I want to say yes. I know the blessing of obeying Jesus is way more beneficial than the selfishness of following my own desires.

Let me ask you some questions. If you have made a decision to follow Jesus, are you open to what he says?

Are you listening to what he says?

Do you seek to know where he wants you to go?

Do you live life like Jesus is accessory or do you give him control of your heart?

It's always scary to let go of control, but with God it's always worth it. A life following God's plans is always more fulfilling than a life ignoring his plans.

Once you get the new operating system then the question to ask is, "What am I doing to advance the kingdom?"

Application: To focus more on Jesus and less on yourself, think about one practical way to advance the kingdom of God today. Pray for an opportunity and then do it.

Questions:
1. What is your biggest takeaway from this chapter?
2. It may be hard to admit, but what is an area where you may want to resist God? Is it finances, forgiving someone, grace, etc.?
3. What can you do to resist making Christianity all about you?
4. What is God saying to you from this chapter?

YOU MISSPELLED CHRISTIAN

CHAPTER 4

THE BATTLE FROM WITHIN

The greatest battles you will ever fight are the battles within.

Every human is wired with self-interest. We are wired to seek pleasure. So much so that we will focus on pleasure even at the expense of the rest of our lives.

If I touch a hot burner I feel the effect of it immediately and take my hand off. We often wrongly believe that sin is like a hot burner. The truth is we don't always see the impact of our poor choices until a later date.

Because of that we are all tempted to seek momentary pleasure at the expense of the rest of our lives. We think we got away with it, when in reality sin always has a way of finding us out.

It's why so many humans abuse their bodies. We are addicted to pleasure even at the expense of the quality of our lives.

THE COMFY CHAIR

One of the greatest inventions in the history of mankind is the comfy chair. Do you have a chair at home that is your comfy chair? It doesn't matter if I'm tired or not, I will fall asleep in my comfy chair. I love the comfy chair.

There is a great quote by Academy Award winner Robert De Niro,

"If it's the right chair, it doesn't take too long to get comfortable in it."[1]

And isn't that the goal of our lives? To get comfortable?

Whether or not you have defined that as the goal of your life, research shows that humans are geared to find what is comfortable and to resist any form of pain or discomfort.

So, anything that stresses us, causes anxiety or discomfort, we are wired to avoid. So we seek to live life in the comfy chair. I love the comfy chair.

Now, we truly are wired to spend some time in the comfy chair, but there is a danger in hanging out here. If we aren't careful the comfy chair becomes a way of life. We have all heard the phrase *comfort zone*. The comfort zone, according to author Brené Brown:

"Where our uncertainty, scarcity and vulnerability are minimized—where we believe we'll have access to

1   Robert De Niro, *Brainy Quote*, https://www.brainyquote.com/quotes/robert_de_niro_460676.

enough love, food, talent, time, admiration. Where we feel we have some control."[2]

—Brené Brown

So, our comfort zone or the comfy chair is where we go to feel some control. It's where we go to escape. It's also where most of our bad habits hang out. You see, the problem with the comfort zone is that we are also wired for some sort of stimulation. So the comfort zone removes the stress we feel, but then we get bored. According to psychologist Phil Stutz and psychotherapist Barry Michels,

"Merely escaping pain isn't enough for us. We insist that the pain be replaced with pleasure. We do this with an endless array of addictive activities. Examples include internet surfing, drugs and alcohol, pornography, the aptly named 'comfort food.' Even gambling and shopping are pleasures of a sort. All these behaviors are widespread—our entire culture is looking for a Comfort Zone."[3]

—Barry Michels

Did you catch why this is such an important topic? The comfort zone is a place we go to escape, but escaping isn't enough. We

2   Brené Brown, a research professor at the University of Houston Graduate College of Social Work and author of *The Gifts of Imperfection: Let Go of Who You Think You're Supposed to Be and Embrace Who You Are* (Center City, MN: Hazelden Publishing, 2010). Quote accessed online.

3   Barry Michels, "The Comfort Zone: Hiding in Plain Sight," *Psychology Today,* May 8, 2012, https://www.psychologytoday.com/us/blog/the-tools/201205/the-comfort-zone.

need pleasure, so we fill the need with stuff that is bad for us. When we live in the comfort zone, we get bored and seek out pleasure. That's not the way God intends life to be lived. The comfy chair was meant to be a temporary place to rest.

It doesn't matter who you are, if you are living in the comfy chair you don't look ready for action. In the comfy chair, if God comes along and asks you to do something really hard, your first response will be "No!"

So much of the American dream is based off getting comfortable. For a lot of us, that's what we're really after—comfort, safety, security. But you were meant for something more than life in the comfy chair. We were meant for adventure. We were meant to make a difference. And when you follow Jesus, he will lead you to take steps that scare you in order to help you grow.

Comfy chairs are amazing, but when it comes to the kingdom of God, the comfy chair is a vacation and not a final destination.

If you stay in your comfort zone you will never leave your current view of life.

The book of Acts starts with Jesus spending forty days with his disciples. He has just risen from the dead, which is a pretty big deal. He gathers them outside and gives them this one last challenge.

> But you will receive power when the Holy Spirit comes on you; and you will be my witnesses in Jerusalem, and in all Judea and Samaria, and to the ends of the earth." After he said this, he was taken up before their very eyes, and a cloud hid him from their sight. (Acts 1:8–9)

Did you catch what Jesus said to them? He promises they are going to get the Holy Spirit. The Holy Spirit is the redheaded stepchild of the Trinity. He's often left out of conversations about God. We talk a lot about God the Father and Jesus the Son, but we diminish the significance of the Holy Spirit.

Today, because of what Jesus said, we have the ability to experience something that the great heroes of the Old Testament longed for. People often say how cool it would be to experience the miracles that God did in the Old Testament. It would be cool to be Moses and experience the waters parting in the Red Sea. It would be cool to be Daniel and experience God's protection in the lions' den. It would be cool to be Joshua and experience God's miracle of making the sun stand still. If you read the Old Testament, there are some phenomenal miracles and it is easy to get somewhat envious of the men and women who lived them. But we get to experience something they would have been envious of. We get to experience the Holy Spirit of God. In the Old Testament the Holy Spirit was around but his power was only known by certain select people. Today, because of Jesus we get the Holy Spirit of God. That's exciting. And you can tell if you have the Holy Spirit inside of you because he is somewhat annoying. No offense. The Holy Spirit is constantly nudging followers of Jesus outside of their comfort zones. The Holy Spirit will allow seasons of rest, but eventually the Spirit gets antsy and starts moving and shaking.

I love the phrase Christians have used for centuries to describe a relationship with God. It's called a walk with God. I think that's so appropriate because walking indicates forward motion. You don't walk in the comfy chair.

Sir Isaac Newton's First Law of Motion states, "An object at rest stays in rest and an object in motion stays in motion."

Isn't that true. I get exhausted from sitting around in my comfy chair all day. I just want to take multiple naps.

The Holy Spirit is active. The Spirit is in motion and is constantly moving in our lives to stretch us. And Jesus says when the Holy Spirit arrives on the disciples they are going to receive power and get to moving.

Walking with Jesus is scary as all get-out because he constantly leads you to places that you would never go without him. It's scary, but it's where the magic happens. The true magic of life is found in the adventure. When we are at a place where we desperately need God, that's one of the best places to be. Think about it...

Did you ever do something you were really proud of when you were in autopilot mode?

The comfy chair leads to autopilot. It leads to just existing and walking through life. There is no adventure in that. In fact, there is exhaustion there. If you are feeling burnout in your job or in life, it's a sign that you are not living in the zone God has created for you. We get more tired and worn out when we are bored and in autopilot. We don't get energy from doing work without a purpose. You know you have the right job when you come alive doing it. And if you are walking with God, the Holy Spirit will constantly be leading you away from what's comfortable, and the truth is you'll thank him for it.

Jesus tells the disciples the Holy Spirit is coming, but let's see what he says they are to do after the Holy Spirit arrives.

"[W]hen the Holy Spirit comes on you; and you will be my witnesses in Jerusalem, and in all Judea and Samaria, and to the ends of the earth."[4]

—Jesus

The disciples go to Jerusalem and wait on the Holy Spirit. The Holy Spirit comes and brings the power. Three thousand people are saved in one day. After that another five thousand people are saved. The Holy Spirit starts moving and people start becoming Christians left and right. I love this idea. I want to be a part of a move of God. I want to see lives radically changed. How cool would it be to be a part of God transforming thousands of lives?

Well, if you keep reading in Acts, the Holy Spirit is moving but the disciples aren't. Jesus told them to go to the ends of the world and to tell people about him. They don't. They hang out in Jerusalem.

The movement of Christianity gets some success, and so often in life success brings complacency. When we achieve what we feel like is success, oftentimes we start to coast because we have now reached the comfort zone.

You read through seven whole chapters of Acts and not one disciple obeys Jesus' command and goes to Judea, Samaria, or the ends of the earth.

You get to chapter 7 and a guy by the name of Saul starts persecuting the Christians. He has an extremist view of God and believes that the Christians are wrong. He approves of the death of one Christian and then seeks to arrest many others. That's where our text picks up.

---

4   Acts 1:8

On that day a great persecution broke out against the church in Jerusalem, and all except the apostles were scattered throughout Judea and Samaria. (Acts 8:1)

Jesus tells the disciples to go to spread his message to the ends of the earth, but first they are supposed to go to Judea and Samaria. They don't. Now, a persecution breaks out and did you catch where the followers of Jesus fled to? Judea and Samaria.

Now, we don't know the exact reason why the disciples didn't go to Judea and Samaria, but we do know about Judea and Samaria. They were near Jerusalem where the disciples were staying, but they were different. Especially Samaria. Samaritans did not like the Jews and the Jews didn't like them back. The Samaritans were not considered pure Jews because they had married non-Jews. There were racial lines drawn and Jews did not associate with Samaritans. Judea is a little better than Samaria for the disciples, but not by much. Most of the disciples were from Galilee. Judeans despised Galileans because they didn't see them as being as sophisticated as them. Galileans spoke a distinct form of Aramaic and the way they spoke was the butt of Judean jokes. I don't know about you, but I don't want to go to places where I know I'm going to be made fun of.

Stick with me on this one. Jesus' disciples were Jews, and the Jews didn't like the Samaritans. Jesus' disciples were from Galilee and Judeans didn't like them. Jesus says, "Go to the people you don't like and tell them about me, and then go to the people who don't like you and tell them about me." And what do the disciples do? They stick around where it's more comfortable. I don't blame them. I don't want to be around people I don't like or people who don't like me. The disciples stayed with what was comfortable.

And that's the same thing you and I are tempted to do. We stick to what is comfortable even when we know there is something better for us.

So how do you know where you've settled in the comfort zone?
1. **Look at what you are avoiding.**
2. **Listen to your excuses.**
3. **Pay attention to your negativity.**

LOOK AT WHAT YOU ARE AVOIDING

When we are avoiding what we need to do, we are in dangerous territory. The pull of comfort is so strong that it leads us away from our responsibilities.

Who are you avoiding talking to? What problems are going unsolved because you are too afraid to confront them? What chores need to be done but you cannot muster the energy? What are you avoiding? Now, the harder question is why you are avoiding it.

When I first felt led to plant a church, I buried the thought deep down. The reason was I was comfortable. Fear of change, fear of leaving, fear of being rejected, and fear of failure were all very real. Six months after first feeling the pull to start a church, I went through a three-week period of depression. I had never experienced depression before. I knew it was depression because I was not motivated by the things I love. I'm a big TobyMac fan and from time to time I like to pretend to rap. At the church I was serving at, I had the opportunity to do a few TobyMac songs with the band. Every time I would feel a sense of energy and excitement. During this period of depression, I had a chance to do a song and it was miserable. The band was on point. The song was hot like fire. But I was miserable.

I went away to a conference called Catalyst. It's an amazing conference that I have attended thirteen times. As soon as I got to Catalyst, the depression left.

When I got home from the conference I felt like myself for the first time in three weeks. On Sunday morning I got up early to pray before heading to the church. My prayer that day was simple. I prayed, "God, please don't let the depression come back."

As soon as I stepped into the doors of the church, I felt the depression come back over me like a thick cloud.

I knew I needed to do something.

The problem was there was nothing wrong.

At that time, I thought depression was linked to an event. I thought depression was the result of being hurt. Nothing was wrong. In fact, life was the best it had ever been.

After ten years of infertility, my wife was pregnant with twins. The church I was working at was growing, and seeing hundreds come to know Jesus. I had job security and truly loved my job.

My amazing boss paid for me to go see a counselor. I was scheduled for four sessions, but after the third session the counselor told me I'm good to go. Wait! What?

I walked to the parking lot after that third session incredibly confused. How was I good to go? Why didn't he want to see me for the fourth time? We hadn't solved any problems. In fact, I didn't even know what the problem was.

As I was standing outside the counselor's office, I reflected on what I talked about. I talked about my fears. My fears of leaving my comfort zone. My fears of leaving when it was way easier to stay.

After that revelation the depression went away instantly. I now had my answer. I was afraid. Most of the time, we know the right answer, but fear causes us to freeze. We often look for other people to give us the answer. We don't need answers. What we need is someone to believe in us. We need someone to inspire us to overcome our fears.

From that moment on I knew I was going to plant a church. There was one problem. I didn't have a fat clue how to plant a church. I did what so many Christians do. I prayed about it.

I believe in prayer. Often, though, Christians use prayer as an excuse to stay when they know they should go. That was me. I prayed that God would open a door. It bought me some time to remain comfortable. If God opened a door then I didn't have to do any of the hard work.

Remember in the first chapter the pastor I got to meet, Andy Stanley? Well, my friend Chad Johnson asked me to go out to Catalyst West in California to help him. I viewed it as one last hurrah before my twins were born. That trip was life changing. Not just because I got to meet Andy Stanley. After I picked him up from the airport, I got to hear him speak.

Andy started his sermon by talking about a time where he went through a season of depression. He talked about the fears he had leaving his dad's church. The depression was linked to the thought of leaving what he thought he would never leave. He was set for the rest of his life to take over at the church in which his dad was the pastor. His dad is pretty famous. Charles Stanley is one of the most loved and respected pastors in America. When Andy was feeling a pull to leave, he went through a season of depression. He went to see a counselor. All of this resonated with me because of what I went through a few months earlier.

Andy's sermon was on courage. In the sermon he challenged us by saying, "Have the courage to leave when it would be easier to stay."[5]

Are you joking me?!

What are the chances that I fly out to California from Virginia to help my friend Chad out at a conference and the sermon is a direct punch in my throat.

I'm sure God used that sermon in a lot of other people's lives, but it was the reason God sent me to California.

Often new experiences bring change because we are forced out of our comfy chair. I went home from that conference and told my wife we were planting a church. It took me a total of two years from the original idea to actually leaving to plant a church. Leaving was so difficult because it was so comfortable. Fear paralyzes us.

But the Holy Spirit has a way of leading us to the uncomfortable. And look at what happens next in the book of Acts.

Those who had been scattered preached the word wherever they went. (Acts 8:4)

Now, the sad thing is Jesus' disciples were told to go and they stayed. They ended up missing out on being a part of the next movement of God. In fact, in the first eight chapters of Acts Jesus' disciple Peter is a major player. But he decides to stay in Jerusalem. So, God raises up someone who will go to the ends of the earth. A guy by the name of Paul. Paul goes on to become the featured person God uses in the rest of the book of Acts. He goes on to be a

---

5   Andy Stanley, "Take Courage" (sermon, Catalyst West 2012, Orange County, CA, April 2012).

missionary to the ends of the earth. He goes on to write half of the New Testament. You want to talk about momentum?

For the first few chapters Peter is a central figure. For the rest of the New Testament he becomes a bit player. I'm not trying to judge Peter, but I wonder how many adventures he would have experienced if he obeyed Jesus and left the comforts of Jerusalem? He was there when Jesus said to go to the ends of the earth. And yet he stayed.

Listen, God will use someone to accomplish his will. He doesn't force you to. If you want to stay in what's comfortable then you are free to do that, but just know you miss out on God experiences when you live in the comfy chair.

I know it's scary to make changes. I know it's scary to do things that are not comfortable to you. But…

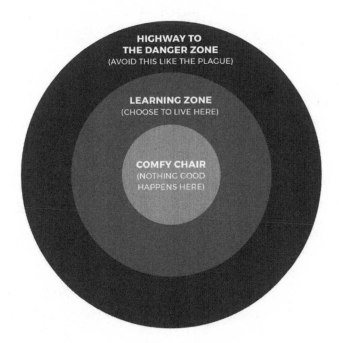

If you stay in your comfort zone
you will never leave your current view of life.

So how do you leave the comfort zone? You have to walk toward some things you fear.

Even if it's a baby step.

We often miss out because of our addiction to comfort.

The majority of people live in the comfort zone. Depending on whose research you read, on average 70 percent of people live in the comfort zone of life. Nothing productive happens there. Only 20 percent of people live in the learning zone. Ten percent of people live in the danger zone. That's the people who may be addicted to adrenaline, jump out of airplanes without a parachute, or do other potentially harmful experiences.

The learning zone is where we want to live. This is where people walk toward challenges. It may be baby steps, but taking steps toward growth means you are learning.

If you are not growing, you are dying. It may be a slow death, but it's still death.

The old operating system is so comfortable it becomes the go-to when life gets hard. We would rather live in the comfort of selfishness than walk through the discomfort of growth.

As a Christian you have never arrived. There is always more growth to happen. That's exciting. I'm not a finished product. Until I'm dead I get to fail into learning more about the grace of God. But I don't learn if I don't grow and I don't grow if I don't move.

The kingdom of God is on the move. It's filled with constant growth, movement, and change. There is nothing comfortable about following Jesus, but it leads to the greatest joys humans can experience.

I love what pastor and author Mark Batterson says,

"Quit living life as if the purpose is to arrive safely in Heaven."[6]

The kingdom of God is to be experienced here on earth. Now. What are you avoiding? Walk toward it. Take a baby step. You don't have to overcome your fears in one day.

The funny thing about fear is that as massive as it is, the way to defeat it is by taking little steps.

Massive leaps are too scary to take. The way to consistently overcome fear is one step at a time.

LISTEN TO YOUR EXCUSES

Excuses are like a child's blankie. Often when a child is scared they will cover their face with their blanket. It provides some sort of imaginary protection. The truth is the blanket isn't going to protect you from much more than a sneeze.

What are your excuses?

I'm not successful because _____.

I'm not happy because _____.

I'll never do something significant because _____.

What are your excuses?

The hardest battles you will fight are the battles within. Until you are willing to stand toe-to-toe with your excuses, you'll never take a step toward your fears.

---

6   Mark Batterson and Richard Foth, *A Trip around the Sun: Turning Your Everyday Life into the Adventure of a Lifetime* (Grand Rapids: Baker Books, 2015). Quote accessed online.

One way to change your perspective is to add "yet" to your excuses.

Whatever your problems are, they aren't solved...yet. Whatever is holding you back hasn't been overcome...yet.

PAY ATTENTION TO YOUR NEGATIVITY

I'm convinced when a person lives an amazing story, they don't have time to criticize someone else's story.

Negativity is often a result of inactivity.

So often in life we think that the people who are great are great because they were born that way. That's just not true. Anyone great is because they refused to settle for less than.

> **"If you want to make a difference, step over the line and into that second mile, because magical things happen there. There's joy and fun and reward in that second mile."**[7]
>
> **—Dan Cathy**

I love that quote. The second mile is what separates great people from everyone else. If there is an area in your life that you are not happy with, it is because you have settled. We've settled for good enough when God has called us to be great. We've settled for okay when God has called us to be excellent. We've settled for less because it's easier than going the second mile. But the real magic of life happens in the second mile.

---

7   Dan Cathy, Chick-fil-A Customer Service Book.

We stop living our story when we complain about someone else. Negativity has a way of interrupting the chapter God is writing in our lives.

If you are bored, there is a great chance you'll have time to criticize others.

When you are fulfilling your mission for God there is no time to complain. You are too productive doing what God wants you to do.

Application: Take one step out of your comfort zone. Embrace the fear that comes with it. It's okay if it's a small step. Just take a step.

Questions:
1. What is your comfy chair of life?
2. What are you avoiding currently?
3. What excuses do you make?
4. What is one way you can eliminate an excuse?
5. What are some common things you go negative about?
6. What is God saying to you from this chapter?

CHAPTER 5

YOUR ATTITUDE DETERMINES THE QUALITY OF YOUR DESTINATION

A bad attitude can turn paradise into a punishment. The truth is whatever you are looking for, you will find. If you are looking for negativity, you'll find it. If you are looking for problems, you'll find them. If you are looking for God, you'll find him. Even in tough circumstances you can find him.

In order to bring the kingdom of heaven to earth, we have to get over ourselves. It's not easy. But nothing worth having ever is.

What if the reason we miss God is because of our attitude and not our reality?

It drives me crazy when one of my kids says, "I'm bored." That is not a reality...it's a choice. You don't have to be bored. There are a bazillion toys in your room. We own a Ms. Pac-Man arcade game from the 1980s. It's glorious. We have an iPad. We have cable television. We have hundreds of movies. We have a playground in our backyard. We live in a neighborhood close to some school friends. Boredom is a result of an ungrateful heart. It's a choice.

My point is we often miss out on what God has given us because we are focused on what we don't have. We can miss God when we focus on ourselves.

Exodus is the second book of the Bible. It is the story of God's people, the Israelites, exodusing from slavery in Egypt into the promised land. Where we are going to pick up in the story is after Israel miraculously escapes from Egypt with the help of God and they are now in the wilderness. There are a million people in the wilderness and their leader is a man named Moses. The Old Testament of the Bible was written in Hebrew. In Hebrew the name Moses is pronounced Charlton Heston. I'm kidding. For those of you who don't get that joke, Charlton Heston played Moses in the very famous movie *The Ten Commandments*. I digress.

> In the desert the whole community grumbled against Moses and Aaron. The Israelites said to them, "If only we had died by the Lord's hand in Egypt! There we sat around pots of meat and ate all the food we wanted, but you have brought us out into this desert to starve this entire assembly to death." (Exodus 16:2–3)

Your attitude is incredibly powerful. We often think that some people are dealt better circumstances than others. The truth is everyone you know has some difficult circumstances. And it's not a competition. If someone has overcome their difficulties it has to do with their attitude and not their circumstances.

Have you ever heard of the placebo effect? The placebo effect has been around since the sixteenth century. It's the idea that humans have the potential to find healing based off how they think. Patients would be given a placebo, which was a pill or medicine that had no healing ingredients in it. They were told the pill would heal whatever sickness they had. Because patients believed this, at times up to 80 percent of the patients were healed. Now, from this research has come the nocebo effect. Nocebo is the interesting impact of the potential symptoms of the fake medication. Some of the placebo patients who read the labels saw there were potential side effects, such as nausea, stomach pains, itching, bloating, depression, sleep problems, and loss of appetite, and as a result they developed the side effects mentioned. The nocebo effect shows the power of our attitude. More research has shown that when studying to become doctors, oftentimes medical students get sick...

"One study showed 79% of medical students report developing symptoms suggestive of the illnesses they are studying. Because they get paranoid and think they'll get sick, their bodies comply by getting sick."[1]

This is powerful stuff. A few months ago, my doctor put me on some medication and said he wanted to watch me because it can affect some people's hearts. The first two days I took the medication I convinced myself I had sixteen heart attacks. It was like Fred Sanford from the TV show *Sanford and Son*, "This is the big one. I'm comin' to join you, Elizabeth!"

---

1   Henry K. Beecher, M.D., Boston, "The Powerful Placebo," *J.A.M.A.*, December 1955. Quote accessed online.

Your attitude is incredibly important. It might be more important than anything else in your life.

Your attitude determines the quality of your destination.

In the text you just read from Exodus, the Israelites have escaped from Egypt and they are now in the desert called Sin. Some of you have been there. It's also known as Las Vegas. I'm kidding. The point is the Israelites have experienced God do some amazing miracles. They have been delivered from slavery. It's an amazing story, but moments later this happens...

In the desert the whole community grumbled against Moses and Aaron. (Exodus 16:2)

In the desert the whole community grumbled. Today, we live in a culture of complaint.

Everybody is complaining. Everybody is grumbling. The issue is that based off science and research, what we complain about has very little to do with our circumstances and a lot to do with our attitude.

Rational Emotive Behavior Therapy—"How people react to events is determined largely by their view of the events, not the events themselves."[2]

—Albert Ellis

In other words...

---

2 Albert Ellis developed REBT in the mid-1950s and is considered the second-most influential psychotherapist in history.

Your attitude determines the quality of your destination.

If you are not enjoying life, don't blame your circumstances, blame your attitude. That doesn't mean that things don't need to change in your life. You may have to make some changes, but grumbling doesn't change your life. Grumbling wrecks your health, makes you not enjoyable to be around, and makes you miss out on God.

Let's keep reading and see what happens next.

> The Israelites said to them, "If only we had died by the Lord's hand in Egypt! There we sat around pots of meat and ate all the food we wanted, but you have brought us out into this desert to starve this entire assembly to death." (Exodus 16:3)

This is grumbling at its best. Ultimately, they are saying they wish they were still in slavery. Do what?

Why would they want to be enslaved?

Sometimes it's easier to stay in the comfort of slavery than in the uncertainty of freedom.

The Israelites are grumbling against God. When you grumble it's about God. When you grumble it's not to fix the problem. It's selfish. Grumbling is about trying to find someone who agrees with your perspective.

A RABBIT TRAIL

Stick with me on this. I want to address something really quickly that is incredibly important to this understanding.

There is a difference between grumbling and groaning. I once taught this in a sermon and a group of high school students giggled at the word *groaning*. It's a funny word out of context. But stick with me on this. Scripture is filled with people who struggle. Scripture is filled with people who go through difficult times. Often, we think that if we have a relationship with God only good things will happen. That's not true. The struggle is a part of it. In fact, there is as much struggle, pain, and hurt in Scripture as there is victory. The difference is, for people who have God, we have someone who hears our groans.

God heard their groaning and he remembered his covenant with Abraham, with Isaac and with Jacob. (Exodus 2:24)

Groaning comes out of difficult circumstances and is to God. Grumbling is out of not getting our way and is about God. There is a major difference.

God hears our groans. In fact, God is often the closest when we are in the valley. I hate the pain of life. Life hits hard sometimes. Being a Christian and living for God's kingdom doesn't remove you from the difficulties of this world. But walking with God is what gets you through the difficulties of life.

Groaning doesn't scare God, it often draws us into his presence. In fact, God is big enough to not only handle our groan, he responds to it.

A relationship is not truly a relationship unless you walk through the highs and lows of life with someone. When life hits hard look to the people who stick around. Those are the ones who didn't just like you for something you could offer, but truly love you. God is one who sticks around. He loves you. It's okay to bring hurt, pain, and disappointment to God. Groan.

Grumbling is about not getting our way. Whenever someone grumbles they don't really want to take care of the problem. They simply want someone to agree with them. It's why we grumble about people to people who cannot do anything about the problem. Very rarely does someone bring a complaint to a person who can actually solve the problem. We grumble because we want sympathy.

Grumbling is a negative attitude that does not honor God.

We often grumble because we don't trust that God's plan is best for us. When we don't get our way, we respond like toddlers.

When you walk with God he will walk with you through every season of life. If you have a problem or a complaint, bring it to God.

It's a good thing to practice in life.

When you have a grumble, go to someone who can do something about it. A principle that I try to live by is "Talk to people and not about people." Talking about people doesn't solve a problem. It makes you feel better, but the problem isn't solved.

Jesus gave the system for how to deal with conflict. It's found in Matthew 18. I try to use Matthew 18 like a verb. When there is conflict, I have to choose to Matthew 18 it.

Because we are fearful creatures, we often avoid having tough conversations. We stuff our feelings down. Your frustrations will come out somewhere.

I love the quote from my ministry coach...

"A frustration is never content until it's expressed."[3]
— Chris Sonksen

That quote is so true. A true frustration will come out. Sometimes we vent to people simply because we cannot keep the frustration in. The problem is venting a frustration doesn't solve it. In order to move on from a frustration we must express it to someone who can do something about it. We need to work hard at making sure when our frustrations do come out it is to the right person. A person who can do something about our frustration.

You will have frustrations in life. You will be tempted to grumble about them to people who cannot help solve the problem.

Whenever you are frustrated you will complain to someone. Living to build God's kingdom means we deal with problems and not run away from them. We talk to people instead of about people. We lean in when we want to run away. It's radical.

And when you hurt it's okay to groan to God. It's okay to let God know you have hurt. God's big enough to take our emotional breakdowns. Cry out to God. Groan. In any relationship there are difficulties and that includes our relationship with God. We are fragile humans who can't see what God is up to. When life hits us just right, groan to the one who can actually do something about it.

AND NOW TO OUR REGULARLY SCHEDULED CHAPTER

The problem with the Israelites' complaint is they had forgotten who they were talking about. The same God who delivered them

---

3   Chris Sonksen is the founding pastor of South Hills and founder of ChurchBOOM, a resource for pastors.

from slavery is the one they were complaining about. Instead of complaining they should have been praying. Instead of complaining they should have offered a solution. This is why this is so important.

Your attitude determines the quality of your destination.

You are going somewhere. Whether you enjoy the journey is based off your attitude.

Instead of celebrating the type of God they had, they found a way to complain about him. Not only that, they insult God by saying they had it better off in slavery. The same slavery they groaned about they are now saying they want to go back to. Are you joking me? And that, my friends, is what grumbling is. It's insane. When you go negative it causes you to miss out on the miracles God has given you and it causes you to reimagine the past.

Let's see what happens next.

> The Lord said to Moses, "I have heard the grumbling of the Israelites. Tell them, 'At twilight you will eat meat, and in the morning you will be filled with bread. Then you will know that I am the Lord your God.'"
> That evening quail came and covered the camp, and in the morning there was a layer of dew around the camp. When the dew was gone, thin flakes like frost on the ground appeared on the desert floor. When the Israelites saw it, they said to each other, "What is it?" For they did not know what it was. (Exodus 16:11–15)

This is such an awesome verse. In a way that only God can, he provides a miracle for them. At twilight God provided meat and in the morning, God provided bread. It was a miracle that was supposed to not only stop their complaining but help the Israelites know who God is. At night God provided quail to eat. In the morning they literally woke up to Frosted Flakes on the ground. They're great. When the Israelites saw the frosted flakes they didn't know what it was, so they said, "What is it?" They named the frosted flakes "what is it." Missed opportunity. They should have patented it Frosted Flakes. They didn't know the joys of cereal, so they named it "what is it?"

Can you imagine this with your kids at the breakfast table?

Child: "Mama, what is it?"

Mama: "It's what is it."

Child: "Mama, that's what I'm asking. What is it?"

Mama: "Baby, I heard you, it is 'What is it.'"

Child: "No, mamma, what is it?"

Mama: "It is what it is, child! It's 'What is it.' That's the name. Don't ask me again. You ask me one more time and so help me God! It's 'What is it.' Now go to your room without any 'What is it'!"

They named it manna, which means "what is it." This was such an amazing miracle they stored some of the "what is it" in a jar so they could show future generations this amazing miracle. They grumble, and God provides something so amazing they don't even know how to name it, so they name it "what is it."

Now, if you continue to read on in this you'll see that a lot of the Israelites weren't following God. God gave them very specific instructions and they weren't willing to follow them. I'm convinced whenever there is a Christian complaining it's because they have a heart problem. They aren't willing to do what God has told them to do. Maybe it is to talk to a person one on one. Or maybe it is to make a difficult change. I'm not saying Christians don't have things to complain about. There is a lot of brokenness in the world. What I'm saying is that when a Christian complains it's pointing to a deeper issue. It's easier to complain about others than to love them. It's easier to complain about life than to live in such a way you don't have time to complain. It's easy to complain about someone than it is to talk to someone about a complaint. Complaining doesn't solve anything. Where you see complaining you'll soon see signs of disobedience in other areas of a person's life.

God provided manna, and for a while it was amazing, but after a while the very miracle God provided became a source of their complaint.

Have you ever been there?

Have you ever started something and at first it was amazing, but over time the very thing that you loved became a source of your grumbling? It's like this in marriage. Before marriage, opposites attract. After marriage, opposites attack. It's like this at churches. A person goes to a church and loves everything about it. Then after about a year, maybe two, they start to find some issues. What they used to love they now don't like very much anymore. People jump from church to church and then eventually decide it's too hard to keep leaving. They find a church, settle down, and just stay miserable because the church can't meet their needs. People sit around complaining about the miracles that God is doing in their presence. It's so broken.

Let's fast-forward a little over two years after the manna miracle.

The rabble with them began to crave other food, and again the Israelites started wailing and said, "If

only we had meat to eat! We remember the fish we ate in Egypt at no cost—also the cucumbers, melons, leeks, onions and garlic. But now we have lost our appetite; we never see anything but this manna!" (Numbers 11:4–6)

This is so powerful. Did you catch where the complaint started? With the rabble. The riffraff. The rabble is a reference to a group who decided to go with the Israelites. They were not Israelites. They had seen the amazing miracles of God in Egypt and jumped on board to be a part of the excitement. In essence they were the first bandwagon fans. This group were spectators. Spectators turn to critics.

It's like this in the church world. If you take on the role of a spectator, you will consume. As you consume, you will eventually reject the very thing that once gave you life. You will leave a church feeling spit out and used because it no longer meets your needs.

The way to avoid this is to invest in an unchurched/de-churched person and invite them with you to church. Through the eyes of an unchurched person you will see church differently. You will care about things that you didn't use to care about. You will want everything to be just right. Investing in others and then having them come with you to church is not the only answer to protect yourself from consuming. But it's an answer.

Spectators find things to complain about. It's easier to complain than it is to play the game.

Complaints started with the rabble because they began to crave something other than the "what is it." The complaining of the small rabble ended up impacting the entire Israelite community. And once again they lie to themselves and say, "Remember how great we had it in Egypt?"

Negativity breeds negativity.

This kind of thinking happens all the time in churches. Someone will leave a church and go to a new church. They will love it at first, but after a few months they start to grumble. They say things like "Well, at my last church we did _____."

Wait a second.

Didn't you leave your last church because you had issues with it? Then why do you want to bring that into this church? Don't let someone grumble to you about the place God has you in. It will impact how you see the miracle God has given you.

Negativity breeds negativity. You have to resist it like the plague or you will catch it.

If you love your job, don't let someone grumble to you about the boss. Shut it down. If you love your friends, don't let someone grumble against them. Shut it down.

Just know, if someone is going to talk about someone else to you they will talk about you to someone else. So, shut it down. Don't let someone else's grumble become your story.

One way to shut it down is by simply saying, "That's not my story. I'm happy to set up a meeting for you to talk to the person you are talking about." It's not rude. You are not telling them they are Satan's spawn. You are simply protecting yourself from the rabble.

This is so important. Negativity breeds negativity. If you are around it you will catch it like the plague.

It's an incredibly contagious thing. Pretty soon everybody is whining. See, the thing is, the reason I grumble is it reinforces my sense of superiority. When I'm grumbling about something else, I don't have to look at myself. I don't have to look at my problems. Grumbling is incredibly toxic. It can destroy a family. It can destroy an office. It can mess up a church.

You have some manna in your life. There is something God has given you, and because of your attitude you are missing the blessing of it. If you are married, your spouse may be God's manna from heaven. Sure, your spouse isn't perfect, but don't miss the miracle because of what you don't have. Of course, there are abusive spouses that need to be separated from. There are deadbeat spouses out there. This isn't about them. This is about the spouse who is trying, but still falls so short because of your comparisons or unrealistic expectations.

If you have kids, they are manna from heaven. That doesn't mean they are perfect. Ask anyone who is infertile, and you'll see that having kids is a miracle.

If you have a job that pays you money, it is a gift from God. If you have a church where the leadership is sound, and they teach the Bible, it's a gift from God.

Don't you dare let complaining happen!

Don't you dare!

Don't listen to it. If it's a real complaint do something about it. If it's a real issue help find a solution. If it's sin, then read Matthew 18 and muster the courage to do something about it. Just don't complain.

You've got some manna in your life. It's easy to get tired of the manna God gives, and then complain.

You have got to get creative or you are going to curse the blessing God sent you. The Israelites may have been a little tired of manna, but that just meant they needed to be creative. It was time for them to be to manna as Bubba from *Forrest Gump* was to shrimp. You can barbecue it, boil it, broil it, bake it, sauté it, pan-fried, deep-fried, stir-fried. There's pineapple manna, lemon manna, coconut manna, pepper manna, manna soup, manna stew, manna salad, manna and potatoes, manna burger, manna sandwich. That-that's about it.

If God has given you manna, you've got to make the most of it.

Your attitude determines the quality of your destination. You have something God has given you. Whether you enjoy it or not is up to you.

Let's keep going…

Moses heard the people of every family wailing at the entrance to their tents. The Lord became exceedingly angry, and Moses was troubled. (Numbers 11:10)

Okay, now why is God angry? He is angry because this is a heart issue and not a provision issue. No matter what God does, the Israelites will find a way to grumble. Your attitude determines the quality of the destination.

When you have a bad attitude, you have two choices.
1. Change the circumstance.
2. Change your attitude.

We cannot always change our circumstances. At least not right away. It takes some time to find a new job. It's not the smartest thing to leave a job before you've found a new one. You cannot change circumstances when they are out of your control. We cannot control traffic, or the weather, or other people. If your bad attitude is because of something you can change, then change it. Do the work to find a solution to the problem.

If you cannot change the circumstance, then change your attitude.

It's difficult to complain about the things you are thankful for. I'm not thankful for every circumstance, but I can be thankful in every circumstance.

The apostle Paul wrote,

Rejoice always, pray continually, give thanks in all circumstances; for this is God's will for you in Christ Jesus. (1 Thessalonians 5:16–18)

Giving thanks isn't a suggestion, it's a command. If you are a Christian today you are to give thanks in every circumstance. Now, I need to point out something incredibly important. Paul does not say give thanks for every circumstance. That would be masochism.

Masochism is the enjoyment of pain or pleasure in being subjected to pain or humiliation.

God is not masochistic, and you shouldn't be either. Paul says give thanks in every circumstance, not for every circumstance.

When my wife and I had a miscarriage, we weren't thankful for that situation. We were thankful in that situation. When our twins had to have surgery at six months old to fix hernias, we weren't thankful for that, we were thankful in that. We were thankful for the doctors and hospitals that took such great care of our kids.

This week you are going to have something unfortunate happen to you...some of which you are not thankful for, but unless you train yourself to become thankful in all circumstances, you will have a miserable time.

It is in thanks that God transforms difficult situations into lessons to learn. There is always something to be thankful for. We either choose to be thankful or we allow difficult circumstances to master us.

As Christians we are allowed to hurt. We are allowed to struggle. It's okay to admit that you don't have your junk together. It's okay to admit that you are sad.

We are thankful in every circumstance, not for every circumstance. The way to remain thankful is to thank God continually. I'm not thankful for a headache, but I'm thankful for the medicine I have to help it go away. I'm not thankful for a child's tantrum, but I'm thankful this is just a phase. I'm not thankful for traffic, but I am thankful to have extra time to think, pray, or listen to music. Be thankful in every season.

You may not have the money you think you need. You may not have the family you think you need. You may not have the looks you used to have. Life may not be what you want at this moment, but you can still find something to be thankful for.

I love the quote by author Max Lucado:

"What if you woke up this morning and had only the things you thanked God for yesterday?"[4]

ATTITUDE MATTERS

Your greatest limitation in life is your attitude, not your ability.

A bad attitude stops you from going the second mile in life. It wrecks the miracle manna God has given you. Change your circumstance or change your attitude.

We cannot control everything that happens to us, but we can control how we respond to what happens to us.

---

4   Max Lucado (@MaxLucado), Twitter, 2011.

Viktor Frankl was a Holocaust survivor who wrote about his experiences in a Nazi concentration camp. Everything was taken away from these prisoners. They were stripped of their clothing, their pictures, and their personal belongings. They even took away their names and gave them numbers. Frankl was number 119,104. Everything was taken away except one thing.

Frankl said,

"Everything can be taken from a man but one thing: the last of human freedoms—to choose one's attitude in any given set of circumstances. When we are no longer able to change a situation, we are challenged to change ourselves."[5]

It's so easy to blame others for our problems. It's easy to think, "I am unhappy because of _____." The truth is that some people have found happiness in worse conditions than you. Giving thanks may not change your circumstance, but it will make it more bearable. You cannot control everything that happens to you, but you can work on controlling your attitude.

Application: Spend time thanking God. If you are currently going through a difficult situation, how can you be thankful in that situation?

Questions:

    1.   What was your biggest takeaway from this chapter?

---

5   Viktor E. Frankl, *Man's Search for Meaning* (New York: Pocket Books, 1997). Quote accessed online.

2. How have you seen negativity change your perspective of something good?

3. Based off this chapter, what is God saying to you?

4. Where do you think God is leading you right now? If you don't know, ask him.

5. Who do you know that doesn't have a relationship with God? How can you love them with no agenda? How can you invest in them? How can you bring heaven to earth?

CHAPTER 6

WORRY IS NOT A SIN

This chapter is all about worry. Now this is a tough subject to write about. It's not tough because the Bible is silent on it. The Bible has a lot to say about worry. In fact, I'm betting that you've heard a sermon or twelve on worry. You've heard a sermon on it and yet you still have moments when you worry. This is a safe place. I won't judge you. Be honest with yourself. You worry. There are times where I worry about things. Worry happens to the best of us.

I want to start by clearing up a few misunderstandings about worry.

Worry Is Not...
1. **Sin**
2. **Easily solved**

First off, worry is not sin. Worry is an emotion. It's a response to our perceived circumstances. Worry is a response in the same way that laughter or crying are. In fact, worry is a natural response. I worry my kids will get hit by a car, so I don't let them play in the street. I worry that my house might get robbed, so I lock my doors. I worry that my hair might look like a bad comb-over, so I shave it off. Worry is a response to our perceived circumstances.

The problem is that most of us worry about things that will never happen. We worry about the what-ifs of this life. What if I don't get the job? What if I make a bad choice? What if I never get married? What if my kid is born ugly and I have to tie a pork chop around his neck to get the dog to play with him? What if? Even when it's not justified, worry is not a sin. It's what we do with worry that becomes the sin.

At times the Christian community has communicated that if you worry it means you don't love Jesus. I do not think Jesus ever communicates that. Worry is a natural thing that God put in our brains. We do have to manage it but should not put shame on an emotion God gave us.

Because we are broken we often need a little help. When my head hurts I don't think, "I just don't love Jesus today. If I loved him more this headache would go away." That thinking is super spiritual. When I'm tired I don't think it's because I don't love Jesus. I know it's because I didn't get enough sleep. The human body is built in with warning systems to help us stay on track. When one goes off we must seek the proper help to get it working right again. Worry is like that. God gave us worry to allow us to show caution or inspire us to take action. When worry becomes paralyzing we must seek some help.

Feel free to disagree with me, but I'm convinced that worry is not a sin. That's the first thing we need to clear up. The second thing we need to clear up is worry is not easily solved. It's not. It's not something that a thirty-minute sermon will cure us of. It's not something that memorizing one verse will make us impervious to. Worry is tricky. Why? It's tricky because of what it is. Look at the definition of worry.

wor·ry
ˈwərē/

verb:

give way to anxiety or unease; allow one's mind to dwell on difficulty or troubles.[1]

The definition states that worry is where we give way to anxiety by allowing our mind to dwell on difficult situations. Worry is thinking about a difficult situation. That's it. The simple antidote to worrying is to simply stop worrying. Right? But that's not really helpful. Worry is not that easily solved.

---

1   Google Dictionary.

Praying is important. Prayer is a crucial part of controlling worry. Far too often we use prayer as an excuse to not take action. At times the answer to the prayer is to simply take action. We pray and ask God to remove a situation or to quickly fix it, but God rarely removes barriers. He often gives us strength to get through them. What most often causes worry are the bombs of life we cannot control.

It's kind of like this.

Imagine you are holding a string tied to a balloon filled with helium. In fact, you are holding a balloon for everything that you worry about. And what are you worried about? The big ones probably include the job, family, health, the economy, safety, how people are going to respond to you, and are you good enough. Now, because each thing that you worry about is represented by a helium-filled balloon, you now have a bunch of balloons dangling over your head. Now as long as you are holding on to those balloons, you can't help but think about them. They are there. No matter how much you try to not think about it, you can't because they are all up in your business. You can't go to the bathroom comfortably because you are holding so many balloons. You can't drive safely because the balloons are in your way. You can't talk to another person without the balloons becoming a major part of the conversation because they are all up in your face. They are hanging over you. It's annoying because they won't go away.

It's the same thing with worry. Worry is "allowing one's mind to dwell on difficulty." As long as worry remains in the think stage, the balloons won't go away. Translation? The worry won't go away as long as you are simply thinking about it. The key to stop worrying is to take action. Make a decision. Do something. Make a choice and watch the pressure go away.

> **"Unless we are occupied with other thoughts, worrying is the brain's default position."[2]**
> **—Dr. Mihaly Csikszentmihalyi**

The default position for the brain is worry. Unless you occupy the mind with something else, your brain's resting place will be worry. That's why it's so crucial to do something with your worry.

---

2   Ray Williams, "Are We Hardwired to Be Negative or Positive?" *ICF,* June 30, 2014, https://coachfederation.org/blog/are-we-hardwired-to-be-negative-or-positive.

Don't think that there is something wrong with you because you worry. You are better than that. Worry is God's way to tell you to take action. I know that worry can be paralyzing, but you must take action. To do nothing is to misuse the gift of worry.

Telling you not to worry is like telling you to forget there are a bunch of balloons floating around your head. The more that you try to not pay attention to the balloons, the more you become consumed with them. The things that I worry about aren't going away. The things you worry about aren't going away. Worry is when our thoughts take us captive.

But that's the funny thing about worry.

A GREAT QUOTE BUT AN EVEN BETTER POINT

"Worry is like a rocking chair, it gives you something to do but it takes you no where."

—Author unknown

Now, a lot of us know this and yet we worry. We know our worry is not doing us any good, but yet it's still there. Hanging over our heads. Again, just telling you not to worry doesn't fix the problem. According to stats, 85 percent of what we worry about never happens. And yet we still worry.

A BETTER SOLUTION THAN TO SIMPLY STOP WORRYING

Thankfully for us worry isn't a new thing. It's something that Jesus' audience struggled with so much that he addressed it. I want to look at what Jesus had to say and see what we can do about it. Let's dive in.

"Therefore I tell you, do not worry about your life, what you will eat or drink; or about your body, what you will wear. Is not life more than food, and the body more than clothes?" (Matthew 6:25)

Now whenever you see the word *therefore* in the Bible you should ask yourself what's it there for. Because in order to get what Jesus is about to say, you have to understand what he just said. And Jesus just finished telling his audience that they cannot serve two masters. Look at it with me...

"No one can serve two masters. Either you will hate the one and love the other, or you will be devoted to the one and despise the other. You cannot serve both God and money." (Matthew 6:24)

Jesus talked about storing up for ourselves treasures in heaven as opposed to treasures on earth. And Jesus' point is that money can be a god. It can be an idol. It's something that can control our thoughts. It so often controls our actions. Now there is nothing wrong with having money. The problem is when your money has you.

And so, Jesus says money will have a hold on you. For example, what would your first thought be if God called you to go on a mission trip to Africa for one month? My thought would be about money. How am I going to raise the funds? How am I going to provide for my family while I am over there? Those are great questions to ask. Those are questions that would have to be answered. And this is where worry comes in. We start asking questions that we don't know the answers to and it stops us from doing what God wants us to do. Therefore, we don't go to Africa because our god is money and it says no. What if God wanted you to give more to your local church? If you don't have the money it becomes stressful to give it. Money is one of those things that can have a crazy power over us.

Now that we have that, let's go back to our first verse.

"Therefore I tell you, do not worry about your life, what you will eat or drink; or about your body, what you will wear. Is not life more than food, and the body more than clothes?" (Matthew 6:25)

Now if this verse stopped here we'd all be in trouble. Jesus says don't worry about your life. Well, that is easy to say when your life is going great. But what is worry? Worry— "Allow one's mind to dwell on difficulty or troubles."

So, let's say that you have a tough situation. Let's say that you don't have enough money to pay your bills. Is Jesus saying that you are just to dismiss that concern and not do anything about it? No!

Jesus isn't calling us to be pacifist hippie lazy faces that don't take any action or care about anything.

Worry is a gauge that should cause you to take action. If the worry is your power is about to be shut off because you can't pay your bills, then maybe the action is to take another job. Or maybe it's to sell your house to get something you can afford. If your worry is remaining happy in your marriage, then your action is to date your spouse and keep the romance alive. If your worry is about living an insignificant life, then your action might be to invest in one person to make a difference. If your worry is about being fired, then your action might be to work harder or to have a backup plan. If your worry is about what others think about you, then I wrote another book about that called *Even If You Were Perfect, Someone Would Crucify You.* I kid, I kid.

The point is that the problem with our worry is that we do nothing with it. We are so paralyzed by our worry that we do nothing. We do nothing but worry. We freak. We dwell on it. We analyze it. And then the worry balloons just hang over our head like a constant reminder.

WORRY IS NOT SIN. WHAT YOU DO WITH WORRY IS.

Jesus points us to take a specific action. Don't just think about your problems. Do something. Let's look at what Jesus says next.

> "Look at the birds of the air; they do not sow or reap or store away in barns, and yet your heavenly Father feeds them. Are you not much more valuable than they? Can any one of you by worrying add a single hour to your life?
> "And why do you worry about clothes? See how the flowers of the field grow. They do not labor or spin. Yet I tell you that not even Solomon in all his splendor was dressed like one of these. If that is how God clothes the grass of the field, which is here today and tomorrow is thrown into the fire, will he not much more clothe you—you of *little faith*?" (Matthew 6:26–31, italics mine)

This is the key for our worry. It's not just to not worry about anything. It's to allow your worry to increase your faith in God.

The bottom line with our worry is that we do not trust that God's got this. Ultimately, it's a control issue. We believe in God, but we don't want to give God control. We worry about what we have to do. We worry about the results of things. We worry about what people will think of us. We worry. Stress. Freak out. And ultimately if your worry doesn't lead you to action, it will lead you to anxiety.

Anxiety is worry on steroids. When you don't take action with a real concern or worry, then the fact there is an unknown ending will drive you crazy. If worry was a balloon with helium, then anxiety is going to fill the balloon with concrete, chain itself to your neck, and throw you in the river.

Look at what Jesus says next.

> "So do not worry, saying, 'What shall we eat?' or 'What shall we drink?' or 'What shall we wear?' For the pagans run after all these things, and your heavenly Father knows that you need them." (Matthew 6:31–32)

Did you catch what Jesus said? He said don't worry about it in the same way that the pagans do. A worry that acts as if we are in control. A worry that acts like it's our kingdom. A worry that acts like God is not in control. A worry that acts like it's all about us. A pagan doesn't have God to help with worry. A Christian does.

OUT OF CONTROL

Now, what I am about to write might cause some to have an anxiety attack.

You are not in control. In fact, there is very little that you do control.

You don't control who you were born to. You don't control what your birth name is. You can't control other people. You can't control the economy. You can't control the weather. You can't control when you die. Now, worry should cause us to try to eat healthy, exercise, and take care of ourselves. We should be concerned with our health in a way that causes us to be healthy. But you can be the healthiest person on the planet and still drop dead in a second from a brain aneurism. You can only eat kale, carb-free, salt-free, taste-free foods and still die in a car accident. I am not trying to scare you, but it's true. We are not in control. Those who try to be in control are never satisfied. We weren't meant to bear the weight of the world.

It's easy to feel stressed, worried, and anxious when you feel like the entire world rests on your shoulders. Your worry often comes from things that you cannot control.

Signs We Love to Be in Control

1. **We do not delegate.** It won't get done if you don't get it done. How's that working out for you? How's that working out for your worry? Delegation is about letting go of the control.

2. **We feel that we can do it better alone.** Not only do you not delegate but you don't delegate because you feel like you can do it better. You are a control freak.

3. **We freak out when others are in the driver's seat.** This is both figurative and literal. This is the wife who grasps the side of the car while letting out a *huge* gasp when her husband is one hundred yards from another vehicle. This is also the person who freaks out when their presidential candidate does not get elected. We love to feel like we are in control, and whenever we are not we *freak*!

This is why it's so easy to freak out about the government. We aren't in control. When your political party is in control, you feel some sort of ease and peace of mind. But when your party is not in control, you freak out. You freak out because you are not in the driver's seat. You say things like "I don't think our country can survive four more years of this president."[3] So far, in America, it has survived. God bless 'Merica.

This is why some of you freak out about storms and weather. Now, should we be safe? Yes. Should we buy flood insurance and get in the bathtub when a tornado is bearing down on us? Yes. Should we take a selfie when we are in the bathtub being safe from the tornado? Yes. That's just what people do these days. Should we be stupid and drive in really bad weather? No! We should be smart. We should do our part, but anxiety is more about control than it is about solutions.

When you feel worried, look at what you can control. If you can do something, then do it. If you are worried about something out of your control, then you have to try and let it go. Do what only you can do and let God do what he can do.

I cannot control the future, but I can control what I do while I wait. I cannot control people, but I can control how I respond to others. I cannot control when I'm going to die, but I can choose how I'm going to live.

We cannot control other people. We cannot control everything that happens to us. To control worry we must do something we can control. I cannot control my circumstances, but I can work on controlling how I respond to my circumstances. I can pray for wisdom when I don't know what to do. I can pray for courage when

---

3   Millions of people after their candidate loses an election.

I do know what to do but I'm too scared to move. There is always something you can do. Do that.

JESUS ISN'T DONE

Jesus isn't done. He closes this section by making a kingdom challenge. Look at what Jesus says.

"But seek first his kingdom and his righteousness, and all these things will be given to you as well. Therefore do not worry about tomorrow, for tomorrow will worry about itself. Each day has enough trouble of its own." (Matthew 6:33–34, italics mine)

Did you catch that? But seek first God and all the rest will follow. Do you spend more time worrying or seeking God? The key to popping your worry balloons is not to stop thinking about it. It's to allow your worry to make you take action. Specifically, the action is to seek God first. Seek God, and the rest will follow. What is the rest? The answers. The solutions. The peace of mind. The ability to walk around without the pressure of worry balloons.

What if we took Jesus' words literally and sought God first? What would that look like?

We often do not seek God first because we love to be in control.

You see, your worry is a gauge that something is not right. And the Christian's response should be to seek first God's kingdom. That is to say God, you are in control. God, I don't understand this, but I trust you. God, this is difficult but I'm going to seek you. Being a Christian isn't about being impervious to the worries of this world. When my kids aren't with me I worry about their safety. When my wife is on a trip I worry about her safety. When I fly I worry that the plane comes with flotation devices but no parachutes. I'm not sure if they know this, but planes crash from the sky. What good is a seat flotation going to do me when we are crashing down in Texas? I've lived in Texas. Everything is bigger in Texas except for the bodies of water. Texas is an entire state made up of concrete. Buildings everywhere. Thanks for the flotation seat but I want a parachute. I digress.

The point is that our worry should cause us to take action. Our action should be to pray to God. Our action should be to seek God. To find God. To trust God in the situation. Our action should be to do whatever God tells us to.

We trust God with our future. We get our hustle on in the present and trust Jesus with the future. I have found when I work on what I can control and trust God with what I cannot control, my worry level shrinks.

Seek God first means when we worry we ask God what to do with our worry. God may lead us to see a counselor. God may lead us to find a medication that will help balance what is off in our brains. God may lead us to realize we aren't seeking God. Worry is complicated. There isn't one answer for worry. There is one starting place. We start by seeking God and then we trust that the rest will follow.

LET'S MAKE THIS PRACTICAL

A very helpful way to seek first God's kingdom is to simply pray through your calendar each day. What do you have to do that day? Start your day before you get out of bed seeking God. God, I have three loads of laundry to do and it's freaking me out. God,

I have to cook for a bunch of people tonight, I need you. God, I'm about to start my new job and I'm a mess. God, I have to talk to someone and I'm worried how she is going to take it. God, I have too much to do and not enough time. God, I'm about to fly to Texas and my plane didn't come with a parachute. God, I have to confront someone today and I'm freaked out about how he might respond.

Seek God first.

First thing. Give him your concerns. Ask him for wisdom. Seek his righteousness, and that is to seek to follow God and do what he says. Seek God and the rest will follow.

A REAL-LIFE EXAMPLE

I'm a pastor. Pastors tend to worry about things. There are not many jobs in the world where one person is supposed to come up with new material each week in an inspiring manner, oversee a staff, oversee a building, raise funds, feel the brunt of people that he loves leaving, wrestling with the hurt of those that come under his care, be a leader, teacher, friend, counselor, all while trying to maintain an amazing family life. I'm not whining. I love my job. I love what I'm called to do. I write all of that just so you know that pastors have a lot on their brains, which so often leads to the balloons of worry. The following story was my worry balloon.

In 2012 I made the biggest faith jump of my life. I left an amazing church and position to start a church. There was no guarantee of people or money. It was scary and exhilarating at the same time. I was in desperate need for God to help me see that he was leading me.

My parents, my brother and his wife, my wife's best friend, our best married couple friends, and a newer couple that we had become really close with had committed to help us start. There were eleven of us total including me and my wife. From there we needed to get word out about this new church.

Our church started from a blog post. I posted that I was planting a church and invited anyone who felt that God might be calling them to help start a church to join me for an interest meeting. It was on a Tuesday. We had it all planned out. We were going to meet in my friend Dan's house. We could seat thirty comfortably if we moved out all of the chairs. I remember talking to a friend and being really excited about the possibility of thirty people showing up. In my mind I thought fifteen to twenty was realistic. Our goal was to meet in homes until we got to fifty people. From there we would officially launch by holding public meetings in a rented clubhouse or school.

Well, by Thursday we had ninety-six people RSVP for the interest meeting. The vast majority of them I didn't know really well. I had to act fast to find a new place for us to meet.

Two weeks earlier I had gone to a meeting at Reservoir Community Church. It was located a few miles from my house. I knew we could not meet in a house with ninety-six people, so I had to find a church to meet at. Because I had recently gone to a meeting at Reservoir, I thought of them. I Googled the church, found the phone number, and gave the pastor a call. I had never met him. The next thing I know their pastor, Chris, had opened his doors for us to have our interest meeting. Not only that but he came and ran sound for us. It was a good thing he did because none of us knew how to turn on the soundboard.

After that first interest meeting, I knew we needed a church building to meet in. I had heard about a local church that was extremely kingdom minded. So much so that they shared their resources with other churches. Once again, I had to Google a church because I knew no one there. This church was an answer to prayer. They had sound equipment, computers, screens, fully furnished children's rooms, and comfortable chairs in the auditorium. We had zero dollars, so there was no way we could afford any of this stuff on our own. This church, though, allowed other churches to rent their space and use their stuff for a very tiny fee. Not only that, they offered to let us meet there for our first three months rent free. I'm not sure if they felt really sorry for me because I had no money, but next thing I knew we were meeting in a fully furnished modern-day church building. For free.

The only problem was there were eight other churches who called this facility their church home. That meant that we had to meet on Sunday nights. Sunday nights are like a death sentence to church planters. The only churches I knew of that hold services on Sunday nights are churches that are full on Sunday mornings.

So, I was stuck.

I couldn't find a better deal than the one we were getting, so it was financially the wise thing to do. It was just on Sunday nights.

I had hoped that God would be moving in such a powerful way that it wouldn't stop people from coming to our service. It didn't stop a lot of people from coming. In our first year we averaged 115 people. That's great for a church plant. The problem was we were losing families quicker than we could gain them. On a regular basis I would receive emails from core members who said they could no longer hang with Sunday nights. I heard from many people at our church who would say, "I keep inviting my friends to church but they can't make Sunday nights."

This worried me. Now before you accuse me about being all about the numbers, let me tell you that no one starts something for it to die. When you started a family, you cared about the numbers.

One wasn't good enough, so it led to two. For many, two isn't good enough, so they add to it with a child. The church is the family of God. I don't apologize for wanting to add to it.

It doesn't mean that we were striving to be a church of millions, but we were and are trying to reach people for Jesus. And every number represents a person. For crying out loud, there is a whole book of the Bible called Numbers. Someone counted. Every number represents a person.

Right away our members started telling me that we needed to get a building of our own. I felt like I explained why we couldn't 1.8 million times that first year. I feel pretty strongly that we need to be setting a good financial picture for our church. It is not wise to get into millions of dollars of debt for a building that you hope to one day afford. It's also impossible. In Virginia a church has to exist for seven years before a bank will give them a loan. So not only did I not want us to get into debt, we couldn't even if we did want to. So, my worry led me to pray. It led me to seek God.

I didn't like what God said. After praying, I felt led to keep praying. This time it was to pray specifically for a free church building. I dismissed the thought, but it kept coming back. Over and over when I would pray, I would feel led to pray for a free church building.

I felt crazy. I felt insecure praying for a free church building. If it was up to me I would have dismissed this crazy thought. It kept coming to my heart, so I knew there was something to it.

Close to six months into being a church plant, I told our church that I felt that God was going to give us a building of our own. Fully furnished. I invited the church to pray and ask God with me.

For almost two years we prayed. There were moments where I didn't worry about it. There were days and even weeks where I didn't think about it. But then I would get one of those emails. The ones that told me they love what God is doing at our church but they can no longer hang on Sunday nights.

I felt stuck. I prayed. I prayed some more.

In the meantime, I met with every person who had a church for sale. I asked the tough questions. Would they consider a lease to own so we could stay out of debt? I prayed and sought. I sought God first and then took action. For a little over a year I got doors slammed in my face. And then…

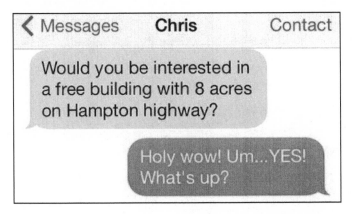

One early March morning in 2014, I got a text that said, "Would you be interested in a free building with 8 acres on Hampton highway?"

Splat. That was the noise of me pooping my pants. What the what? Are you joking me? Nope.

A pastor friend was giving me a church building. A fully furnished church building. It came with sound, kids' equipment, and those really comfy chairs. It was a miracle that we cannot explain away. It was a God-sized miracle. It did not come quickly but it came. Why? Seek God, and the rest will follow.

Oh…one more bit of info. The pastor who gave us the building was the same one who opened his building to us for our interest meeting. The place where we first met is now our home. That's a God thing!

Now this doesn't mean that every time you pray, God's going to say yes to you. But what is better than an answered prayer? God! Seeking God is what it's all about. You seek God in the process. You seek God when you worry. You seek God when you think you have an open door. You seek God when the door is slammed in your face. You seek God and find a peace that surpasses all understanding. For a little over a year I sought God. When my worry would grow, God helped diffuse my worry. And now every Sunday we have a reminder, in the form of a church building, that God does answer prayers.

Ultimately, worry is about control. We like to be in control. In control of our kingdom. But following Jesus is saying, "Your kingdom come, your will be done, on earth as it is in heaven." Following Jesus is about trusting that he is in control and that he will do what he says he'll do. It doesn't mean that life won't come with disappointments or heartache. It just means that we can trust Jesus through it all. Seek God, and the rest will follow.

Now, before we leave this let's address one thing. Sometimes the thing God leads you to do is to go see a counselor, or a doctor. There is no shame in using the resources God has given us. When I get a headache, I pray that God will heal it. I also take some medicine to relieve the pain. Seeking God is not exclusive of getting help. Sometimes God uses others to help us. Seek God through the process. When I went to see a counselor, I prayed that God would give him wisdom. When I see a doctor, I pray God gives him or her wisdom. I pray for healing and I accept healing in the form of God's creation/people. The worry in this chapter is more about the everyday worries we all face. If there is something more serious, please seek God...and get help.

Application: In light of what you are most worried about now, take one step of action to solve the worry. Whether it is talking to someone, saving some money, making a plan, asking for help, etc.

Questions:

1.   What are some things that you currently worry about?
2.   What are some things you worry about that will most likely never happen? These can be somewhat silly.
3.   What are some practical action steps that you can take to fix what you are worrying about?
4.   What is stopping you from taking those steps? If it's a job, what's stopping you from applying? If it's a spouse, what's stopping you from making a move? What is stopping you from taking those steps?
5.   Do you agree or disagree that worry is not a sin? Why or why not?
6.   What does it practically mean to seek God first?
7.   What if we took Jesus' words literally and sought God first? What would that look like?

CHAPTER 7

A HOLY RISK

Sometimes people ask me why I don't do altar calls each and every Sunday at church. If you are not familiar with an altar call, it's where the pastor gives an invitation to receive Jesus at the end of the service. It's essentially "the prayer." The prayer to ask Jesus into your heart. If you grew up in church then you probably know what I'm talking about. I think the altar call is fine, but I don't find it in the Bible. In fact, there is not one instance of Jesus or any other major players of the Bible doing an altar call or leading someone in what is traditionally known as the sinner's prayer. Now, I do think that there is some value in the prayer. It can lead people to have some comfort. But it's not the prayer that saves you. And that's the problem that I have with the altar call and the prayer. Please don't use this as ammunition against your church or pastor. It's okay for churches to do altar calls. I have just made the decision to only do them on special occasions. And if you disagree with me then know we can still be friends. Don't let this hang you up from the point I'm making.

The first church I worked at did an altar call every single week. Whenever there was a teenager I would go to the front to meet with them. I remember meeting a teenager by the name of Paul. He had gotten into some trouble and his parents made him go to church. He came forward to receive Jesus. I did what I was supposed to do. I led him in the prayer. He never came back to our church. I never saw him again. Now I don't know what God did with that moment in his life. It could have gone down one of two ways. Maybe God used that prayer and did awesome things through Paul's life. Or maybe Paul thought the prayer was a get out of jail free card. Maybe Paul didn't want to go to hell and saw this as a chance to get out of trouble. And if that's the case then maybe Paul is banking on one day going to heaven, but he doesn't even know Jesus. That scares me.

I might be wrong about this, but I think if people do what Jesus said to do, it's a better sign of them being a Christian than a prayer. In fact, what Jesus did say about getting to heaven is something that is seldom talked about. Jesus never said anything about saying a prayer to become a Christian. He did talk about building his kingdom. In fact, Jesus talked about building his kingdom more than any other subject. And this is something that we all should be talking about. This is what we should be asking about. What does it mean to build Jesus' kingdom?

In one of Jesus' most famous sermons, he talks a lot about the kingdom.

Now when Jesus saw the crowds, he went up on a mountainside and sat down. His disciples came to him, and he began to teach them.
He said:

"Blessed are the poor in spirit, for theirs is the kingdom of heaven." (Matthew 5:1–3)

I want to give you a little bit of context from this verse. If your Bible has titles before each section, then it will say "Beatitudes." What in the world is a beatitude? When I hear that word I can't help but think of…

Maybe you've played the game Angry Birds, but have you ever heard of the bee attitudes? These are bees with attitude. *Ba dum ching.* That's the sound of a drum after a bad joke. I digress.

The beatitudes actually have nothing to do with angry bees.

The Beatitudes are the set of teachings by Jesus that begin "Blessed are…" and appear in the gospels of Matthew and Luke. The term *beatitude* comes from the Latin adjective which means "happy," "fortunate," or "blissful."

I'M SO HAPPY

The best way to explain beatitude is with the word…

Happy.

As in "If you're happy and you know it clap your hands." Did you clap? Come on. Aren't you happy? If you are happy I want you to get your clap on. Here we go. Let's try this again. "If you're happy and you know it clap your hands." (Clap, clap.)

If you are reading this in a public place and actually played along, please Tweet me to let me know (@robshep). I want to celebrate with you. You, my friend, are full of awesome!

Sometimes you just have to get your happy clap on. I think most people in this world want to be happy. I bet if you ask most people what they want in life, they would say "to be happy." And Jesus gives a sermon on happiness. Now this isn't a fleeting happiness that leaves whenever you do not get what you want. This isn't a happiness that you feel while eating three Krispy Kreme doughnuts only to have the happiness leave the next morning when you step on the scale. Wait. Is that just me? I mean, I have a friend who did this once. Yeah. I don't know anything about happily eating my face off only to wake up the next morning feeling shame. Nothing. At. All. Let's move on quickly. This is getting personal.

This is a happiness that is supernatural. It's a happiness that you can find even in the midst of great suffering. It's not cheesy. It's not fake. It doesn't mean that you always walk around with a smile on your face. It does mean that you can be happy. Jesus gives a list of things. It's called the Beatitudes. We read how it starts, but let's read it again.

"Blessed are the poor in spirit, for theirs is the kingdom of heaven." (Matthew 5:3)

Notice what Jesus said? He didn't say blessed are those who say a prayer after a church service, for theirs is the kingdom of heaven. He said blessed are the poor in spirit. That seems to go against everything that we know. The words *poor* and *happy* don't seem to go together. But Jesus says that the key to the kingdom of heaven is to be poor in spirit.

We already know that the word *blessed* means happy. Happy are the poor in spirit. What does that mean?

I love how one commentary puts it.

"To be poor in Spirit is not to lack courage but to acknowledge spiritual bankruptcy. It confesses one's unworthiness before God and utter dependence on Him."[1]

I love that wording. To be poor in spirit means to be spiritually bankrupt.

HOW DO I BECOME SPIRITUALLY BANKRUPT?

The question is, how do you become spiritually bankrupt? As a pastor I've observed that you become spiritually bankrupt one of two ways.

---

1   D. A. Carson, *The Expositor's Bible Commentary* (Grand Rapids: Zondervan, 1976). Quote accessed online.

1. Circumstances force you.

Sometimes life stinks. People die. People that you love die. A bad doctor's report can lead you to become spiritually bankrupt. A breakup of a relationship can lead you to become spiritually bankrupt. In fact, many of you who are reading this picked up this book because you became spiritually bankrupt. That is, you had a situation that was so painful you didn't have the means to fix it. You had to look to God. It was when the words "I want a divorce" were uttered. It was when you got a broken heart. It was when you lost your job. You were finally forced to rely on something other than yourself because you were spiritually bankrupt. I have never heard a story of a person getting rich and then finding God. In the history of lottery winners, I don't think there is one person who won and then ran straight to the church to find Jesus, and then give 10 percent to that church. Maybe they are out there, but it's not the norm. What is, unfortunately, the norm is people hitting rock bottom and because of their situation humbling themselves to rely on God. Have you been there?

When I was in college I went through an extremely lonely time. I transferred to Liberty University and because I was a little bit older they put me in the senior dorms. My floor only had two groups of people, seniors who already had their friends, and the basketball team. My first day on the campus was awesome. I got my room set up. I surfed the World Wide Web using AOL and dial-up Internet. I killed a lot of time listening to the noise the computer made while waiting for my Internet to connect. Some of you are too young to remember that. If you do remember dial-up Internet, you should go hug your high-speed Internet right this second. Don't you ever take it for granted.

All of a sudden, my door opened. It was a gigantor man who poked his head in my door and said, "Hey, I'm your roommate." It startled me at first, but then I quickly became excited because up to this point I had had very little human interaction. He said he needed to go get his stuff, closed the door, and then never came back. I don't know if he didn't like what he saw or what, but this guy never came back. Not even for a visit. I never saw him again. Ever. So, there I was four hours away from home with no roommate and few interactions with humans. I knew friends would eventually come, so I wasn't sad at first. That was until I had to eat dinner by myself. I went back to my empty dorm room and didn't see anyone else until I was changing clothes for bed. All of a sudden, my door swung open while I was standing in nothing but my underwear. It was my RA, Blake, who apparently had to do room checks every night at 10:00 p.m. Liberty is a private school. With rules. We had a curfew. We had room checks. Somehow no one remembered to tell me about said room checks at 10:00 p.m. I would have waited to drop down to my tighty-whities. This was B.B. As in Before Boxers. How embarrassing.

I would have tried to strike up a conversation with him if it weren't for the fact that I felt really awkward standing there in my tighty-whities. The most embarrassing part is this same thing happened for the next three days. It took me three days to figure out that I was going to get a nightly visit from my RA at 10:00 p.m. I started changing for bed at 9:55 so I'd be fully dressed when my RA visited at 10:00.

Finally, after three days, classes started, and I couldn't wait! I drove my car to class and parked in the only parking spot that I could find. It was near the cafeteria. I thought this would be perfect. I could go to class, then walk to the cafeteria where my car would be waiting for me. When I came out of class I saw a little yellow piece of paper on the windshield of my car. It was signed by LUPD or

Liberty University Police Department, telling me that I had parked in the commuter parking lot and that I owed them twenty-five dollars. That's a lot of money for a college student.

The next week not much had changed. I was still eating meals by myself and feeling really lonely. I saw a friend from high school who invited me to have lunch with her and her friends. I was so excited. There was no parking anywhere, so she told me to park my car in front of the cafeteria. I told her that it said no parking, but she was a junior and told me that it would be okay. When we got out of lunch there was a little yellow piece of paper on the windshield of my car. It was signed by LUPD and it said I owed them twenty-five dollars for illegally parking. I was bummed, but not too upset because I actually had some human interaction and didn't have to eat by myself for lunch that day. Two days later I came back to my dorm only to find there were no parking spaces anywhere. I pulled into this dirt parking lot that was really far away from my dorm and found a little corner to park in. The next day when I went to my car I had a little yellow piece of paper on my windshield. It was signed by LUPD and it said I owed them twenty-five dollars for "inventing a parking space." Are you joking me?! I was pretty upset at this. Of course, I invented a parking space. It was a dirt parking lot. Everyone invented parking spaces!

Well, a few days passed and that meant more meals by myself. I had been waiting to get to my second weekend at my school because that was when I started my new job as a youth pastor at a little country church in Farmville, Virginia. Yes, it is a real place. So, Saturday came and I got a message from my church asking me to pick up some flyers for an upcoming conference coming to my school. I pulled my car in front of the building with the flyers, and it looked like the building was locked for the weekend. I wanted to double check, so I pulled my car up next to the curb, left my car running and my door open, and ran to the door to the office. It was locked. I ran back to my car and as soon as I sat down LUPD pulled up behind me. The officer walked up to me and handed me a little yellow piece of paper. It was signed by LUPD and it said that I owed them one hundred dollars for illegally parking. I tried to reason with him, but he wouldn't have any of it. I'm pretty sure LUPD weren't real cops. I think they only gave them one bullet for their gun, aka Barney Fife. I thought about peeling out and seeing if he could catch me, aka *The Dukes of Hazzard.* Then reality struck me, and I realized that I drove a Dodge Neon and not a Dodge Charger like in *The Dukes of Hazzard.*

I was crushed! In fact, I cried the whole way to Farmville, which was about forty-five minutes. I got to Farmville and one of the first people I met was a girl named Monica. She wasn't too happy to see me on that first encounter. Apparently, she was a big fan of the last youth pastor. It wasn't just her. It was all the leaders and students. I did the event and was reminded about 125 times about how awesome their last youth pastor was. His name was Chris. I know this well because for the first year I was often called Chris from people at the church. It was not the night that I had envisioned.

I drove back forty-five minutes that night to my dorm. Alone. And while alone in my dorm thinking about the $175 that I owed to LUPD and thinking about how lonely I was, I cried out to God. I was spiritually bankrupt. I had tried everything in my power to be happy and nothing was working. I was lonely. In fact, the only people who paid attention to me kept giving me little yellow pieces of paper saying I owed them money, and an RA who had impeccable timing to see me model my tighty-whities. Oh me! It was sad. I was sad.

You see, sometimes life forces you to feel spiritually bankrupt. God ended up using that experience in my life. The youth group ended up being one of my favorite experiences. The pastor of the church is an amazing mentor. The girl, Monica, that I mentioned ended up marrying me. The RA ended up being my best friend in college. Overall the entire experience was amazing, but it wasn't easy.

It wasn't the only time that life has forced me to feel spiritually bankrupt. When we had our miscarriage, I felt spiritually bankrupt. After praying for six years to get pregnant, we finally did. It was a miracle. In fact, we found out the day before we were going to visit an infertility specialist. I never dreamed we would lose that baby. When we did I was crushed. So much so I thought, "What's the point of living for God if he isn't going to protect me from this type of hurt?"

When I lost a job that I loved, I felt spiritually bankrupt. The loss felt more like a divorce. It was crushing.

When some of my favorite people of all time left our church, I felt spiritually bankrupt. Sometimes life hits you hard and leads you to need Jesus. Some of you have experienced that all too well. The pain of loss cost you more than the $175 I had to pay in tickets. It broke your heart. It wounded you. It made you hit rock bottom.

But there is a promise with this short verse. Blessed are the poor in spirit because theirs is the kingdom of heaven. And though you may have experienced all sorts of pain and struggle on this earth, the spiritually poor are promised eternity in heaven where there is no pain, suffering, or little yellow pieces of paper signed by LUPD. And no tighty-whities. Thank God. The key when life hits you hard is to make sure that you rely on God. Seek God. Talk to God.

It's okay to get angry, but don't push God away. Don't stiff-arm God in your pain. Run to him. Ask him to hold you. Allow him to make you blessed. It will not instantly take the pain away, but I can tell you through experience that there is healing in the arms of God. Sometimes you need to hit rock bottom in order to be desperate enough to reach up.

After our miscarriage I asked God, "What's the point of living for you?" The response I heard rocked me. In a quiet whisper I heard, "You don't live for God to change his perception of you. You live for God to change your perception of him."

Often, we get it wrong and think that we do good things to earn something back from God. Then, when life goes wrong, we wonder where God is. That day what I heard was I don't need to do good to change God's perspective of me. He loves me. I pray, give, read the Bible, go to church, serve, etc. to change my perspective of God. Doing spiritual practices helps my heart and mind focus on God. When I doubt, or feel God is distant it is not because he is. It's because I've moved away. Being in the presence of God allows me to see God past my circumstances. I do not do spiritual practices so that God will bless me. I do them to get to know God.

After the miscarriage, I didn't feel like praying, but praying during that difficult season changed my perspective of God.

We don't serve a God who is distant when we struggle. We serve a God who meets us in the struggle.

Struggle is a part of life. Almost nothing brings us close to God like struggle or pain. Often the very thing we need is the one we blame. I don't know why bad things happen, but I do know that I have a God who understands pain.

SECOND WAY TO BECOME SPIRITUALLY BANKRUPT

That leads to the second way that people become spiritually bankrupt.

2. Take a holy risk for God.

Sometimes life makes you spiritually bankrupt. When life doesn't, what can you do? Take some holy risks for God.

Poor in spirit = being dependent on God

When life doesn't force you to depend on God, it can become easy to be prideful and think that we don't need God. And the only thing I've found that helps this is to do something that is way bigger than yourself. To take a holy risk. A holy risk is to attempt something so big that you will fail without God's help. And it's a risk that is about building God's kingdom and not yours. A holy risk could be telling someone you love about Jesus. There is risk in this. What if they say no? What if they call you a Jesus freak? What if it starts a fight?

A holy risk could be going on a mission trip. It's not easy to raise the funds for a trip, but with God's help it's possible. A holy risk could be following a leading that you think is from God. For me I felt like God wanted me to plant a church. I didn't know all of the details. What made it worse is I never heard God say, "Plant a church." I just sensed it inside. I felt like it was what I was supposed to do. I had heard planting a church was incredibly difficult. I was scared. What made me even more scared is that I knew that if I left my job to start a church, I would be leaving without any financial support. That was a risk. A holy risk. But it's a risk that has paid off. It was so much bigger than myself that it forced me to rely on God.

Maybe for you it's taking a risk and trying to publish that book that is inside of you. Maybe for you it's taking a risk to ask her on a date. Maybe for you it's taking a risk to start a new business. Maybe it's a risk to move. Maybe it's a risk to restore a broken relationship. I don't know what your risk is, but it's worth it if it makes you spiritually bankrupt for God. Even if you don't succeed in the way you think you should, it's still worth it. It's worth it to rely on God.

Sometimes I miss those early days of church planting where I fell on my knees in desperation for God. Sure, it was scary, but an even more scary thought for me is to rely on my own strength, gifts, and talents in a way that causes me not to rely on God. Whenever I feel a lack of zeal for God, to pray, or to read the Bible, I seek God to ask him, "What's next?" What's the next thing that is going to push me out of my comfort zone, and toward desperately needing you? My dreams and desires are so small I can achieve them. God's dreams and desires are God-sized. God laughs in the face of risk. A God-sized risk may seem big for you or me, but they are still small because he's so big. That adventure that scares the pee out of you is a walk in the park for God.

We serve a God who called a stutterer (Moses) to lead a group of slaves in Egypt to freedom, a shepherd boy (David) to slay a giant, a religious fanatic (Paul) on his way to imprison Christians into a missionary who wrote half of what is our New Testament. So, what are you scared of?

HOW DO YOU TELL IF IT'S A HOLY RISK?

Now the question you should be asking is, "How do I tell if it's a holy risk for God?" This is an important question. I don't want anyone reading this to put God to the test. That is, I wouldn't want anyone to blindfold themselves and run down a major interstate yelling, "This is my holy risk for God!" That's not a holy risk. That's a holy stupid.

A holy risk is "a risk that stretches you to rely on God while honoring God in the process."

Here are some questions to ask to help you figure out if it's a holy risk or not.

1. Does it push you to serve someone else? If it's a yes, ask the following question.
2. If you succeeded, would it be more about how great you are or how great God is? If it's more about God, move to the next question.
3. Does it go against what the Bible teaches? If so, then it's a no. If it doesn't go against the Bible, move to the final question.
4. Does it make other people nervous?

Big dreams that are a holy risk make other people feel uncomfortable in their mediocrity. If God is pushing you to do something, expect some naysayers. But *do not* allow a few negative voices to stop you from doing what God is stirring inside of you.

I don't know about you, but I want to be spiritually bankrupt before God. I want to be desperate for him. I can build my kingdom based off my dreams, but it will leave me feeling tired. Building God's kingdom by taking a holy risk energizes you. Relying on God's strength to get you through something is better than an adrenaline rush on steroids. If you currently do not feel spiritually bankrupt for God, ask him to stir a dream or desire in you. He put you here for his glory and to accomplish something for him. Watch how you come alive when you discover what that is. Watch how your view of God grows as he smashes your fear into tiny little pieces.

Some of you are being forced by life to become spiritually bankrupt. Others of you are living large on your own power. If I were you I'd ask God what he wants you to do with your life. Where does he want you to go? Here's a question to get the ball rolling.

What would you try for God if you knew you could not fail?

Potentially that desire that you have is from God. Spend lots of time praying and seeking wise counsel and then take a holy risk for God. Watch how he stretches you as you trust him.

AN EXAMPLE OF POOR IN SPIRIT

There is a great verse in the Bible that shows what it looks like to be poor in spirit versus what it looks like to rely on yourself.

To some who were confident of their own righteousness and looked down on everyone else, Jesus told this parable: "Two men went up to the temple to pray, one a Pharisee and the other a tax collector. The Pharisee stood by himself and prayed: 'God, I thank you that I am not like other people—robbers, evildoers, adulterers— or even like this tax collector. I fast twice a week and give a tenth of all I get.'

"But the tax collector stood at a distance. He would not even look up to heaven, but beat his breast and said, 'God, have mercy on me, a sinner.'

"I tell you that this man, rather than the other, went home justified before God. For all those who exalt themselves will be humbled, and those who humble themselves will be exalted." (Luke 18:9–14)

How can you know if you are poor in spirit? Are you utterly dependent on God? If the answer is yes, then you have the promise of heaven. In the verse you just read the "sinner" was spiritually bankrupt. He humbled himself. He relied on God because he knew he didn't have another choice. He was at the end of his rope. He was at the bottom. When you are on top of the world it's difficult to be humble. You feel unstoppable. But the type of faith that causes us to be spiritually bankrupt starts with humility.

It starts with admitting that life is better with God. Life may be good now, but it's better with God. In order to live a godly life, we have to humble ourselves to admit we will never get there on our own. Either life is going to force you there or taking a risk will. Either way the end result is a God-honoring place. And that, my friends, is the secret to being happy.

You see, happiness does not come from anyone but God. A person can make you feel joy or excitement or sadness or pain, but a person is not responsible for your happiness. As long as we look to others for happiness, we will constantly be disappointed. Let's live lives that are so full of spiritual bankruptcy that no one can steal our happiness away.

When you are truly at peace with God, you bring happiness to life. You don't wait for happiness to come to you.

The truth is we want people to give us happiness, but it's not their job. You can work a less than amazing job and still be happy.

You can go through difficulty and still be happy. Happiness starts with God. When you are happy your circumstances don't tell you how to live. You tell your circumstances whose you are. As a child of God, you may have sadness at night, but joy comes in the morning. If you are happy and you know it clap your hands.

Application: Do you know what you would do if you could not fail? Take a step toward making a dream become a reality.

Questions:

1. What is it that you ultimately want from God?
2. After reading this chapter, how would you explain to someone that being happy equals being poor in spirit?
3. Has there ever been a time where you have felt poor in spirit? Explain.
4. What is one thing that you would do if you knew you could not fail?
5. Have you ever taken a holy risk for God?
6. Realistically, will you spend time tonight seeking God in order to become spiritually bankrupt? Why or why not?

YOU MISSPELLED CHRISTIAN

158

CHAPTER 8

I HATE GRAMMAR

The hardest thing about life is that it's so daily.

Let me ask you a question. If you only had one day to live, what would you do? Your answer will reveal whether or not you are on the path to living a truly extraordinary story for God's kingdom.

You see, for most of us when we think about what we would do if we only had one more day to live, we instantly think about what we could do to better our lives. We'd go skydiving, rocky mountain climbing, we'd go 2.7 seconds on a bull named Fu Man Chu. Am I right?

We make the majority of our decisions because we live as if we have eternity. Most of us are selfish creatures who develop selfish habits that we wish we could change. I don't know about you, but I feel like I repeat the same day over and over again, but it's in my struggles. I say I'm going to do better tomorrow only to find myself in the same place again and again and again. So often when it comes to my struggles it's as if I'm in an eternal Groundhog Day. Do you remember that great movie?

As a dog returns to its vomit,
so fools repeat their folly. (Proverbs 26:11)

I hope I'm not a fool, but I sure do have some foolish tendencies. A fool is a person who knows the difference between right and wrong and chooses to do wrong anyway. A fool chooses to do what's wrong over and over and over again. A fool says, "I'm going to lose weight tomorrow," "I'll never drink like that again," "I will be more faithful tomorrow," but then doesn't take steps to change. We lie to ourselves over and over again hoping that tomorrow will be different.

It's like the famous quote "The definition of insanity is doing the same thing over and over again and expecting different results."[1]

A fool is insane. A fool thinks they have forever to change. A fool puts off what needs to be done until Monday. You ever notice how everyone wants to start a diet on Monday? Then when Monday comes around we say, "I'll start it next Monday."

Why do we put off what we need to do? It's because we are ultimately building our kingdom and even though we know we need to change, we like doing things our way. But how is that working out for you?

Ultimately, if you want to get the most out of your life, it has very little to do with you. It has very little to do with your goals. It has very little to do with what will make you happy. If you want to make the most of your life, you'll have to learn a lesson from Jesus' example.

---

1   This quote is often attributed to Albert Einstein, but it is a misattribution. The original author of the quote is unknown.

Do nothing out of selfish ambition or vain conceit.
Rather, in humility value others above yourselves, not
looking to your own interests but each of you to the
interests of the others. (Philippians 2:3–4)

Eventually, everything we pursue in life will become meaningless
unless we learn to live this verse. Making money is great, but it will
not satisfy you. Intimacy is great, but ultimately if it's all about your
needs it will not satisfy you. Church is great, but if it's all about you
then it will not satisfy you. When you live to build your kingdom, you
end up sucking out all the good from something and then when it no
longer benefits you, you walk away.

One of the first things that God does when he enters a person's
heart is change his or her perspective. Building God's kingdom
starts with God and then he quickly starts messing with you.
He messes with you in the best way possible, but it still messes
with you. It messes up how you view the world. He messes up
how you view others. To follow Jesus is to love God and to love
others. Life often messes with our ability to do that. Hurt people
hurt people. When we struggle, the natural pull is inward. The
answer is found outside ourselves. The further we go inward the
more issues we find. No matter the situation, God leads us back
to loving him and loving others. It's how we get over the pain we
feel.

I HATE GRAMMAR

I hate grammar.
It makes no sense.

I was taught that an *e* + *a* = a long *e* sound. Like *beat*. So when you work out and perspiration starts dripping from your body, it should be spelled *swet*. But NOOOOOAH! It's sweat. You say, "What does Noah have to do with this?" I say, "Even my puns are biblical." But back to the word *sweat*. That should be the word we use to drink the only acceptable form of tea. Sweat tea. But if you do that then you are saying you want a glass of perspiration from tea. That sounds gag nasty! But sweat is really confusing to the word sweet.

What's this word? *Live.*

If you said *live* as in "I want to live in a house with a tub full of Nutella," then you would be wrong. I meant *live*. As in "Did you go to the live taping of that show?"

Grammar makes absolutely no sense to my brain. People have tried to come up with all sorts of rules to help make sense of grammar. I think a better system would be to come up with a new grammar system that actually made sense. Who is with me?

One rule that my dad taught me when I was in elementary school is when it comes to the letter *i* it is "*i* before *e* except after *c*." Translation: when you are spelling a word that has an *ie* combo you put the *i* before the letter *e* unless the letter that precedes them is a *c*.

This is a great rule until you come to science. Science is always throwing everything for a loop. What's up with that science? I love you, but why can't you play by the rules? You should be spelled *sceince* and I want Pluto back as a planet. He was always my favorite and you came along and took him away. What's up with you, science! Or should I write *sceince*. I digress.

I was randomly thinking about the *ie* rule and thought, "That's a better rule for Christians than grammar."

Most of us make decisions based off what is best for "I." I know it should have been "me," but I'm going somewhere with this. Stick with me.

"I" is what we are all about. We live in a world full of people focusing on "I."

If you do not realize how bad it is, take a look through Instagram. We've invented a term called *selfie*. Pictures that focus on "I."

Focusing on oneself is fine and dandy for everyone except Christians.

Jesus modeled that we are to put the needs of others ahead of our own. With Jesus it's "I before E (everyone) except after C (Christ)." When Christ enters the scene it's C (Christ) and then E (Everyone) followed by I.

Let's look at the verse that kicked off this chapter again.

"Do nothing out of selfish ambition or vain conceit. Rather, in humility value others above yourselves, not looking to your own interests but each of you to the interests of the others. In your relationships with one another, have the same mindset as Christ Jesus:" (Philippians 2:3–5)

Jesus was all about building God's kingdom on earth as is it is in heaven. He built God's kingdom and modeled what that looked like for us. When a person becomes a Christian, Jesus puts in them a desire to live like him. Specifically, to put other people first. Think about this, Jesus left the perfection of heaven for the calamity of earth. He left the comforts of his heavenly throne to be born in a stinking manger. He gave us his life by dying on a bloody cross when it would have been way easier to rule. Why? Because he put others ahead of himself. Christians are called to follow Jesus' example. To humbly build God's kingdom by putting other people ahead of ourselves. When you seek Jesus and look to build his kingdom, he leads you to put others first. I before E except after C.

THIS ISN'T EASY

It is so difficult to build God's kingdom without seeking God. By so difficult, I mean impossible. The power of self is too strong. And yet we try to live day by day relying on our own strength. Seeking God first radically changes the way we view other humans. Putting others first is a sign that God has made us whole.

Wholeness is giving more than you take.

Christians should constantly be giving more than we take. When we hang out with people, they should feel refreshed because we've poured into them more than we've taken. Churches should be full of life and energy because every Christian is giving more than they take. Christian marriages should be based off trying to out-give each other.

When we are whole we are at our best. When we are not whole the pull is to look inward. The more we look inward, the more lost we become.

WHY IS IT SO DIFFICULT TO BE WHOLE?

Christians have one thing going for them that most other religions don't. We even have something that science doesn't offer.

Christians offer an explanation to why we are all broken. It doesn't mean that we can't do good. We were created in God's image, and after he created humans he said we were good. It is easy to be self-reliant because we are so good. We can accomplish a lot of good without God. Because of sin we may be good, but we are far from perfect. Even our goodness is tainted. At times we settle for good when God wants something great.

We all have the ability to do good, but don't let that cover over the fact that we all bear the effects of being broken.

There are times in my life where I have doubted God, doubted a biblical explanation, and allowed my mind to wonder, and it's in those times that I come back to this explanation.

We are broken. Not just some of us. All of us. Not a single human is perfect. We all have struggles. As amazing as science is, it has yet to explain why we are all born broken. When our instinct should be to survive, we self-destruct.

No one has to teach us how to lie, steal, or be selfish. Being born comes with the ability to suckle and suck at life. I threw in the suckle because it's a funny word and I wanted to see if you were still paying attention. The point is that we are only born knowing how to do a few things and being selfish is one of them.

We are all born broken.

The question that not many people are asking is how to become whole.

The temptation is to say you just need Jesus, but you can have Jesus and still not truly be whole. Don't stone me. Keep reading.

The definition of wholeness is *giving more than you take*. You can find Jesus and remain broken because you take more than you give. You can take more from God than you give to God. You can continue to show your brokenness by taking more from others than you give. Now, God still loves you, but you can still feel the effects of being broken. If that shocks you then I'd recommend a dose of humility.

> Do nothing out of selfish ambition or vain conceit. Rather, *in humility* value others above yourselves, not looking to your own interests but each of you to the interests of the others. In your relationships with one another, have the same mindset as Christ Jesus: (Philippians 2:3–5, italics mine)

The process to becoming whole starts with Jesus. Accepting what Jesus did and allowing him to change you. That often comes after brokenness. It often comes when we have no other option. It often comes when we want something from God like a ticket out of hell or for him to complete us by making us whole. But it doesn't end there. From there it moves to humility. Humility is...

> "Not thinking less about yourself, it's thinking about yourself less.[2]
>
> —Rick Warren

True humility puts us at a place where we can invest in and then lead others. A true leader is a servant.

Can you imagine living a life where pride did not interfere in your relationships? Can you imagine a life where you weren't worried about your status or what people thought, and where you made a difference because you helped people? Really helped

---

2   Rick Warren (@RickWarren), Twitter.

people. Helped people who could not help you back. That sounds like Jesus. Maybe that's the point.

Jesus doesn't just want us to be mindless drones that obey. He wants us to be whole. He wants us to be so healthy we are at a place to help others.

Most people do not give more than they take. In fact, most people, even well-meaning Christians, take more than they give. Why? Because we are broken and desperately seeking something to make us whole. We are so focused on "me" that we cannot even fathom "we."

Show me a person who takes more than they give, and I will show you a broken human. Show me a person who gives more than they take, and it will point you to Jesus.

A NEW REVELATION FOR ME

There is a lot of talk about building a platform. There is a lot of talk about fulfilling a dream. There are a lot of social media posts, conferences, and books that teach us how to make our dreams come true.

I think that's good.

I also think it can be exhausting.

I had a breakthrough two weeks ago. It's still new to me, so I don't know if it will stick.

There is a chance this idea that I'm about to share will end up being the equivalent of an obese man writing a diet book based off the fact he lost two pounds after eating at Taco Bell last night. I love Taco Bell, but let's be honest, it is the best-tasting laxative.

Being consumed by my dream can cause me to get frustrated with others who aren't helping my dream become a reality.

My dream also is never satisfied.

Once I fulfill one level, I just start dreaming of the next level. I'm all for having dreams, but I think what really makes humans come alive is helping others fulfill their dreams. Maybe that's not a new idea to you reading, but that's the idea that has been smacking me in the face for two weeks.

I'm reading a great book called *Creating Magic* by Lee Cockerell. It's a leadership book from one of the bigwigs at Disney. Disney is an amazing dream come true. It's brought lots of money to those who run it. But every page of this book points to how Disney works tirelessly to make other people's dreams come true. What separates Disney from so many other companies is that their business is people. They are in the business of making people's dreams come true.

Instead of saying what can others do for me to make today awesome, what if we said what can I do to help others become awesome?

Do nothing out of selfish ambition or vain conceit. Rather, in humility value others above yourselves, not looking to your own interests but each of you to the interests of the others. (Philippians 2:3–4)

I'm so familiar with that verse it's like it's an attached body part. But what would it look like to live this out?

I come alive when I help my kids discover a new truth, accomplish a goal, get something they've been dreaming of. I love Christmas, but since having kids I really love Christmas. It's energizing to watch them come alive.

In relationships I come alive when I've had a great conversation. A great conversation involves listening and not just doing all the talking. My energy level gets drained when I've done all the talking. When I help someone, when I listen, when I pour into others with my words…I come alive.

What if we set out to make someone's dream come alive once a week?

What if we asked what would help others have a better day?

"You can get anything in life you want, if you help enough people get what they want."

—Zig Ziglar

Isn't that what it means to sow and reap? We sow into others by taking a genuine interest in who they are, and in return they make our lives better. We don't sow into them so we will get something. That's selfish. We sow into them and the byproduct is energy, excitement, and fulfillment.

The vast majority of relationships are based off half-selfish people. A half-selfish person is one who gives as long as they benefit. As soon as they are giving more than they are getting in return, they terminate the relationship.

Two half-selfish people make one whole selfish situation. As long as we are half-selfish we will help, but it will be conditional.

As long as we view people as owing us something, we will never receive what they can give.

Think about it this way. If I owed you ten dollars and one day offered to give you two dollars, you wouldn't view it as a gift. You would view it as paying off the debt I owe you.

So many relationships are based off a barter system. I'll give as long as I get something in return.

Way too many marriages are based off a barter system.

Way too many friendships.

Way too many churches.

Way too many relationships.

As long as we are keeping track of how much we give versus how much we get, we will never be whole.

Helping people come alive with excitement is life-giving for my soul.

It's easy to forget that when I am so focused on building a platform or a dream or fulfilling a mission.

I once asked my staff to put a number to how they were feeling. On a scale of one to ten, one being on the ledge and ten being doing awesome, where would you put yourself in this moment? Most of my staff landed on an eight. That's a pretty good number.

I then asked what I could do to help them go up to the next number.

Two of my staff members started talking about if they saw a real-life unicorn it would help their number to go off the charts.

A real-life unicorn?

I left that meeting with the goal to make that happen. Even if it was a crazy dream I wanted to find a way to help make it happen.

After a little brainstorming I came up with an idea.

I presented them with a really old translation of the Bible. I told them I couldn't come up with a real unicorn, but this was the best I could do. I had them read the following passage from the old Bible.

God brought them out of Egypt; he hath as it were the strength of an unicorn. (Numbers 23:22 KJV)

It created excitement because a couple of the staff had no idea a unicorn was in the Bible. Now, I didn't spend time telling them that it wasn't a real unicorn. It's a bad translation and most likely a rhino, or goat, but that's not the point.

The point is seeing them get excited made me feel excited.

What if we found out what made others come alive and we tried to do something about it? What if we took a genuine interest in others? What if we accomplished more than we could ask or imagine by helping others accomplish more than they could imagine?

What Is Selfish Ambition?

Do nothing out of selfish ambition or vain conceit. (Philippians 2:3)

Let's talk about selfish ambition.

Selfish ambition—a lifestyle based on "get"

The natural question all humans ask is, "What do I get out of it?"

In our minds we then weigh the pros and cons. Is it worth the effort to get what I want?

We live for the get.

When it comes to going to church we often ask, "What am I going to get out of it?" They say every church has 20 percent of the people doing 80 percent of the work.

Before we join a small group, volunteer, give back even in the church, we ask, "What do I get out of it?"

And yet, most of us don't truly think we are all that selfish.

According to a recent study, when surveyed, 74 percent of people identify with unselfish values. That is, they see themselves as unselfish. When it comes to how we see others, 78 percent believe others are more selfish than what they really are.

Something is broken in us. We view ourselves as less selfish than we are and others as more selfish.

This is what psychologists call fundamental attribution error.

Fundamental attribution error is the belief that when someone does something wrong, it is because they are defective. There is something wrong with them. But when you do the same thing, it's because of a good reason.

So, if someone doesn't return your phone call, you say, "They are so selfish. All they care about is themselves." But when you fail to call someone back you say, "I've just been extra busy." You see, we attack others while we often give ourselves the benefit of the doubt. When Paul writes do nothing out of selfish ambition, right away in our brains we start to think, "I can't wait to give this book to _____. They are so selfish."

We demand that others live selflessly so we can continue to live selfishly.

We want Chick-fil-A service while we offer McDonald's service. McDonald's may be known for their fries and Big Macs, but low customer service is pretty much accepted by most of us who eat there.

This is why we demand good service but then often serve like we are employees at the DMV. We demand the best, but we stop at giving our best. We want to get more than we want to give.

We see selfishness in others but we can't see it in ourselves. So, what do we do?

Jesus' brother James has some amazing insight on what we can do.

For where you have envy and selfish ambition, there you find disorder and every evil practice. (James 3:16)

I love what James writes because we are all blind to our selfishness. If James just said, "Stop being selfish," we would all say, "I'm not that selfish." James doesn't say just knock it off. Instead he challenges us to look at our disorder.

You may not be able to see your selfishness, but you can see the disorder.

I know I'm selfish, but I struggle to see it. Disorder on the other hand is easier to spot.

WHY ARE WE BLINDED TO OUR SELFISHNESS?

Often selfishness is birthed out of a wound. When we are hurt we have a hard time seeing how our actions impact others. All we see is our pain. It's why hurt people, hurt people.

We often give ourselves permission to live selfishly because of the wounds we have experienced. Because everyone is selfish, everyone causes wounds in others. At some point you have been wounded by someone you love. It might have been a relative, a friend, or a loved one.

When we are wounded we think we deserve to feel happy. If something is selfish but makes us happy, we justify it because we have a wound. If you have a trail of damage caused by your selfish ambition, you'll never be able to fix it until you allow Jesus to heal your wound.

To be whole we must be healed.

So as difficult as it might be, look at the disorder in your life. What part do you play in it? Being a victim never wins any battles. You have some wounds. I have some wounds.

Jesus has some wounds.

By his wounds we are healed.

When speaking of Jesus, the Scripture says…

"He committed no sin,
and no deceit was found in his mouth."
When they hurled their insults at him, he did not retaliate; when he suffered, he made no threats. Instead, he entrusted himself to him who judges justly. "He himself bore our sins" in his body on the cross, so that we might die to sins and live for righteousness; *"by his wounds you have been healed."* For "you were like sheep going astray," but now you have returned to the Shepherd and Overseer of your souls. (1 Peter 2:22–25, italics mine)

By Jesus' wounds we find healing for our souls.

Will you let Jesus in? Will you let him heal the pain you've felt from others? Will you let Jesus work on your insecurity? Will you let Jesus work on the wounds caused by your parents? Will you let God work on the wounds caused by others?

WHY DOES THIS MATTER?

No matter what your wounds are, in Jesus you can always come back home. This is important because as Christians we represent Jesus. Our wounds will continually get in the way until we allow Jesus to heal them.

Christians should have the healthiest relationships around. Being a Christian doesn't mean you won't have drama in your relationships. It does mean you need to deal with your drama in a Christ-like way. Christians should have the healthiest families around. When we struggle we should be an example to the world on how to struggle. By Jesus' wounds you are healed, but he won't heal you until you bring the wounds to him. When you do, God starts to put your life in order.

I love the quote by Andy Stanley…

> **"Following Jesus will make your life better
> and make you better at life."**[3]

The church should be the healthiest organization on the planet. Christians should strive to have the healthiest families on the block. Christians should be the best friends. We often fall way short, but the more we find healing in Jesus, the more like him we will become.

The more we allow Jesus to forgive us, the more we can forgive others.

The more we allow Jesus to truly love us, the more we will be able to truly love others.

DISORDER WARNING

When everyone is focused on "get," you have disorder. Whenever a relationship struggles, it is because one or both people

---

3   Andy Stanley, Catalyst Conference, Atlanta, GA, 2016.

are holding on to selfishness. We don't see it because of the wound. Wherever you find disorder you'll find selfishness.

Let's wrestle with this.

Where is there disorder in your life?

Where is there relational disorder? Every fight is because of selfishness of one or both people. We can't see it in ourselves, but it's true. We fight with others because ultimately, we aren't getting our way. So where is there disorder in your life?

What choices are you making that have a negative impact on those that you love?

It's like this.

My wife is difficult for me to buy gifts for. In her family she grew up picking out her own gifts. Her mom would still wrap them, but she knew what every gift was.

I can't handle that. I love the surprise.

I'm constantly trying to surprise Monica with gifts.

On Valentine's Day we take turns planning whose year it is to spoil the other. One year I'm completely off the hook. I don't have to worry about a gift, a date, or any details. The next year the pressure is on. It's a lot of fun for us.

A few years ago, we were on a really strict budget. It was my year to plan Valentine's Day and I wasn't going to let a budget stop me from planning something amazing.

I went to Pinterest.

I know I'm getting judged for going to Pinterest. Before you jump to a judgment, think about why I went to Pinterest. For my wife! A site called Manterest wouldn't help me make the perfect gift for my wife. I'd end up with a rack of ribs, a chainsaw, and the entire *Rocky* movie series on VHS.

On Pinterest I found a very romantic gift. It was a real-life message in a bottle. I had to buy the supplies and make it, but I knew it was going to get me some.

Some social media love. Get your mind out of the gutter. In today's world it didn't happen unless it's posted on social media. I knew this idea would inspire a share to the masses.

I went to the craft store, bought a glass bottle, a little chain that I had to cut, and a piece of felt to cut a heart out of. Felt. I bought felt.

I connected the chain, cut out a heart from the felt, and wrote a personalized note and rolled it up. I attached it all and it came out perfect. Have you ever heard of Pinterest fails? This was a Pinterest Fabulous. It was amazing.

I also bought doughnuts, and flowers.

I presented it to Monica. She said, "Thank you."

That was an okay response, but I was hoping for more. I told myself it would come later that night via social media. Around bedtime I didn't see any social media love.

I asked her how she truly felt about the gift. She said, "It was nice, but not really my style."

She liked it. But…

You know what the issue was? The issue was I was focused on myself. Focused on doing something that would make me look good, and not doing the difficult work of finding out what my wife would love.

Even if it was only half-selfish it was still partly focused on me. I was so busy trying to make myself look good that I never thought to ask what she would really want.

Since then I've tried to do better. It's not that the message in the bottle was bad. It was good. It just wasn't great for Monica.

So, I've tried to do a better job at listening. I try to do the hard work to figure out what my wife needs.

For Mother's Day this year my gifts were based around what Monica truly wanted. With her job, our twins, and the busyness of life, she often mentions how she doesn't enjoy planning dinner. She does an amazing job, but with all she has going on she doesn't enjoy it.

My gift was a meal delivery service. Once a month a recipe and the meal are delivered to our home. Not only that but I made dinner for her on Mother's Day. I went to Pinterest again. Chicken Cordon Bleu Pasta. It was glorious. In fact, Monica said it was her favorite Mother's Day to date.

And...

I got some.

Some social media love.

What's my point with all of this? My point is that so often even when we do something nice, it's tainted with self. We still think about "What am I going to get?" We think about "What's in it for me?" We think about "How can I benefit from this?" We often get in our own way from truly blessing others.

So, what's the answer to this? If we are all a little selfish and if the natural question is to ask what am I going to get out of this, what are we supposed to do? I believe the answer is found in the following statement...

Life has meaning when you focus on serving and giving.

What happens if you have ambition?

What do we do when we want to succeed at life? Having ambition is not wrong. In fact, it's right. If you have a job, you are called to work your job as unto the Lord. If you have a home business, you should set big goals. If you have a dream, make it big. Ambition isn't wrong. Selfish ambition is. We fight this when we intentionally plan on serving.

Life has meaning when you focus on serving and giving.

If you are great at something, you should work hard to become the best at it. But the way to stay humble is to ultimately do what you do to serve others.

Your talents that God has given you are not meant to be spent on your pleasure alone. The greatest pleasure in life is when you take the gifts that God has given you and you use them to serve other people. If you can bake then don't fall into the trap of baking for applause. You bake to serve the people in your life. That means you have to go the second mile and find out what they love to eat. It's not about you. If you are a leader then you are called to serve those you are leading. It's not about being the top dog. It's about serving those who God has entrusted to you. Do nothing out of selfish ambition.

So how do you do something great and not do it for selfish ambition? You serve.

That's how you do nothing out of selfish ambition. You start with wanting to help people get what they want. Serve others.

Service is finding practical ways to show people they matter even when they can't return the favor.

That's the calling of following Jesus. To find practical ways to show people they matter even when they can't return the favor.

The temptation in every relationship is to fight to show why you matter. As Christians we have to flip the script and fight to show why they matter.

What did Paul say? Don't look to your own interests all the time. Look to the interests of others.

Here are some questions to help us think about others first.

Do you understand before trying to be understood?
Do you take the time to listen and learn about others, or are you focused more on your own agenda?
Do you know your friends' favorites?
Do you have anyone in your life that you serve even though they can't pay you back?

Listening to your family, friends, and the people you meet is a huge way to show second-mile service. The other day at the gym one of my coaches was feeling tired. A lot of days he drinks an energy drink. On that day he didn't have one. When I heard he was tired, I thought, "I can do something about that." After my workout I drove to the store and bought him an energy drink. No big deal, right? Except for the fact that listening shows people you care about them. It made his day.

Amy is a person who was very plugged into the church I pastor. She invited more people to our church than any other person. She moved to Arizona for school and it wasn't the easiest transition. She was flying back to Virginia for a quick layover before traveling overseas. She was only going to be here for a couple of nights. My wife uses the app Marco Polo and you record video messages to each other. I was lying in bed listening to Amy's Marco Polo and she said that she wanted her visit to be low-key here. She just wanted to see a few friends. But she said she was really sad because what she wanted most was to go to church on a Sunday and she wasn't going to be able to make that work. So, I listened. And we decided to throw a church service on a Thursday night. We had worship, I wrote a special talk, we had ushers and greeters. It was a small gathering of her friends that she had been in groups with or had invited to Next Level. She said it was one of the best things anyone had ever done for her.

It's so easy to only focus on self. It's easy…and destructive.

Ryan Leaf is a former NFL quarterback who ended up throwing away his career due to a drug addiction. In an interview Ryan said, "I was a drug addict long before I ever took a drug. Spoiled entitled athlete is what addict behavior looks like."[4]

In prison his cellmate spoke some truth into his life. His cellmate said, "You don't understand your value. We are going to go down to the library and teach guys who don't know how to read, how to read."

While reflecting on teaching other prisoners in the library, Ryan said, "That was the first time in my life I had been a service to someone that wasn't selfish in any way."

Simon Sinek is one of my favorite authors. I love his quote…

"You can easily judge the character of a man by how he treats those who can do nothing for him."[5]

4   Ryan Leaf, interview on *Mike and Mike*, ESPN, 2017, http://www.espn.com/espnradio/play/ /id/18965845.

5   Simon Sinek, *Leaders Eat Last: Why Some Teams Pull Together and Others Don't* (New York: Portfolio, 2017). Quote accessed online.

We all have some areas in our lives where we have some selfishness.

We also have some amazing areas in our lives. Don't beat yourself up about the selfish areas. Let the love of Jesus transform you so you can move away from them.

In your relationships with one another, have the same mindset as Christ Jesus: (Philippians 2:5)

What was Jesus' mindset? It was to serve. Think about that. The most important man to ever live didn't come to be served, but to serve. That's our inspiration.

A JESUS EXAMPLE

I love that Jesus didn't just preach at us how we are supposed to live. He modeled it.

As Jesus and his disciples were leaving Jericho, a large crowd followed him. Two blind men were sitting by the roadside, and when they heard that Jesus was going by, they shouted, "Lord, Son of David, have mercy on us!" The crowd rebuked them and told them to be quiet, but they shouted all the louder, "Lord, Son of David, have mercy on us!"
Jesus stopped and called them. "What do you want me to do for you?" he asked.
"Lord," they answered, "we want our sight."
Jesus had compassion on them and touched their eyes. Immediately they received their sight and followed him. (Matthew 20:29–34)

Jesus was incredibly busy. He had things to do. He knew he only had a little over three years to get all of his work done. Think about that. We run around stressed and busy and we aren't doing anything quite as noble as saving the world. Jesus had three years to save the world and yet during the busiest time of his life he stopped what he was doing to help some beggars.

What really makes this significant is the common thought in Jesus' day was that sinners, beggars, outcasts, etc. were the reason why the Jews were under Roman rule. The thought was it was their fault. To associate with the less-than was a slap in the face of the religious elite. Simply by spending time with "sinners" Jesus was destroying the class system of his day. Loving those who were deemed unlovable was a radical shift in society.

And yet, Jesus constantly stopped what he was doing to serve the least of these.

I love the quote from Pastor Rick Warren...

"Being a servant means giving up the right to control your schedule and allowing God to interrupt it any time He needs to."[6]

Being busy is a major sign that we are consumed with ourselves. We are all busy. We are busy being consumed with self. The second mile is where the magic happens, and in relationships that's when we take time to listen to others, serve others, and take interest in other people.

When it comes to family we often think, "What am I going to get?"

---

6   Rick Warren (@RickWarren), Twitter.

If you look for your family to make you happy and you constantly look to see what you can get from them emotionally, you will be royally disappointed. That is not their role. Instead of asking what you can get from your family, ask what you can give.

Let's talk about friends. It's easy to feel left out and think, "I wish they would have included me." I hear people talk to one another all the time, and so much of the conversation is based off what they are or are not getting. When we don't get what we want, we use guilt to try to get it. We say things like "Why didn't you call me?" or "Why didn't you invite me?" or "You know, I would have really liked to go?"

In our hurt we think giving a little hurt will teach them a lesson.

The problem is no one is motivated to be friends by guilt. The very thing we often do to have our needs met is the very thing that pushes people away. As long as we focus on "get," we will always fight to get what we think is ours. Jesus modeled a better way.

Instead of seeking what you can get, see what you can give. When you feel left out, give a phone call and plan a get-together. When you feel lonely, seek to give a friendship. When you feel like you aren't getting what you deserve, seek to give someone what they don't deserve. Isn't that what Jesus did with you and me?

What about with church? We so often ask, "What am I getting?" We only join a group if we think we are going to get something out of it. Add to that the times people bail on a group after one or two weeks because they don't think they will get anything out of it. We only volunteer if we think we get something out of it. It's easy to consume the church and ask, "What am I getting out of it?" So often people consume the church and then leave to find something new.

One of the clearest ways to tell if someone is a church consumer versus contributor is if they say thank you.

Many times, people seek to have their needs met at a church. It's an expectation. I'm all for finding a church where you can grow. What stings is when a pastor gives counseling, prayer, time, etc. to someone and they leave the first time one of their needs isn't met. Of course, not everyone who leaves a church is a church consumer, but I am friends with enough pastors to know it happens often. I don't help people because I want a thank-you, but when I receive one I know the person is not just looking to consume.

Whether it's with your family, friends, church, or job, remember...

Life has meaning when you focus on serving and giving.

You want to know how to get the most out of church? I mentioned this in an earlier chapter, but it's so important.

If you are a Christian, invite an unchurched person to church and you'll start getting more out of church. Until you do that the temptation is to only look at what you are getting. When we don't invite, we tend to view the service through our own personal lens. We ask questions like "Did I like that song?" "Do I like that sermon series?" "Is it worth my time to volunteer?"

Invite an unchurched person to church and you will start to see church through their eyes. All of a sudden you start to see why volunteering is so important. You start to want things to be just right because you are concerned about someone else.

APRIL FOOLS' EASTER

Easter of 2018 was on April 1. Because Easter is the Super Bowl for churches, I figured most people wouldn't be thinking about pulling pranks. Our Easter services often double in attendance. It was a little scary, but on the biggest day of the year we decided to pull an April Fools' prank on our church. The service went along as normal, but when it came time for the sermon we pulled a fast one. I started the sermon by giving an introduction to the topic and series. From there I said, "For this topic I recruited a little help. Back in 2001 one of my seminary professors taught on this very subject and did an amazing job. Today, for the next thirty-five minutes we are going to listen to his sermon."

People were not expecting to hear from a guest preacher on Easter. Some gave me the benefit of the doubt, but then the video started. It wasn't a video. It was a picture of my seminary professor and the audio of the sermon. It was dry. We played the video for a little over two minutes. It felt like two hours. A little after the two-minute mark, the words "In honor of April 1st…April Fools'" came on the screen. There was loud laughter. And a deep sense of relief.

After the service I heard the same thing over and over again. The general message was the same. "I was so frustrated with you! I have been begging my friend/family member to come to church and they finally came! I had no idea how I was going to explain this video to them."

The point is, when you invite you expect. When you invite you see things differently. When you invest in others and they come with you, it pulls on your heart. You want everything to be perfect. We all know that God is bigger than any of our mistakes. We all know that God is bigger than a boring sermon or a mess-up in the service. We know that, but because people matter to God we desperately want to show them they matter to us. When someone matters to you, the desire is to give them your best.

My hope is that you get a lot of Jesus every week at church, but if you don't invest and invite someone else in, eventually you will consume all that's good here and move on.

That's what spectators do. Spectators look to be entertained, and when it's no longer entertaining they complain.

Contributors look to give back to make things better.

Consumers complain when their needs aren't met but are annoyed to help.

So many people serve to get something in return. We serve to feel good about ourselves. We serve so that someone will accept us. We serve to get noticed.

True service starts when you allow your needs to be met fully in Jesus. You are accepted in Jesus. You don't serve to get him to notice you. You don't serve to get him to love you. You are loved by Jesus. When you allow Jesus to serve you, you grow to understand what it means to serve without wanting anything in return.

So, you serve your spouse without wanting something in return. You serve your kids without feeling drained. You serve your church without expecting a bonus. We serve others without expecting anything in return because all of our needs have been met in Jesus' service to us. And while you serve it's amazing to see your needs being met.

Find your joy in making others joyful.

But in order to truly do that you must get past your "me."

THREE PHASES OF ME

I've found that there are three phases of "me."
Phase 1: Me
Phase 2: Me to You
Phase 3: You to Me

We are born into Phase 1. So many of us have never graduated to Phase 2. Phase 1 is about me, myself, and I. It's about doing what feels best. It's about building your kingdom no matter what it costs you. It's about avoiding self-discipline. It's about spending now. It's about doing what feels good. It's about me. This phase is self-centered, selfish, and all about me. Common characteristics of this phase are one-sided conversations that never turn back to the person you are talking to, destructive behavior that hurts yourself and others, and overdramatizing your problems.

Now the ultimate struggle that people in the "me" phase deal with is it becomes really lonely. After a while me-only living pushes others away. Often me-only living leaves a person with such desperation they will find a way to include others. Either that or they will accept isolation and blame others for their loneliness.

That takes us to Phase 2: Me to You.

This phase is where most of us land. We get to a point where we realize that we need other people to feel whole. The problem is that we still have such selfishness in us that we only like people who mutually benefit us. A lot of friendships can last for a long time in this phase. A lot of marriages can as well. The problem with this phase is that as soon as the other person is no longer benefiting you, you drop 'em like it's hot. Two half-selfish people create one whole selfish mess.

Phase 2 is still all about "me," but because we are so desperate for relationships we include "you." Phase 2 says, "I'm still going to do what's best for me, but I'm going to include you." Phase 2 can last for a lifetime because the relational need is met. Phase 2 is the person who only calls when they need something. Phase 2 is the person who looks to see what they can get back from giving to others. Phase 2 says, "I'll be nice to you as long as it's mutually beneficial." As soon as a relationship gets too difficult, a Phase 2 person moves on. Now because a relational connection is there, people get stuck in Phase 2. Phase 2 never leaves us feeling fully satisfied. We live in Phase 2 and it leaves us wanting to know if there is anything more to this life. Phase 2 has relationships, so it has moments of contentment and fulfillment, but ultimately it fails to create great purpose in life.

Very few people move to Phase 3. This is where wholeness comes from. In order to get to Phase 3, it takes humility. It takes humbly admitting that you need Jesus.

True meaning and significance comes from giving more than you take. Jesus was perfect and is the ultimate goal for us to live. In his perfection he considered our needs greater than his own. He put us before himself by ultimately dying. When we become like Jesus, we become whole because we give more than we take from others. Phase 3 is only accomplished by those who are whole. When a person becomes whole in Jesus, he starts to push them through the phases until he or she becomes like him.

Jesus was the Phase 3 architect. Jesus put you before himself. Jesus loves you even when it doesn't benefit himself. In fact, how does loving humans benefit him? He died for us and we do exactly what for him? Jesus loves the dirty, the down-and-out, the sinner, the self-righteous, the lost, the misguided, the confused, the rich, the poor, the American, the anti-American, the sinner, and the self-righteous. Jesus loves the world and the world does jack squat for him. Jesus puts us before himself and as Christians we are to consider his example and allow God to lead us into Phase 3 living.

Phase 3 says, "It's you first, then me." Phase 3 happens when we become whole in Jesus.

"The greater the brokenness, the less a person contributes to the relationship and the more they demand. Emotional wholeness is seen in what you can contribute to others. The spiritually whole consider others more important than themselves."[7]

—Erwin McManus

If you have ever wondered why someone can hurt you so, it's because they are broken. Hurt people, hurt people. They are in need of your prayer and not your anger. They are in need of your pity and not your spite. They are in need of your forgiveness and not your bitterness. They might be so broken that they need you to leave them. Never ever allow a broken person to damage you. You can love someone from a distance. The more broken a person, the less they will contribute to the relationship.

The greatest meaning to this life is found when we are a blessing to others. And not a blessing that somehow is still all about us. I'm writing about a blessing that considers Jesus' example. I'm writing about a blessing that leaves the comforts of home for more than a photo-op on a short-term mission trip. I'm writing about a

---

7   Erwin R. McManus, "Broken People Can Become Whole Disciples," *Christianity Today*, 2000, https://www.christianitytoday.com/pastors/2000/spring/8.48.html.

blessing that gives even when there is nothing to get out of it. I'm writing about a person who looks like Jesus.

Not too long ago, I went to Haiti on a mission trip. It was an amazing trip. It was at times a very difficult trip. Our first stop was an incredibly poor orphanage. I went there to feed orphans, but I wasn't prepared for just how poor these kids were.

These were kids who desperately craved love and attention. For the first hour I had to battle out of Phase 2. You see, at first it was fun because we took pictures with needy kids that we could post on Facebook or Instagram. For the first few minutes it was comfortable. But then...

Then the kids wanted to more than be our photo-ops. They wanted hugs, to play, to laugh, to be wanted. One kid came right up to me and grabbed my hand. It was incredibly cute until I noticed that he had peed his pants. I'm a borderline germaphobe, so this was stretching my mental capacity. He was looking for time and attention and all I could think of was how I was going to have to drink the hand sanitizer just to make sure all the pee germs were off of me. After a brief gut check and prayer, I moved out of Phase 2 and into Phase 3. It was a good thing too because the next kid that attached himself to me was pant-less. I felt something like a spider monkey crawl onto my arm. When I looked over I saw this really cute kid. He was a really cute kid with no pants. I jokingly yelled, "Where are your pants?" He didn't speak English. He smiled. He smiled and kept holding on like this was normal.

This orphanage pushed me. I like serving until it costs me something. Serving these kids was costing me my comfort. It was costing me my time. It was costing me sweat. It was pushing me. It was no longer about me. It was about those kids. It was about showing strangers love. It was about feeding the hungry. It was about helping people who could never do anything for me in return.

I so often teeter between Phase 2 and Phase 3. I love people. I also love serving myself. I'm a work in progress. Building Jesus' kingdom pushes you to follow Jesus' example. It was a kingdom built on service. It was a kingdom built on sacrifice. It was a kingdom worth dying for.

I don't know about you, but I want to live a life worthy of King Jesus. I want to live a life full of purpose, meaning, and significance.

COMING FULL CIRCLE

It's Phase 3 that leads to overcoming our foolish decisions. This chapter started by looking at what it meant to be a fool. A fool knows the difference between right and wrong but chooses to do what's wrong anyway. A person who is whole chooses to do what's right.

Becoming whole in Jesus is where we move from accepting God in our hearts as long as he helps build our kingdom, to following Jesus to build God's kingdom. Becoming whole in Jesus is where we move from relationships that simply benefit us to relationships where we pour our lives into others. Becoming whole is where we follow Jesus' example and in humility consider others better than ourselves.

Let me write you a question. I know technically it should be "ask you a question," but you're reading what I'm writing. I digress.

Let me write you a question: whose needs do you put ahead of your own? Not in a mutually beneficial way or in a way that is based off circumstances. Who can you serve?

I am by no means perfect. There are lots of areas in which I struggle. There are times where I put my needs ahead of everyone else's. There are times where I ask God what he can do for me and don't care what I can do for him. But there are times where I've lived in Phase 3 and it's been those times where I've experienced amazing growth. One of those times was when I was nineteen years old.

I felt called to ministry when I was eighteen years old. As soon as I said yes, my church threw a ministry opportunity at me. For three years I was in charge of a boys' middle school small group. They were in sixth grade when I started. Around this same time, I started attending college. With college came access to this newfangled thing called the Internet. It was awesome.

It came with this really fun buzzing, clanging, beeping sound and about four hours of wait time every time you had to dial up the Internet. Dial-up Internet, if you remember, not only took forever but would tie up the house phone line. I can't tell you how many times I got disconnected because someone picked up the house phone from another room. *You've got to be kidding me! I just waited five whole minutes for this thing to connect!* It is honestly a surprise how families made it out intact during the dial-up days.

The Internet also came with cool things like email. In college I lived for hearing my AOL tell me "You've Got Mail." I also loved Instant Messenger. I'm showing my age.

With the Internet also came easy access to images of women with next to no clothing on. For the most part I was a sheltered Christian school youth group kid. Porn wasn't something that was in my home or a temptation for me. Sure, I appreciated an attractive woman, but I had zero access to porn and no desire. With the Internet, doing a search for something innocent would oftentimes lead to images that would steal your innocence. The first couple of times I closed the page immediately. I then found that I delayed closing the pages. I then found myself searching for images. I would feel all sorts of guilt, ask God to forgive me, vow to never do it again, only to stumble a few days later. One time while feeling tempted I heard a still small voice that said, "What would you do if your students saw you?" I loved the guys of that small group. I wanted to set an example for them. I didn't want to let them down. It was what I needed. In fact, that shift of wanting to serve those guys became so much greater than my selfish desires on the Internet. A true change happened that day. The love for that small group propelled me to live differently.

Today, I have to be extremely careful because temptation is everywhere. I have to be careful about what I watch on TV and in the movies. I have to be careful with what I read. I have to be careful! I have website accountability and filters through a great browser called Covenant Eyes. When I see an attractive woman in too-little clothing I bounce my eyes. That is, I look the other way. When I watch TV I only watch shows without nudity. Before I go to a movie I look up why it's rated what it's rated. If it has nudity in it, I pass on the movie. I don't write any of that to brag. I write that to give hope. Whatever your struggle is, you are not alone. There are lots of others who experience the same type of temptation.

Ultimately, what caused me to change my habits was focusing on who I served. I didn't want to let them down.

Jesus offers a way out.

Serve.
Help others.
Live for something greater than yourself.

It is incredibly easy to move backward from Phase 3 to Phase 1. It's easy to forget Jesus' example. It's easy to forget to put others ahead of yourself. But easy isn't what building Jesus' kingdom is about.

Building Jesus' kingdom is about following his example. An example that loved people so deeply he put their needs ahead of his own. What would your world look like if you followed this example? What would your relationships look like? It'd probably look a lot like Jesus.

Application: If you do not already, find a volunteer position at your church. Seek to make a difference by intentionally serving.

Questions:
1. What are some daily routines that make life difficult and mundane?
2. Read Philippians 2:3–4. What are some practical ways you can put the needs of the others in this group or in your life ahead of yourself?
3. Read Philippians 2:5–6. What stands out to you about these verses?
4. Out of the three Phases mentioned in this chapter, which one do you spend the most time in?
5. What would compel you to move up to the next phase?
6. Moving to Phase 3 is not about behavioral modification. It's about spiritual transformation. It's about following Jesus and allowing his love to propel you to love others more than you love yourself. What are three areas

where you would like to be more like Jesus? Spend time this week praying and asking God to specifically help you in those areas.

CHAPTER 9

HOW TO TICK JESUS OFF

Now, I am about to make an assumption. My assumption is that most of us think we tick Jesus off pretty often. I know you probably wouldn't word it that way, but I'm betting I'm right. Jesus is perfect and therefore all of us know we can't reach his status. Jesus is also loving, so there is this conundrum of "I know Jesus loves me, but he has to be a little bit ticked off at me."

I think our culture at large feels like it's pretty easy to tick God off. For example, when I invite someone to church it is not uncommon for me to hear, "If I come the roof may cave in." Maybe you have even said that. In the history of our church we have had a lot of "sinners" visit church, and so far, the ceiling has only collapsed once. Now before you panic and think that it collapsed because a really bad sinner came to church, you should know that it collapsed because of a staff member. When we were first given our church building, we had five weeks to do a lot of work and get it ready for our first service. The week of our grand opening I was walking around just looking at everything. I was taking it in. I was thanking God for the miracle of giving us a building. I walked into the auditorium, and I saw a hole in the ceiling. I thought it must have been a leak from the rain we had that week, so I ran to go talk to the other staff. When I started talking to the other staff, they casually dismissed it by saying, "It's not rain, JoJo fell through the ceiling." JoJo is not his real name. I changed it to not embarrass him.

After they told me he fell through our ceiling, I thought, "Do what?!" That's kind of a big deal. Why didn't anyone tell me about this? And a distant second thought was, was JoJo okay? He was okay. And he didn't fall through because Jesus was judging him and his sin. He fell through because he misstepped. He was running cable and accidentally took a step off the support beam and through the ceiling. Apparently, his legs were dangling through the ceiling of our auditorium. In a day and age of cell phones I still don't know why no one got a picture of this. I digress.

Now there are some of you reading this who might not feel like you tick Jesus off, but I'm betting even you think that from time to time Jesus looks at you and does a facepalm. If you are not familiar with a facepalm, it is the ultimate sign of disbelief and frustration.

Most of us believe that our actions frustrate Jesus. Sure, he loves us, but because he is perfect and we are not, he must get frustrated with us.

It's funny to me that we've come to this conclusion because I've read through all four of the accounts of Jesus' life multiple times and I don't see that Jesus. I see a Jesus whose heart breaks for sinners. I see a Jesus who is loving and patient and views people like sheep without a Shepherd. That is, he views them as needing direction but from a loving guide. I see a picture of Jesus who runs to sinners when they come home. I see a picture of Jesus who hangs out with sinners and is actually their friend. It's not that he approves of their sin, but he knows in order to truly convince them of his love, he can't be distant. He can't love sinners from the comforts of heaven. He has to be with them. To show them who he is. To show them love is near.

When we strive to build Jesus' kingdom, we must care about what he cares about. We must learn to love what he loves. We must learn to be more like him. That includes learning what truly does tick Jesus off. If it bothers him, it should bother us.

Is Jesus face-palming every time we mess up? Is he disappointed with us? No!

Now, if you think Jesus is a complete pacifist we are going to see later that he is not. Jesus does get ticked off. What ticks him off is different than what you might think.

I want to give a little context about what we are going to read. The text is one that makes it into two of the four gospel accounts. The New Testament of the Bible starts with the four gospels of Matthew, Mark, Luke, and John. We are going to read this account from Mark's perspective. Mark wrote this section with a non-Jewish crowd in mind. You will see Mark takes time to explain a few things and he does this specifically to help the non-Jewish readers understand what is going on. Remember Jesus was a Jew. So were his followers. The movement of Jesus became a worldwide phenomenon. Mark writes for those who did not grow up in Jewish households.

With that, let's dive in.

The Pharisees and some of the teachers of the law who had come from Jerusalem gathered around Jesus and saw some of his disciples eating food with hands that were defiled, that is, unwashed. (The Pharisees and all the Jews do not eat unless they give their hands a ceremonial washing, holding to the tradition of the elders. When they come from the marketplace they do not eat unless they wash. And they observe many other traditions, such as the washing of cups, pitchers and kettles.) (Mark 7:1–4)

Okay, let's stop there for a second. Some Pharisees came from Jerusalem and saw some of Jesus' disciples eating food with hands that were defiled, that is, unwashed. Then Mark goes into an explanation of this. All the Jews do not eat unless they give their hands a ceremonial washing. Now that tells us a lot. That tells us that this wasn't about hygiene. This was about something far greater and deeper.

In the Jewish culture there is the idea that certain things were ceremonially clean and unclean. Translation: there are certain things that you could do that would make you holy or unholy. In Jesus' day, before you would eat a meal with bread, it was incredibly important to wash your hands.

The hand washing before meals has nothing to do with hygiene. It is not about cleanliness. It is about holiness. Cleanliness is a physical state. By removing dirt, you become clean. But holiness is an entirely spiritual concept. Holiness means a sense of something beyond, something higher, something with a higher purpose. You can be completely clean, but that doesn't mean you're holy.

The ceremonial washing would look something like this. It involved a special cup with two handles. The cup is filled with water and starts in the left hand. Taking the cup, you pour water on your right hand three times. Then the cup is passed to the right hand, but it is important to have a towel in your hand to now hold the cup. This is where the two handles come in on the cup. After you pour water on your left hand three times, you then rub your hands together while saying the following prayer.

"Blessed art Thou, O Lord our God, King of the universe, who has sanctified us with Thy commandments and has commanded us concerning the washing of the hands."

Okay, so this process was to signify that a person was now ceremonially clean. And this was a big deal.

One Jewish rabbi said...

"Holiness means connecting to something higher. It means living with an awareness that not all dirt is visible, and we don't always see the effect of our actions. So before engaging in physical activity, before consuming the fruit of our handiwork, we wash our hands. They may be clean already, but we must ensure that they are pure and holy too."[1]

—Rabbi Moss

Now even though this was all done in the name of God, this wasn't something that God told them to do. There isn't a verse in the Bible that said to do this ceremony. This was something that was instituted by the Rabbis.

The obligation to wash the hands was instituted by the Rabbis more than two thousand years ago. Jews follow Torah. It's the first five books of the Old Testament. Jews also follow the oral teachings of Rabbis passed down from generation to generation. They explained that the "Oral" Torah commands to obey the Rabbis and by obeying the Rabbis you are indirectly obeying God. So, the blessing that God commanded us to wash our hands is really a declaration of our obedience to the God-given authority of the Rabbis to enact new commandments.

Okay, you still tracking with me? This wasn't something that was instituted by God, but it was done by all the Rabbis. And Jesus

1   Rabbi Moss, "Are Your Hands Clean?" *Rabbi Moss* (blog), July 15, 2010, https://rabbimoss.blogspot.com/2010/07/are-your-hands-clean.html.

is a rabbi. When the Pharisees see that Jesus' disciples aren't ceremonially clean, they freak out.

Orthodox Jews considered the breaking of this tradition to be as serious as, for example, sexual immorality.

Jesus is being called out for not obeying a religious custom and look how he responds.

> So the Pharisees and teachers of the law asked Jesus, "Why don't your disciples live according to the tradition of the elders instead of eating their food with defiled hands?"
> He replied, "Isaiah was right when he prophesied about you hypocrites; as it is written:
> "'These people honor me with their lips,
> but their hearts are far from me.
> They worship me in vain;
> their teachings are merely human rules.'
> You have let go of the commands of God and are holding on to human traditions." (Mark 7:5–8)

Oh snap! Jesus just got ticked off. But notice what he got ticked off about. He wasn't ticked because someone sinned. He was ticked because there was a culture of caring more about man's customs than God's.

In other words, Jesus was ticked because the people thought as long as they checked off a few boxes, they were good to go with God.

Today, it would be like thinking if you go to church, or if you give money to the church, or if you volunteer, then it is a sign that you are close to God.

That's like thinking if you walk into a Pizza Hut you'll automatically become a large pepperoni stuffed crust pizza.

Ultimately, Jesus got ticked because religious people were blind to their own sin.

Jesus doesn't get ticked when Christians sin. He gets ticked when Christians pretend not to.

And that is the problem with religion. Religion is all about checks and balances. The thought is if you do a few religious things then you are good to go with God. If you take communion, if you've been baptized, if you've been confirmed in the church, then you are in. If not, then you are out.

If you are new to Christianity, then you are in a great place. It's those of us who have been Christians for a while who need to be concerned. Because the longer you are a Christian, the easier it is to forget just how much of a sinner you really are. And when you forget how much of a sinner you really are, you become prideful. And when you become prideful you start to overlook the sins in your life.

I once read a fascinating blog post on Jerry Sandusky. You might remember him as one of the Pen State coaches who for years sexually abused kids. He did all sorts of evil things and many people even saw signs of it, but they ignored it. Why?

"He actually rescued young, neglected kids. He changed lives. He quoted the Bible. He was known as a man of prayer and a deeply religious man. Before he was caught, he'd do interviews promoting his organization and nearly come to tears talking about the needs of the underprivileged kids in the community."[2]

---

2   Donald Miller, "How Do So Many Good People Get Away with Bad Things?" *Storyline* (blog), May 11, 2015, http://storylineblog.com/2015/05/11/good-people-bad-things/.

It's scary to think that in some regards Jerry Sandusky was a better Christian than most Christians while at the same time he had this secret life that was horrific.

And as much as we don't want to admit it, we all have more in common with Jerry Sandusky than we'd like to think. We may not commit the same type of crimes as he did, but it's easy to play the same game. It's easy to believe that if you go to church, read your Bible, say a prayer, volunteer, give a little money that your works have made you into a good person. And Jesus got ticked at this type of thinking.

Jesus got ticked at religious people who were prideful. Let's see what he says to end this section.

> He went on: "What comes out of a person is what defiles them. For it is from within, out of a person's heart, that evil thoughts come—sexual immorality, theft, murder, adultery, greed, malice, deceit, lewdness, envy, slander, arrogance and folly. All these evils come from inside and defile a person." (Mark 7:20–23)

Jesus doesn't want just your church attendance. Jesus doesn't just want your money. Jesus wants your heart. And if we are not careful we will become religious. We will focus on manmade things and fool ourselves into thinking that we are really living for Jesus. And this is what is so brilliant about what Jesus said.

He is challenging us to look at our actions. Look at the words you use. Look at your attitudes toward other people. Do you look down on other sinners? Do you have a hard time forgiving other people? Do you envy others? Do you look at pornography? Jesus isn't ticked at you because you sin. He's ticked at you because you think doing religious things outweighs your sin. We have to be honest with ourselves, and our words and actions are a reflection of our hearts. When Jesus has our heart, our actions follow.

Jesus is patient with sinners; he gets ticked at religious people who act like they don't sin.

So, what do we do about this?

We seek humility.
We remember that we aren't perfect.
We become honest with our own sins.
We confess.
We repent.
We repeat.

Sin is messy, but hidden sin is explosive.

It's fascinating to me that Jesus only got ticked at religious people. What he started was a movement and it's now become the very thing that he taught against. We turned the movement into a religion. Now that Christianity is established it means we have something to lose. As long as we feel we have something to lose, we will fight to pretend to be better than we really are.

Jesus doesn't want us to pretend. He loves us. He loves the real us. Through his love we can be inspired to change.

LEGALISM TICKS JESUS OFF

The church is always so concerned with God being ticked off at people following the right rules and regulations. God has standards, but God's heart breaks when we sin. We hurt ourselves and others when we sin. What ticks Jesus off is not that we sin but when we become so comfortable that we don't give a rip about our fellow humans.

We are going to look at a time where Jesus dealt with the Pharisees. The verses we are about to read are going to build upon an event. Before we get to the Scripture let's summarize the event.

Jesus and his disciples were walking through a grain field when some of them picked some grain to eat it. The Pharisees saw this and got ticked off. Jesus responds to them and says, "The Sabbath was made for man, not man for the Sabbath." Translation: The Sabbath was made to help men, not to be a stumbling block to men. Then Jesus says, "I'm the Lord of the Sabbath," and he drops the proverbial mic and walks off. It was awesome. This didn't settle very well with the Pharisees. And with that context let's dive into our text for today.

> **Another time Jesus went into the synagogue, and a man with a shriveled hand was there. Some of them were looking for a reason to accuse Jesus, so they watched him closely to see if he would heal him on the Sabbath. (Mark 3:1–2)**

Let's stop there for a second. The verse starts off by saying, "Another time Jesus went into the synagogue." Jesus went into the Jewish synagogue, which was his custom. This would be like a church on steroids. This was a very sacred place for Jews. There were some religious leaders who were envious of Jesus and were looking for a way to trap him. Specifically, they wanted to see if he would heal on the Sabbath. Jesus had just shut them up by saying he was Lord of the Sabbath and now they were looking for a way to take out Jesus. Now it's interesting that the

Pharisees didn't doubt that Jesus could heal. They didn't doubt that Jesus did miracles. They weren't concerned with if Jesus could do miracles. They were concerned with if he would heal on the Sabbath. Now that is just ridiculous. But let's put ourselves in Jewish culture for just a second to try to better understand what is happening.

The Sabbath was on Saturday and was considered a holy day of rest. In the Ten Commandments God tells his people to rest.

> "Remember the Sabbath day by keeping it holy. Six days you shall labor and do all your work, but the seventh day is a sabbath to the Lord your God. On it you shall not do any work, neither you, nor your son or daughter, nor your male or female servant, nor your animals, nor any foreigner residing in your towns. For in six days the Lord made the heavens and the earth, the sea, and all that is in them, but he rested on the seventh day. Therefore the Lord blessed the Sabbath day and made it holy. (Exodus 20:8–11)

So traditionally Saturday was a holy day of rest. It was a day to go to the synagogue and focus on your relationship with God. This is a good thing. In fact, this is something we should practice more today. We are so busy and so active that we actually accomplish a lot less work than in years past.

Our busyness creates stress, and actually causes us to do less work. I love the insight by one author…

> "Busyness serves as a kind of existential reassurance, a hedge against emptiness; obviously your life cannot

possibly be silly or trivial or meaningless if you are so busy, completely booked, in demand every hour of the day."[3]

—Tim Kreider

We have become addicted to being busy. In fact, the number one response that people give when asked how are you doing is "I'm so busy."

Max Lucado is a brilliant writer. I love his insight about busyness…

"Busyness is an expert in robbing the sparkle and replacing with the drab. Busyness invented the yawn and put the hum in humdrum. The strategy of busyness is deceptive! With the passing of time He'll infiltrate your heart with fatigue and cover the cross with dust so you will be safely out of the reach of change."[4]

Busyness creates a feeling as if we are important but leads us to ignore the things that are most important.

Busyness makes us say no to playing games with our kids, going on dates with our spouses, and hanging out with our friends. Busyness will cause us to not work on ourselves. We won't take time to improve because we are so busy doing the same things.

But why are we busy? We are busy because we have chosen to be busy. God created the earth in six days and then rested. We try to do what not even God did when we work seven days a week.

3   Tim Kreider, "The 'Busy' Trap," *Opionator* (blog), *New York Times*, June 30, 2012, https://opinionator.blogs.nytimes.com/2012/06/30/the-busy-trap/.

4   Max Lucado, *Growing the Marriage of Your Dreams: 4 Interactive Bible Studies for Individuals or Small Groups*, Max on Life (Nashville: Thomas Nelson, 2007), CD-Book.

And science is showing us that why so many of us are stressed, worried, and anxious actually has to do with our constant busyness or the pressure we feel to be busy.

The American Psychological Association has published its Stress in America survey since 2007. They find that the majority of Americans recognize that their stress exceeds levels necessary to maintain good health. The most frequent reason they cite for not addressing the problem? Being too busy.

Let that sink in. We know we have a problem, but we are too busy to deal with the problem.

And God knows how we are supposed to function because he made us. God said that we are to work for six days and make sure that we take a sabbath. To make sure that we rest. To make sure we have time to take a nap. To make sure we have time to be idle and think.

> "Idleness is not just a vacation, an indulgence or a vice; it is as indispensable to the brain as vitamin D is to the body, and deprived of it we suffer a mental affliction as disfiguring as rickets."[5]
>
> —Tim Kreider

We need a sabbath. We need time to ourselves to just be. And the Rabbis in Jesus' day understood this all too well. In fact, they took a good rule by God and turned it into a legalistic weight that was almost impossible to carry. In Jesus' day the religious leaders had gone crazy with the rules. They had added all sorts of rules to help the people not sin. What started off as general, do not work,

---

5   Tim Kreider, "The 'Busy' Trap."

became very specific. In fact, it came to mean that you could not take more than three thousand steps in a day. I don't know if they had an old-school pedometer or ancient version of the Fitbit, but somehow, they counted their steps. So what God intended to be a day of rest to refresh became a heavy burden. In fact, the burden was heavy because if you broke the Sabbath law it was punishable by death. The religious leaders considered healing on the Sabbath a sin and were hoping that Jesus would do it so they could kill him. Let's keep going.

> **Jesus said to the man with the shriveled hand, "Stand up in front of everyone." Then Jesus asked them, "Which is lawful on the Sabbath: to do good or to do evil, to save life or to kill?" But they remained silent. (Mark 3:3–4)**

Okay, so there is a man with a shriveled hand and Jesus asks him to stand before everyone. The Pharisees want to see if Jesus is going to heal this guy. Jesus says, "Which is lawful on the Sabbath: to do good or to do evil, to save life or to kill?" Now in Jesus' day you had the written law, which is our Old Testament, and you had the oral law. The oral law for many Jews is on par with the written law. And the oral law is called the Mishnah. It is filled with Rabbis' teachings on the written law. And the Mishnah says,

"Whenever there is doubt whether life is in danger, this overrides the Sabbath."

Jesus is pointing out to the Pharisees that even in their strict understanding of God's laws, they have provided a loophole. If someone is about to die you are permitted to save their life even on the Sabbath. And this is a brilliant move because the Pharisees can't argue with Jesus on this. But after Jesus asks them the question, they remain silent. And this didn't sit very well with Jesus.

> He looked around at them in anger and, deeply distressed at their stubborn hearts, said to the man, "Stretch out your hand." He stretched it out, and his hand was completely restored. Then the Pharisees went out and began to plot with the Herodians how they might kill Jesus. (Mark 3:5–6)

Did you catch that? Jesus got angry. He got angry because there was something worth getting angry over. Jesus asks the religious leaders what is more lawful to do, good or evil? They can't answer that and so Jesus then gets angry. He's angry because they are getting angry over things that don't really matter. He's angry because they have stubborn hearts. He's angry because they care more about looking good than doing good.

The Pharisees are angry because Jesus heals on the Sabbath and Jesus gets angry because they put religious practices over helping people.

We are way more like the Pharisees than we'd like to admit.

About two years ago I was in a meeting and someone was telling me about her complaints about how we do our monthly Make a Difference projects. Every month, our church partners with a local, national, or global organization to make a practical difference in the world. The complaints weren't suggestions. She didn't like what we sponsored. She didn't like how we sponsored them. She offered no suggestions to make it better. She was just complaining about how we were trying to make a difference in the world. I listened, but the more I listened the angrier I got. I wasn't angry that someone was complaining about something at Next Level. I was angry because of what they were angry about. In the grand scheme of things, why are we fighting about something so stupid when there are children dying of hunger every day? Why are we fighting over silly things that don't make a difference in the world? If we are going to get angry, let's get angry over things that lead us to take action and change the world. This conversation was simply about complaining.

Jesus' anger makes the world a better place. What does your anger lead to?

We get angry over the silliest things. We get angry over traffic, and sports teams losing, and spilled milk. Let me pick on Christians for a little while. If you are not a Christian, then this is a good section for you to read because you are off the hook. But if you are a Christian, what are the things that cause you to be angry?

I love the quote by Philip Yancey…

"Christians get very angry toward other Christians who sin differently than they do."[6]

I have yet to see a Christian get angry over the things that actually tick Jesus off. You want to know what ticks Jesus off? Injustice. You want to know what ticks Jesus off? When Christians ignore hurting people, it ticks Jesus off.

How should our hearts respond when someone we know is caught in sin? Our hearts should break. Sin means someone is missing out on God's best.

---

6   Philip Yancey, Homosexuality Q&A, *Philip Yancey*, July 8, 2010, https://philipyancey.com/q-and-a-topics/homosexuality.

I long to be a part of a church where messy people feel welcomed. This won't happen until religious people stop pretending that they are perfect. And that means that we are going to deal with some messiness. We are going to deal with people who sin, and whenever we encounter sin our hearts should break.

I love the quote by Mike Yaconelli...

"Christians do not condone unbiblical living; we redeem it."[7]

You cannot help redeem a culture you are constantly mad at. I've never met anyone who said, "I started to believe in God after I was yelled at and condemned by a Christian." I'm sure there is someone out there who goes against what I just wrote. God is so big he can use anything to win people to himself. The point still stands. Just because we can doesn't mean we should.

I want to be a person whose heart breaks for sinners and who gets angry about things that really matter. I want my anger to change the world. And Jesus gets angry at the Pharisees because they cared more about following a bunch of manmade rules over helping someone.

Would you take a moment to pray the following prayer? You don't have to. It's your choice. If we want to change the world, we have to change. Would you pray the following...

"God, help me to have a heart like yours. Help me to care about what you care about. Help my heart to break for sinners."

---

7   Mike Yaconelli, *Messy Spirituality* (Grand Rapids: Zondervan, 2015). Quote accessed online.

A MISUNDERSTOOD VERSE

As followers of Jesus we are called to live as Jesus did. That means our lives should reflect Jesus. One of Jesus' best friends wrote…

Whoever claims to live in him must live as Jesus did. (1 John 2:6)

Now the author of that verse is a guy named John. He knew Jesus firsthand because he was one of his closest friends. We are to love like Jesus, live like Jesus, and get ticked off like Jesus. So, what ticked Jesus off? Those things should also tick us off. And the same guy who wrote the verse we just read writes about Jesus' most famous explosion of anger. It's an often-preached verse that I think many have misread. Maybe you grew up in the church and you are familiar with this instance of anger, but if you did not grow up in church then put your imaginary seat belt on. This is a wild ride.

When it was almost time for the Jewish Passover, Jesus went up to Jerusalem. In the temple courts he found people selling cattle, sheep and doves, and others sitting at tables exchanging money. So he made a whip out of cords, and drove all from the temple courts, both sheep and cattle; he scattered the coins of the money changers and overturned their tables. To those who sold doves he said, "Get these out of here! Stop turning my Father's house into a market!" His disciples remembered that it is written: "Zeal for your house will consume me." (John 2:13–17)

Jesus went into the temple and gets really upset. This verse says that Jesus made a whip out of cords and then he overturned their tables. Okay, I can tell that me just writing about this isn't really making a point. Jesus went into the temple. Imagine an incredibly nice church. I'm talking about a really proper church. I'm talking about a place with lots of stained glass windows and expensive church furniture. Now imagine that in the middle of a service a guy comes barging in yelling, whipping things, and then flips over tables. Now, this event in history is known as Jesus cleansing the temple.

This event is recorded in all four gospels, which are the four books at the beginning of the New Testament that tell the story of Jesus. In three of the books it happens at the end of Jesus' ministry. In John, the verse that we just read, it happens at the beginning of his ministry. Now many scholars believe that because of the placement of it in John's gospel, Jesus actually hulked out not once but twice. That's huge! Something is going on in the temple that is upsetting Jesus. Now even if this only happened once it's recorded in all four gospels, so I think that it must be incredibly important for us to learn about. So, the question is, what upset Jesus so much?

Well, I need you to stick with me because in order for us to understand this we have to know a little bit of history. Jesus was Jewish, so the temple was the Jewish place for people to worship God. In fact, the word for temple in Hebrew is *Beit YHWH*, which means House of the Lord. The temple was literally known as the footstool of God. God chose to dwell with Israel, and in the Old Testament he tells them to build a house for him. Now, God can't be contained in a house, but it was literally the place where God's presence was felt. It was the holy of holies. The temple was the place where people went to make sacrifices. Before Jesus died, if someone sinned they had to purchase an animal that didn't have any blemishes on it and bring it to the temple to have it sacrificed for their sin. Now the reason that Christians don't have to sacrifice animals when we mess up is because Jesus was the ultimate sacrifice. He was broken for our sin. And thank God for that! I love meat. I'm a meatatarian. But as much as I love meat, I do not want to go to church and see a whole bunch of animals being sacrificed. No, thank you. Can you imagine if we tried that today? It would be such a mess.

The temple served as a place where people went to offer sacrifices for their sins. It was also the place where rabbis would teach about God. You still with me? The temple was a house where God's presence dwelt, and it was supposed to be a holy place. Well, let's look at the temple cleansing from another book of the Bible and see why Jesus got so upset.

> On reaching Jerusalem, Jesus entered the temple courts and began driving out those who were buying and selling there. He overturned the tables of the money changers and the benches of those selling doves, and would not allow anyone to carry merchandise through the temple courts. And as he taught them, he said, "Is it not written: 'My house will be called a house of prayer for all nations'? But you have made it 'a den of robbers.'" (Mark 11:15–17)

In this account Jesus gets upset because when he goes to the temple there are people who are selling all sorts of animals. Now remember that I told you that people had to have an animal sacrificed in order to have their sins forgiven? Well, because there was only one temple, people would come from all over to worship God in the temple. If you traveled a long distance you often couldn't carry an animal to be sacrificed, and you couldn't risk it becoming hurt and therefore imperfect on the long journey. There were men who were selling animals, but they were overcharging for the animals. They were also selling a special temple coin. They would say that the Roman coin wasn't acceptable to God. They were being dishonest and making a huge profit in the church. So, Jesus hulks out on them.

Okay, now traditionally this verse has been accepted in the church as saying we should never sell anything. I worked at a church once where we brought in a special singer. She was on *American Idol* and was also a Christian. She had some copies of her Christian music and we sold it. That upset some people. They didn't turn over tables like Jesus, but they did quote the verse about Jesus flipping tables to us.

But was Jesus really anti selling anything in the church? I think there is a lot more going on here than that. Jesus initially gets upset because they are creating a heavy burden to come to God. It's not just that you had to sacrifice an animal, it's that they created a special coin that you had to have, and they overpriced the sale of animals. Translation: there was a lot of corruption going on in the temple.

Instead of just helping people, they had turned it into a market. And it was very successful. They were making a lot of money. And Jesus goes buck wild crazy. We can understand a little bit better why this upset Jesus so much when we look at what happened after he calmed down. After Jesus cooled off he taught the people and said this...

"Is it not written: 'My house will be called a house of prayer for all nations'? But you have made it 'a den of robbers.'" (Mark 11:17)

Jesus is quoting someone and the question we need to ask is, "Who is Jesus quoting?" That's a great question. Thanks for asking it.

Jesus is quoting Isaiah. Isaiah prophesied a lot about the Messiah and so it makes sense why Jesus quotes from Isaiah so much. Well, in Isaiah he prophesies about who will be a part of the family of God. Now, stick with me on this. This is why Jesus got so ticked off. Look at what Isaiah says…

"And foreigners who bind themselves to the Lord
to minister to him,
to love the name of the Lord,
and to be his servants,
all who keep the Sabbath without desecrating it
and who hold fast to my covenant—
these I will bring to my holy mountain
and give them joy in my house of prayer.
Their burnt offerings and sacrifices
will be accepted on my altar;
for my house will be called
a house of prayer for all nations."

The Sovereign Lord declares—
he who gathers the exiles of Israel:
"I will gather still others to them
besides those already gathered."
(Isaiah 56:6–8)

So, what in the world is going on? Isaiah prophesied that God was going to draw people to himself. Specifically, outcasts and the rejected. Those who had been exiled and those who did not belong.

The temple was a massive building. It sat on thirty-five acres. And on the outside of the actual temple was a place that was open to anyone. This is where Gentiles would gather. They were allowed there but were not allowed to actually go into the temple. In fact, if a Gentile entered the temple the penalty was death. Paul is a guy we talk about a lot because he wrote over half of the New Testament, and Paul was actually arrested and accused of bringing Gentiles into the temple. They wanted to kill him because of this. This is a big deal. This area was called the Court of the Gentiles.

Now when Jesus enters the Court of the Gentiles, there is no room for Gentiles. Let that sink in for a minute. In the area where Gentiles are supposed to be permitted to worship God, the religious leaders have set up a market. And this was why Jesus got ticked off.

I love what Pastor Jonathan Parnell says…

"The great sadness of this scene wasn't so much the rows of product and price-gouging, but that all this left no room for the Gentiles and outcasts to come to God."[8]

Let's bring this home. If Jesus were physically present today and he walked into a church, what would he find? Would he find even a hint of what he was looking for?

If Jesus were to walk into church today, he would look for the misfits, the outcasts, and those who don't belong.

---

8   Pastor Jonathan Parnell, "Jesus Turns the Tables," *Desiring God*, March 30, 2015, https://www.desiringgod.org/articles/jesus-turns-the-tables.

As Christians we have to have a heart like Jesus. It means we must invest in and invite those who don't feel like they fit in.

If we don't, we will eventually either lose interest in church or we will turn the church into something it wasn't supposed to be.

If you've been going to a church for a long time or if you grew up in church, then it's easy to forget what going to church for the first time feels like. It's easy to forget how uncomfortable it can be. It's easy to forget how nerve-racking it can be. For a lot of churches, every Sunday is someone's first time. If it's not, we must wrestle with why not? Have we made church a safe place for Christians, while at the same time an unwelcoming place for those who are new to the church?

What if God is drawing an unchurched person to him, and you are the only Christian they know?

As Christians we have to be safe people for the unchurched to come to. It doesn't mean we have to sacrifice our beliefs. It doesn't mean we have to compromise what we believe.

Welcoming unchurched people into our lives isn't watering down the truth. Being a safe person for unchurched people isn't conflict avoidance. It's the core of who Jesus was. It's serving.

In order to do this, we must believe and live by the fact that we do not have to agree in order to be friends.

Way too often the church has adopted the mindset that in order to belong you have to believe everything we do. There are certain beliefs that we cannot and should not compromise. Accepting a person isn't about changing your beliefs. It's about modeling what Jesus does for us. Jesus doesn't demand that we are perfect before we come to him. If we are honest we all have some bad theology. We all have an idea about who God is that may not be absolute truth. One day God will correct all of our theology.

No matter what you believe, the key is does it help you love God and love people more.

To accept people as they are opens the chance to influence people who are different. In order to do that we cannot rant about unchurched people acting like unchurched people. We can disagree and still be friends.

It ticks Jesus off when religious people make it difficult for outcasts to come to God.

In order to build God's kingdom, we have to be light in a dark world. We have to be intentional about having relationships with those we disagree with.

Jesus said to the religious leaders of his day...

"Woe to you, teachers of the law and Pharisees, you hypocrites! You travel over land and sea to win a single convert, and when you have succeeded, you make them twice as much a child of hell as you are." (Matthew 23:15)

It's amazing to me how Jesus was gentle with sinners and stone cold with the religious. What frustrated Jesus wasn't sin, but when people pretended not to sin.

Unintentionally we create environments for people to pretend to be better than they really are.

I can't expect people who don't know Jesus to act like they do. Truth be told, most of us Christians have a hard time acting like Jesus. Let me rephrase that...Christians have a difficult time reacting like Jesus. We tend to do a decent job of acting. We pretend we have it all together. We hide our issues. Why? Because Christians aren't safe. We have seen way too many people rejected by Christians.

"Sinners" were often drawn to Jesus. They actually liked spending time with him. In order to bring heaven to earth, we have to be willing to step into others' hell.

When we authentically admit that we don't have all the answers, we still struggle, and we aren't perfect, we roll out the welcome mat for others. We communicate that we aren't perfect, but we are safe.

Sounds like Jesus to me.

Application: Who do you know that has yet to accept a relationship with Jesus? Pray and ask God to give you an opportunity to share God's love with them.

Questions:
1. How does understanding Jesus' anger help us better bring heaven to earth?
2. What surprised you most about this chapter?
3. What is one idea that you will apply from this chapter?

CHAPTER 10

IS THIS HEAVEN?
NO, IT'S A JOB

When Good Jobs Happen to Bad People

For most of our adult lives, we will spend a majority of our time at a job. As Christians we are called to bring heaven to earth in every area of our lives. Since we spend so much time at our jobs, I believe it's important to make it a little piece of heaven. So, to start this chapter, let me ask you a question...

How happy are you at your job?

Everyone has a job to do. If you are a stay-at-home parent, you have a job to do. If you are unemployed, your job is to find a job. Whether you work part-time, full-time, or all the time, you have a job.

The question is, how happy are you at doing your job?

According to a Gallup poll, 70 percent of employees hate their job or are disengaged with their work.

That's the majority of us.

There are a lot of bad bosses out there, but are only 30 percent of all the bosses great to work for?

Could it be that we hate to not be in charge?

For a lot of people, it's easy to hate a job because they feel forced to work there. Whenever we feel forced to do something our motivation plummets.

The truth is you don't have to work at your job. It's a choice. Until you realize it's a choice you will always feel like it's a chore.

It may be difficult, but we get a say in where we work. Way too many people have just accepted their penance of work. They live for Friday and can't wait for retirement. What if God wants more for you at your job? What if God wants you to bring heaven to your job?

A lot of people complain about Mondays and love Fridays. I personally love Mondays. I love Mondays because I love my job. I think all people can love their job.

I think all people can love their job and it has very little to do with not wanting to work hard.

Let me flesh this out a little. Some people are much harder workers than others. Some people are lazy. But even the laziest person has shown the ability to work hard at what they are passionate about. It happens when we get in the zone. When we are in the zone we work hard and time flies. When we are in the zone people notice how easy we make hard work look.

The right job equals being in the zone for you. For me the right job does not include construction. Just to help you see how bad I am at anything even remotely resembling construction, let me tell you about the last two times I tried to put something together. The first was hanging curtains in our guest bedroom. I hung them. It took hours. Sweat covered me when I was done. I was so tired I wanted to sleep the rest of the day away. And after all of my way too hard work you want to know what we discovered? I hung the curtains crooked. It was bad. I couldn't fix it. I ended up having to call my father-in-law for help. He fixed it in five minutes and didn't break a sweat.

It's a known idea that I don't fix things. It often becomes a joke. In an attempt to be funny I tried to start a Facebook Live video to show people I know how to change the windshield wipers of my car. The joke was it's not difficult to do, but I was going to play it off like it was installing a carburetor. I don't even know what a carburetor is. Anyway, I started the video and then struggled for fifteen minutes to put my wipers on. I had done it before, but I couldn't remember how. Not only that, but I cut my hand getting the wipers off. It was a disaster.

The right job also does not include being outdoors. I like what comedian Jim Gaffigan says, "I'm what you'd call indoorsy." The outdoors is trying to kill you. Poison ivy, sunburn, hurricanes, tornados, mosquitoes, wild animals, snow, hail, and birds pooping on your head from up above are all signs that nature is trying to kill us all. Some of you reading this might love the outdoors. That's cool. We can disagree and still be friends.

Make me work outdoors and I'll start hating life. I love the indoors. I love the AC in the summer and heat in the winter. I love sitting at a desk where it's nice and safe. My computer has never tried to bite me or give me a rash. Nature has.

Some people like to take their vacation and go camping. That is hard for me to comprehend. I do not have enough vacation days to pretend to be homeless for a couple of them. Not only that, but how insulting is it for the homeless? I kid, I kid. Seriously though, if camping was so great why don't you sell your house and live in a tent? I'm kidding. Feel free to love the outdoors. God didn't invent me to be outside.

What's my point? My point is that for some, working at a desk would make them hate Mondays and feel like their job was hard work because it's not how they are wired. Others are like me and would feel tortured if they had to work outdoors in the elements building things. God has wired us to work. It looks different for each of us. Some are wired to work with their hands. Some are wired to work with their brains. At times I think I'm wired to work with my stomach and would love to be paid to eat. The point is God has wired us to work.

It's a part of his plan since the beginning.

> **The Lord God took the man and put him in the garden of Eden to work it and keep it. (Genesis 2:15 ESV)**

God's original plan was for us to work. I also believe his plan was to enjoy our work. You see, we get satisfaction from working hard and accomplishing something. We also don't mind working hard at something that we love to do. You've experienced it. When you have something you are passionate about, you will work hard on it for hours and love every minute of it.

So Why Don't I Love My Job?

I think the breakdown for our jobs comes from a few areas.

1. We are not having fun. Now stick with me on this one. I'm not saying that your job has to be all fun and games. Hard work can be fun. In fact, when we love something it turns hard work into fun. Remember as a kid how you would

play for hours upon hours. I watch my kids and they just run. I'm not talking about running for exercise. I'm talking about if they have been sitting for more than five minutes their answer is to run. Run in circles. Run up and down stairs. Run. To them it's fun. I'm not sure at what point in life I stopped wanting to run just to run, but I've been there for a while now. If I'm running it's because someone is chasing me or it's because I've heard in advance that someone is going to chase me and I'm training for that. Running is hard work for me. For my kids running is fun.

I think we all have a bit of our kid selves inside us. If you have fun at your job it's like playing on the playground for hours at a time.

Have you ever heard about Pike Place Fish Market in Seattle? It's amazing. They throw the sold fish in the air and then catch them to wrap them for the customers. They've made what could be seen as a boring and mundane job, selling fish, into a tourist attraction. Why? Fun.

One of my first jobs in ministry I instituted Happy Tuesday. Every Tuesday I'd send out a funny email and then our team would go to Sonic for Happy Hour. Happy Hour at Sonic consists of half-priced drinks. Just in case you are feeling like judging me, these are nonalcoholic drinks. It was fun. It became a weekly highlight.

My mom does an amazing job at this. She worked at the writing center at a local college. For one April Fools' Day she made grilled cheese with french fries and ketchup. Only catch was the french fries were made of apples, the grilled cheese was pound cake, and the ketchup was made of strawberries. It looked so real. Fun.

I think there is a reason the Seven Dwarfs whistled while they worked. They were attempting to make the incredibly difficult job of mining for diamonds fun. Or because they had Snow White at home doing all the chores. I kid, I kid. The point is…

You can make your job fun. If you enjoy what you do, then working hard is fun. I hate building things, but I love writing. I spend hours upon hours writing and the time goes by quickly. When we are in our zone, work is fun. Even if we don't have work parties, sleeping pods, or a workplace ping-pong table, we can have fun working.

If you are a boss, you should be making the job of others fun. It doesn't mean that you don't work hard. It doesn't mean that you don't take your job seriously. In fact, it means the opposite. You will work harder when you are having fun and you will stay at your job longer when you are having fun.

Having fun doesn't mean group outings to bowling. Having fun is a mind shift change. Make what you do fun. Another way to say it is to have fun doing your work.

For one Christmas Eve planning service I provided Christmas sweaters, Christmas music, and Christmas decorations, and in order to share an idea you had to hold a toy baby Jesus in the manger. It was October. It was fun.

There are times where you have to put your head down and just work. When you love what you are doing, even those times can be fun. That leads to the second reason we don't love our jobs.

2. We don't feel like there is any value in what we do. Think about all the so-called jobs that people do for free. Gardening is an awful job. You'd have to pay me a lot of money to spend my day working out in the yard. It's not for me. But some people actually choose to spend a Saturday

in the garden. Why? They feel value in what they do. If you feel valuable about it, you'd do it for free even though you are thankful someone is willing to pay you. I see this all the time with people who are gifted at fixing things. I've had some very kind people help me when things in my house broke or when my car broke. Almost every time when I thanked them they replied, "No problem, it was fun." There is nothing fun in putting in someone else's toilet. Nothing. At least not for me. But for those who find value in what they do, not only does hard work become fun, it becomes meaningful.

I was once at the airport in Charlotte, North Carolina. I went to buy an absurdly overpriced bottle of water. Traveling for long periods of time makes me a wee bit grumpy and this was no exception. I walked into the airport store and the cashier was singing at the top of her lungs. She would then stop in between verses to talk to customers. She'd say, "How you doin' baby?" Every person in the store was laughing and smiling. I am betting that she didn't see her job as a meaningless gig in the airport. I am betting that she saw it was her job to bring a smile to someone's face. She seemed to find great value in her job, and ultimately it was because it was about others and not just about herself. Which leads to the final point.

3. You are spending your God-given resources on yourself. Now we are pretty deep into this chapter and so far, we haven't talked much about building God's kingdom. That's about to change. You see, I believe your job is a *huge* part of building God's kingdom.

Not everyone is called to full-time vocational ministry, but every Christian is called to ministry. God has given you gifts and talents that were not meant to be used to simply build your kingdom. At the end of the day, if what you do doesn't bring glory to God, it will leave you feeling empty. What you do matters. It's what brings an income. It's one of the many things that can give you purpose. But what you do is supposed to be done for the glory of God. Whether you are a plumber, rocket scientist, full-time student, stay-at-home parent, CEO, or flipping burgers, your ultimate job is to work for the glory of God. When you view your job as a way to use your God-given gifts to build God's kingdom, it changes your Mondays to Fridays. No longer do you hate going to work because it's a chance to work for the King of the Universe.

I haven't loved every job that I've had. There were some that were under pretty difficult circumstances. Enjoying your job has to do mostly with attitude and perception. You can be happy at a stinky job and you can be miserable at an amazing job. I think a question that far too many people do not ask is if they are called to do their job.

We far too often take jobs based off how we feel instead of what we are called to do.

Whatever you do, work heartily, as for the Lord and not for men, (Colossians 3:23 ESV)

Wherever God has placed you to work is a holy vocation. It's not just a job. It's not just a paycheck. It's a chance to further God's kingdom. In your job you are not just working for a boss. You are working for the King of the Universe.

The way you work your job should point people to who you serve. Christians should be the hardest working, most enjoyable, best team members around.

God has gifted you with specific talents, interests, and passions that the world misses out on when you don't use them for his glory. You were created to do something. You were created to do something more than complain about your job.

HOW DO I FIND MY DREAM JOB?

So maybe you don't have the best job. You can change your attitude. You can make it fun. And ultimately you can leave. Never ever take a job just for a paycheck. Money is nice, but money can't buy having a purpose.

You need to ask yourself what God created you to do. You can tell what he created you to do when you hear others say, "I don't know how you do that," or "You make that look so easy," or "I wish I could be as good at that as you."

If you have a dream inside of you that doesn't match your current place of employment, then please make a note to read *Quitter* by Jon Acuff. Make a note to read it after you finish this book. Jon's first chapter alone is worth the price of the book.

But until you read *Quitter*, and then start your dream job, you are called to work at your current job as if you are working for God. Make your current job your dream job. Make your current job your dream job by doing only what you can do for the team. Make your current job your dream job by encouraging other staffers and refusing to go negative. Make your current job your dream job by refusing to get frustrated when others aren't able to do what you do. You were meant to complete a job. Not everyone has your giftedness.

Now I would never claim to be a perfect employee or a perfect boss. But I will claim to work really hard to honor my bosses and then as a boss honor my employees. Why? Because it's not just about a job. It's about working for God.

HOW DO I TELL IF I'M WORKING FOR GOD?

Here are some signs that will help you tell if you are working for God or man.

1. When something doesn't go your way, you remain nice. People don't always get along. People don't always come through like they say they will. People don't always meet your expectations. None of that excuses being a jerk. When it's all about you one of the first signs is how big of a jerk you are to other people. Find me an employee or boss who yells when things don't go their way and I'll show you an employee or boss who is focused on building their kingdom. Unfortunately, I've lost my cool a time or two at work. Even working at a church can become a disguise for building one's own kingdom. I've had to apologize on more than one occasion for losing my cool.

2. Do you use people to get what you want? I was once stopped at a gas station by a really nice woman. She was friendly and outgoing, and seemed like she just wanted to strike up a conversation. After a few moments of small talk, she turned into a sales pitch. When I told her I was from out of town, she quickly

shut things down, finished pumping her gas, and moved on. She was only nice to me because she thought I could benefit her. When you work for God you care for people, and not just what they can do for you.

3. Your work life is not separate from your church life. It's easy to compartmentalize life. We have our jobs, social life, family, and church life. I've often heard Christians say we should prioritize life by putting God first, family second, and job third. I'd like to push back on that. I think we prioritize by making everything about Jesus. You represent Jesus with your family, your friends, and at your job. This doesn't mean that you cram Bible studies down your co-workers' throats. It does mean you understand that people are watching. In fact, people care more about what you do than what you say. Our lives should match what we say. We should honor God with what we say and how we live. As a Christian you will be the only Jesus someone knows. Your job is a chance to get paid to be a missionary. That's cool!

There are no good jobs or bad jobs. Well, being a nude dancer is not a good job. Neither is being a hit man. Okay, let me rephrase that. There are no Christian jobs. There are only opportunities to get paid to build God's kingdom. That happens just as much outside of the church as it does inside.

Application: Plan one way to make your job fun this week. Thank God for the job you have today.

Questions:

1. What was your first job?
2. If you could go back and change one thing about your first job, what would it be?
3. What are some practical ways you can make your job fun?
4. What challenged you most about this chapter?
5. What is one thing you will apply from this chapter?

CHAPTER 11

LIVING IN THE PAST

If there's something from your past that you are holding on to, there's a great chance you haven't attached yourself to something new in your present or toward your future. As long as you are exposing yourself to whatever that past is, it's going to be really hard to let it go.

According to many psychologists, lots of people are actually addicted to living in the past. You can see this with fashion. Have you ever walked into a store and right away you can tell when their best decade was? Their hair or clothes haven't left whatever decade they thought was the best. They refuse to move on to the future.

> **"The past is nothing more than a story we tell ourselves. Continuing to tell that story, verbally or non-verbally, eventually turns it into a reality."**[1]
>
> **—Tom Ferry**

---

1   Tom Ferry, "Are You Addicted to the Past?" *Huffington Post,* July 1, 2010, https://www.huffingtonpost.com/tom-ferry/self-help-are-you-addicte_b_631620.html.

So much of our future is sabotaged by our past.

When we live in the past it does so much damage to our future. So much of our future is spent trying to cope with our past. Many of our addictions started out as coping mechanisms to our past.

A big idea for this chapter is…

You will miss your future by living in your past.

No matter if you love your past or you hate your past, the truth of the matter is, you cannot change your past. Dwelling on your past only leads to regret. And regret is the number one enemy of happiness.

The Bible has something significant to say about living in the past. The verse we are about to look at is written by the apostle Paul. Now, what makes Paul an expert to talk about what we are talking about is the fact that he had a past. Paul's past included arresting Christians and approving in the execution of Christians. Paul becomes a Christian, but he was such a bad man that many of the first Christians to meet him were afraid that he was going to turn them in. So, Paul has a past. He's not some shiny perfect person who has lived a perfect life. He's got some baggage. But look at what Paul writes to some of his favorite people, his friends in the church of Philippi.

I want to know Christ—yes, to know the power of his resurrection and participation in his sufferings, becoming like him in his death, and so, somehow, attaining to the resurrection from the dead.

Not that I have already obtained all this, or have already arrived at my goal, but I press on to take hold of that for which Christ Jesus took hold of me. Brothers and sisters, I do not consider myself yet to have taken hold of it. But one thing I do: Forgetting what is behind and straining toward what is ahead, I press on toward the goal to win the prize for which God has called me heavenward in Christ Jesus.

All of us, then, who are mature should take such a view of things. And if on some point you think differently, that too God will make clear to you. Only let us live up to what we have already attained. (Philippians 3:10–16)

When Paul wrote this, he was sitting in a Roman prison for simply telling people about Jesus. He was persecuted for his faith in Jesus. He eventually was martyred for his faith. And yet while sitting in a Roman prison, Paul didn't reminisce about the past. Look at what Paul said again.

I want to know Christ—yes, to know the power of his resurrection and participation in his sufferings, becoming like him in his death, and so, somehow, attaining to the resurrection from the dead. (Philippians 3:10–11)

What Paul is talking about is some next level stuff. Paul says he doesn't just want to know about Jesus. That is, he doesn't want to just know some facts about Jesus. He wants to know Jesus. Why? Because there is power in the name of Jesus. Life in Jesus is greater than anything else in this world. It's better than drugs, it's better than any high. And Paul so identifies with Jesus that he actually considered it an honor to suffer for him. That's radical stuff.

How do most people respond to suffering? We blame God. We get mad at God. We say things like "God, why did you allow this to happen to me?" First off, you can't push God away and then wonder where he's at. We are constantly pushing God out of our lives and culture. The second thing is that this thinking is a Western way of thinking about God.

Pastor Andy Stanley says,

> **"The people who want to differentiate God from pain and evil, they're not talking about the Christian God because from the Old Testament to the New Testament, God is in the midst of pain, leverages pain and, here's the key, redeems pain for good because God is a redeemer. That's the essence of the Gospel. The murder of the innocent son of God resulted in the salvation of the world. That's redemption. It's taking evil and leveraging it for something that's good."[2]**

If you have suffered in your past, you are in a perfect place to truly follow Jesus because we have a God who has not only suffered, but redeems suffering.

Paul isn't saying, "Woe is me. My life stinks now. I wish I was back in the past." No! Paul is living in the moment and allowing God to redeem his suffering. Look at what Paul says next...

---

2   Andy Stanley responds to "Why, God?" after the Sandy Hook shooting on Atlanta-based radio show, *The Bert Show*.

Not that I have already obtained all this, or have already arrived at my goal, but I press on to take hold of that for which Christ Jesus took hold of me. Brothers and sisters, I do not consider myself yet to have taken hold of it. But one thing I do: Forgetting what is behind and straining toward what is ahead, I press on toward the goal to win the prize for which God has called me heavenward in Christ Jesus. (Philippians 3:12–14)

Did you catch what Paul said? He said he hasn't already arrived at his goal. That is, he still struggles. He is still imperfect. That is, he isn't dead yet. He might be currently suffering, and he might have had to go through a lot of pain in his past, but let's look at what he says again.

"But one thing I do: Forgetting what is behind and straining toward what is ahead, I press on toward the goal to win the prize for which God has called me heavenward in Christ Jesus."

Paul says, "There is one thing I do. I don't live in the past." In fact, Paul says he forgets what is behind. Now, I don't believe Paul is saying that he has no memory of the past. In fact, just a few verses earlier he writes about his past accomplishments. Paul isn't saying don't have any memory of your past. He is saying forget what is behind. You will miss your future when you live in the past.

"Cleaning up the past is the simple action of facing it. If you don't, you cannot find joy, won't find peace and won't have true happiness if you are firmly planted in old resentment, challenges, stories about your health, your vitality, your income and past relationships that have gone awry."[3]

—Tom Ferry

If you want to clean up your past, you must face it. That means you have to have some tough conversations. It might mean you have to write a letter that expresses your hurt and pain. Now you might need to burn that letter after you wrote it, but you've got to get your past out in the open.

Christine Caine speaks in Tweets. What I mean is whenever I hear her speak she has the most amazing quotes. When talking about facing one's past she says…

"Disappointment is a place we pass through, not a place we stay."

— Christine Caine

I love that! You don't have to stay in a disappointment. You can face it and move on.

"Has it ever occurred to you that, if you'll revisit your disappointment, God can give you a new perspective of it and that it can become a tool to help others?"

—Christine Caine

Drop the mic!

---

3   Tom Ferry, "Are You Addicted to the Past?"

But I saved the best for last.

"We either go through what happens and manage disappointments well, or they manage us."

—Christine Caine

Come on! That's gold.

You must face your past if you want to get on to your future.

In order to forget your past, you must have a future to look forward to.

What is your future?

It's building the kingdom of God on earth as it is in heaven. It's bringing heaven to earth. It's living for something bigger than yourself.

Paul says the reason he can live for the future is because he has a future worth living for. The future for the Christian is heaven. It's a place where we will not experience hurt or pain. Our future is amazing, and when we move on from our past we move toward our future. The Christian is to bring heaven to earth. And in Jesus we have everything we need to move on from our past.

Paul goes on to conclude this section by writing...

All of us, then, who are mature should take such a view of things. And if on some point you think differently, that too God will make clear to you. Only let us live up to what we have already attained. (Philippians 3:15–16)

Listen, if you are mature in your faith you will continually be moving on from your past. You and you alone can control your thought life. And Paul says,

"You are responsible for the truth you currently possess."

In other words, if this is true you are responsible to put it into practice. You must say goodbye to your past and hello to your future.

That means that we have to face our problems. You have to admit that you have a problem and that problem is leading to more problems. We have to be honest with ourselves.

As Christians we don't run away from our problems and pretend they don't exist. We face them and make them obedient in the name of Jesus.

YOU WILL MISS YOUR FUTURE BY LIVING IN YOUR PAST

According to Karen Ann Kennedy, a certified health coach, there are five questions you can ask yourself to see if you are living in the past.

Are You Living in the Past?[4]

1. Is there one particular period from the past that you find yourself clinging on to?
2. Do you feel that you will never reach that level of happiness/status/satisfaction/acceptance/etc. again?
3. Are you frustrated with where you currently are in life?
4. Are you fearful of the future?
5. Does thinking about the past actually make you sad?

If you answered yes to any of those questions, you are living in the past. The past can be fun to think about, but the past is lethal for you to live in.

---

4   Karen Ann Kennedy, "When You're Living in the Past," *Huffington Post*, June 6, 2014, https://www.huffingtonpost.com/karen-ann-kennedy/living-in-the-past_b_5441033.html.

When you try to recreate the past, you end up with a lousy imitation in the future.

Living in the past is a lousy imitation of what life should be. It's trying to go backward.

I love this quote by Pastor Mark Batterson...

"At some point in our lives, most of us stop living out of imagination and start living out of memory. That's the day we stop living and start dying."[5]

Have you ever seen a pink alligator with a yellow tail? I have. It's how my four-year-olds colored a picture of an alligator. Kids live out of imagination. But at some point we grow up and we stop dreaming. We stop creating new memories and we live off our past. We stop imagining what life could be and we start accepting how life is. We no longer dream of pink alligators with yellow tails. We accept our reality and often our reality is marred by our past mistakes and our past failures. It can be marred by our past successes.

And so many of us are impacted by living in the past.

So, the question is, how do we avoid living in the past? How do we avoid rehashing past mistakes that bring guilt and shame? How do we stop living on the glory of old memories?

We have to grow. In order to move on we have to keep moving. At times people think they have arrived. Not me. No matter how old I get I will believe I haven't peaked. There is always growth to happen. This is important to hold on to because...

---

5   Mark Batterson, *The Circle Maker: Praying Circles Around Your Biggest Dreams and Greatest Fears* (Grand Rapids: Zondervan, 2016).

If you are not growing, you are dying.

When you stop growing you start embracing that death is around the corner.

I want to show you how important this is to your life. This is something that you have to constantly pay attention to. The Scriptures actually give us the key to living in the future.

Peter is a guy who had a past. He had some early success when he was chosen to be one of Jesus' twelve disciples. He also had some major failures. On the night Jesus was betrayed, Peter denied that he even knew Jesus. After Jesus rose from the grave, he put Peter in charge of this new movement called the church. Peter writes some amazing words to the earliest Christians that I think can help us move from the past.

> His divine power has given us everything we need for a godly life through our knowledge of him who called us by his own glory and goodness. Through these he has given us his very great and precious promises, so that through them you may participate in the divine nature, having escaped the corruption in the world caused by evil desires. (2 Peter 1:3–4)

I don't know if you ever play the comparison game, but it's easy to do. If I just had what they had then I would be happy. If I just had their luck, then I'd be better. If I just had their circumstances, then I would be better than I am. This line of thinking hits people of faith. You might have even thought something like this. I can't be as good of a Christian as _____. Or the preacher has a special relationship with God. I could never love God like the preacher. Or

I could never pray like her. Her prayers are amazing. I could never do that.

Who told you, you could never do that? Who told you that you could never be more than you are spiritually? Who told you that you can't pray amazing prayers? Who told you that you can't overcome that temptation? Who told you that you don't have what it takes? Who told you that they are special and you are not? Not God!

Peter personally knew Jesus. And Peter is the only disciple to walk on water. Peter experienced some amazing miracles and Peter says that the same God who lives in him lives in you. When you are a Christian the Spirit of God lives in you. This is so crucial because look at what Peter says again.

His divine power has given us everything we need for a godly life through our knowledge of him who called us by his own glory and goodness.

If you are focused on your past, you will never see the future. And you may have been addicted. You may have been selfish. You may have been a soft sissy, but you are not anymore. Why? Because Jesus has given you everything you need to live the godly life. Everything. The key is you have to stop looking at your past and start looking at Jesus.

You are not your past! You are not your past sins. You are not what others have done to you or said about you. You are a child of God! You are God's masterpiece created to do good works for him. Following Jesus means you move from your past. Following Jesus means you move to your future. A future of helping others.

In Jesus the weak become strong. In Jesus the selfish become selfless. In Jesus we have everything we need to live the godly life.

Through Jesus you have escaped your past. But you have to keep your focus on Jesus. And this next part is so important. Peter is about to tell us what all of us have to do. Look at what he writes.

For this very reason, make every effort to add to your faith goodness; and to goodness, knowledge; and to knowledge, self-control; and to self-control, perseverance; and to perseverance, godliness; and to godliness, mutual affection; and to mutual affection, love. (2 Peter 1:5–7)

For this reason. What reason? The fact that you have everything in you to live the godly life. For that reason, make every effort to add to your faith. You have to do something to add to your faith in Jesus. Why?

If you are not growing, you are dying.

Living in the past means you are not growing. It means you are dying. Your current relationships are dying because you are stuck thinking about how things used to be. Your life is not moving forward because you are stuck thinking about how life used to be. If you are not growing, you are dying.

In the 1980s you want to know what was a huge business? Video rental stores. Stores like Blockbuster.

Do you remember Blockbuster? To rent a video it cost almost five dollars, and if you did not remember to rewind it you got charged extra money. Blockbuster was king in the eighties and nineties and today all that is extinct. Why? Because as the times changed Blockbuster got complacent and refused to.

If you are not growing, you are dying.

You can apply this to so many areas of your life. At a job, you want to know who great bosses look to give a raise to? The ones who are hungry to learn. The ones who are growing. If your boss has to push you to grow, you will eventually be passed up. In your family. If you are not growing in learning how to take care of your kids, your relationship will suffer. Your kids don't stay the same. Each phase is different. What you did for your kids at the age of two is not what you need to do for your kids when they are sixteen. You have to continue to push yourself to grow.

And when it comes to your relationship with God, if you don't push yourself and add to your faith, eventually you will grow complacent. Look at what Peter writes next...

> For if you possess these qualities in increasing measure, they will keep you from being ineffective and unproductive in your knowledge of our Lord Jesus Christ. But whoever does not have them is nearsighted and blind, forgetting that they have been cleansed from their past sins. (2 Peter 1:8–9)

I don't know about you, but I don't want to be ineffective and unproductive in my relationship with Jesus.

MAINTENANCE IS A MYTH

"But the Bible teaches that we are always either drawing nearer to God or falling away. There is no holding pattern."[6]

— Jim Cymbala, *Fresh Wind, Fresh Fire*

You don't maintain your faith in God. You either add to it so you can be productive, or you watch it slip into ineffectiveness.

Growth is exciting. We often think that we have to have all the answers. We don't. Growing is the adventure.

I WILL NEVER FIGURE OUT WOMEN

God is a relational being. When we figure out something, we often feel like we control it. God is not to be controlled. God is to be pursued. God pursues you and then you in turn pursue him. You spend your life getting to know him more. You never settle for thinking you have God figured out. You just trust that God is good and God is love and that God will one day correct all our theology. People often act like they have figured God out. As long as I'm growing, I'm still learning who God is. I cannot fully figure him out.

It's hard to trust that man has fully understood God when we can't figure out women.

There are some things that I know for certain about God. God is love. God is good. God is a God of order. God is love.

---

6   Jim Cymbala, *Fresh Wind, Fresh Fire: What Happens When God's Spirit Invades the Hearts of His People* (Grand Rapids: Zondervan, 1997), 163.

I bookend the above descriptions of God with love on purpose. I am 100 percent certain that God is love.

But there is a lot about God that I'm very uncertain about. In fact, I get nervous around people who speak about God as if they have him figured out.

For example, I know that some things are predestined by God. That is, some things are going to happen, and we have no control over them. Jesus is coming back. That is predestined. I also know that it's not God's will for us to sin. I know this because why would God get mad at sin if ultimately it's his fault? If everything is predestined, then we do not have a say in our choices and ultimately it's God's fault. I don't see that in Scripture, so I don't buy into that. There is predestination and there is free will. Many people choose a side. I'm okay with believing both. I don't fully get it. Predestined? Yes. Free will? Yes. I dunno.

I love the grace of God. I know about the wrath of God. Those two things I do not fully understand. How can amazing grace never end and yet at the same time we are warned not to test God's patience by deliberately ignoring God's commands?

I am completely comfortable with believing in a God that I do not fully understand.

A lot of people do not seem comfortable with this.

I am not comfortable with people who act like they have God figured out. In fact, it kind of freaks me out. People have tried to nail God down and figure him out. I wonder if that's because we are uncomfortable with the unknown.

At the same time, 100 percent of men everywhere are very comfortable with the fact that not one man in the history of men has ever fully understood a woman. They are too complex.

I love my wife. She's full of awesome. I love my wife, but I don't have a fat clue when it comes to my wife. My wife is like the Pythagorean theorem; she's impossible to understand. That's not a bad thing. It keeps me guessing.

Monica, on the other hand, has me figured out to a T. She often says to me, "You are so predictable." Men are pretty simple creatures. Men are so simple that when we try to understand women we get brain cramps.

A lot of pastors and theologians treat God like he's a man. Simple. Easy to understand. Men enjoy food, bacon, controlling the remote, bacon, sex, grunting, bacon, being respected, bacon, and action.

Sure, those are gross generalizations but...men. We are simple.

God created man and woman in his image.

So God created mankind in his own image,
in the image of God he created them;
male and female he created them. (Genesis 1:27)

So maybe God is simple in some ways. He is love. And maybe God is complex in other ways. I'm not saying that I have God figured out. If I was I'd start to freak myself out. But maybe, just maybe, we aren't called to figure out God.

Maybe we are supposed to make getting to know God a lifelong pursuit. Maybe we don't have to have all the answers. Maybe we are to continually grow.

Instead of getting frustrated that I haven't figured my wife out, I see it as an adventure. She is complex, and it will take a lifetime to get to know her. I love that. It gives me something to look forward to. I've loved every year of marriage, but it took me fifteen years to start to figure out how to love my wife. She's complex.

In premarital counseling we read the book *The Five Love Languages*. In the early days of marriage her love language was quality time. After kids it swapped to acts of service. Me, on the other hand. I've had the same love language since day one.

So, God is love and God is good. That doesn't change. That also doesn't mean that we have God figured out. You ever notice how God rarely repeats a miracle the same way? Christians tend to take one aspect of God, package it, and then build a foundation on that one aspect. The more I'm alive the more I realize just how much I don't know about God. And that excites me.

In order to move on from our past, we have to grow. The future for you is exciting when pursuing God. The unknown is a part of the adventure.

WHAT IS THE PROCESS TO GET TO THE FUTURE?

We are all tempted to live in the past. We are all tempted to allow the future to pass us by. But no matter how often you revisit the past, there is nothing new there. You don't go to the past to find new insight. You don't go to the past to find healing. The past cannot change, so what can you do to make sure you make it to the future?

I believe the Bible gives us an answer for this. What we are going to read is written by Paul to the church in Colosse. One thing that makes this letter unique is that Paul did not start the church in Colosse. It was started by a guy that we don't know much about. His name was Epaphras. Epaphras had been converted to Christianity and then took it to Colosse. Now the church in Colosse was being attacked by some heretics and it leads Epaphras to go visit Paul, who at this point is sitting in a Roman prison. Paul writes a letter to encourage the church in Colosse and his words are full of awesome. Let's look at what Paul says.

> **Since, then, you have been raised with Christ, set your hearts on things above, where Christ is, seated at the right hand of God. Set your minds on things above, not on earthly things. For you died, and your life is now hidden with Christ in God. When Christ, who is your life, appears, then you also will appear with him in glory. (Colossians 3:1–4)**

Paul kicks off this section by reminding Christians whose they are. You cannot separate whose you are from who you are. If you are a Christian, you belong to Jesus. And if you are a Christian then you must focus your mind on the things above and not on earthly things. This means there are some thoughts that have no place in the Christian life. There are some thoughts and actions that are contrary to who God is.

I love the quote by Andy Stanley...

"While nobody plans to mess up his life, the problem is that few of us plan not to."[7]

---

7   Andy Stanley, *Ask It: The Question That Will Revolutionize How You Make Decisions* (Colorado Springs: Multnomah, 2014).

And Paul is about to give us a plan to not mess up our lives. This is a plan that will help make sure you don't get stuck in the past. Look at what he writes next.

> Put to death, therefore, whatever belongs to your earthly nature: sexual immorality, impurity, lust, evil desires and greed, which is idolatry. Because of these, the wrath of God is coming. You used to walk in these ways, in the life you once lived. But now you must also rid yourselves of all such things as these: anger, rage, malice, slander, and filthy language from your lips. Do not lie to each other, since you have taken off your old self with its practices and have put on the new self, which is being renewed in knowledge in the image of its Creator. Here there is no Gentile or Jew, circumcised or uncircumcised, barbarian, Scythian, slave or free, but Christ is all, and is in all. (Colossians 3:5–11)

There are certain looks that are just not good on people. For example, there is a weight limit that by its very nature means you cannot wear skinny jeans. There are certain things that some people can wear and others cannot pull off as well. Some people can pull off wearing turtlenecks. I am not one of those people. Now when it comes to being a Christian, there are certain actions and attitudes that just don't look good on us. Paul tells us that before we knew Jesus we wore some things that are no longer acceptable for us to wear.

Before an award show celebrities walk the red carpet and are asked, "Who are you wearing?" Then they give name brands that

I'll never be able to afford. As Christians we need to be constantly asking that same question. Who are you wearing?

Paul says there are some characteristics that come with being human. That means it is natural to be sexually immoral. It's natural to lust. It's natural to be greedy. And before Jesus we walked in these clothes. We even celebrated them. "I look good in this." Paul goes on to say things like anger, rage, slander—that is talking bad about people behind their backs—and having filthy language, you have to rid yourself of these things. That is, you have to take them off. That is, no matter how comfortable you are wearing them, you have to make the conscious effort to believe there is a better look for you out there. And Paul says we have to put to death the attitudes and actions that do not reflect Jesus.

We must recognize what attitudes and actions don't represent Jesus and choose to put them to death.

In other words, this stuff is out of fashion for you if you are a Christian. This is not a good look on you.

And here's the thing about fashion—it goes in cycles. What is out of style right now will come back around. Like a bad guy in a horror movie, these characteristics are constantly trying to come back.

And you've got to constantly kill them. Paul doesn't say have a tickle fight with this stuff. He doesn't say be passive and kind of push it away. He says you've got to kill it. That means you have to double tap it. You take it off once, it's going to come back. You've got to kill it again.

But Paul is not done with us. It's not enough to take off certain looks that don't represent Jesus. You must choose to put on certain things that do represent Jesus. Look at what he writes next.

Therefore, as God's chosen people, holy and dearly loved, clothe yourselves with compassion, kindness, humility, gentleness and patience. Bear with each other and forgive one another if any of you has a grievance against someone. Forgive as the Lord forgave you. And over all these virtues put on love, which binds them all together in perfect unity. (Colossians 3:12–14)

Every day you choose what you put on. And you choose to wear what is appropriate for your day. If you have an important meeting or if you are going on a date or if you are doing something special, you pick specific clothes. I used to work out at the YMCA at 5:30 a.m. and every day there was a guy who would get on the treadmill wearing jeans and a polo. I desperately wanted to get him shorts and a T-shirt. Certain outfits are not appropriate for where you are going.

And Paul says that if you are a Christian you are going to heaven and it's important that you choose to clothe yourself in a way that reflects where you are going. So not only do you have to put to death your old self, you must choose to put on your new self. The new self is compassionate, kind, humble, gentle, patient, forgiving, and what holds all of this together is love.

So, if you are a Christian this is the look you must wear. All of this is in your past. You must now dress for your future. So, let's answer the question.

What is the process to getting to the future?

The answer: radical obedience.

If you want to get to the future and out of your past, it means you must choose radical obedience.

It means you must choose to say no to certain places that cause you to dress like your old self. It means you must say no to certain people who influence you to dress like your old self. It means you must say yes to something so much better.

My wife and I are on a diet and it's working pretty well for us. People often ask me if I like the diet and the truth is no, I don't like it. I like to eat pizza. I like to eat a doughnut. Or three. I don't like being on a diet. But as far as diets go this has been great for us. It's a plan and we are doing our best to follow it. Well, the other day I was at a lunch meeting and I was being so tempted to cheat. I just wanted something unhealthy. I was with someone I had never been to lunch with before and he was skinny. I was hoping he was going to be one of those skinny people with a mutant metabolism who eats whatever they want. I let them order first and they ordered healthy. In that moment I felt shame. And I felt inspired. They had no idea that if they ordered unhealthy I was going to follow along in their footsteps. It's the same thing with you. You must place yourself around people who will inspire you to live for Jesus. You must put yourself in circumstances that will inspire you to live for Jesus.

In order to reach people who do not know Jesus, we must have a core group that inspires us to love him. We are called to be salt and light into the world. We should be careful to not fall, but that doesn't mean we avoid all people who do not believe in Jesus. In fact, it's by reaching others that we often grow the most in our faith. Part of radical obedience is reaching people.

If you want to get to the future and leave your past behind, it involves radical obedience.

If you are angry, you've got to do something radical to get over your anger. If it's natural for you to lie, you must do something radical to overcome this. If you are greedy, you must do something radical to overcome this. Radical obedience to Jesus propels us out of our past and into our future.

Application: Identify what areas you live in the past. What would it take for you to move to the future God wants for you?

Questions:
1. What stood out most to you in this chapter?
2. What were your answers to the questions about living in the past?
3. What stops you from moving on to your future?
4. Based off what you read, what are you going to apply?

CHAPTER 12

CROWDED ISOLATION

I often hear Christians talk about their struggle with guilt, shame, and sin. They have tried their hardest, but it has just left them feeling exhausted. Have you ever been there?

Have you ever thought you'll never get over this? This pain. This problem. This issue. This bad habit. Have you ever thought, "Why won't Jesus just take this away?"

Have you ever thought about why you are hiding it from other Christians?

The weight of the world is too much for any person.

One of the reasons we struggle so much comes from isolation. When we make a mistake, shame tells us to hide.

I had a fascinating conversation with one of my friends who has served overseas in Afghanistan and Iraq. War is a horrible product of living in a broken world. One of the lasting issues of war is PTSD. War is awful, but coming home from war can be devastating. My friend who served as a government contractor told me about the issue with leaving war. His insight was fascinating. What he shared was the PTSD comes on so strong because when he comes home he loses the community he had fighting a war. Being alone, he is left with his thoughts. It often led him to go back to war. The community of serving with a team was a powerful bond that could not be found back in the States.

Let that thought sink in.

He felt safer with his fellow troops than he did alone in America. And it is not that he is alone here. He has a family, goes to church, and has friends. But the common purpose is not the same. In America, it's easy to stay in your lane, go about your business, and ignore the world.

We all need some alone time, but with too much alone time we will go crazy. We were meant to live in community with others. We will get further faster with community. We will be able to stand against whatever the world throws at us with community.

Radical obedience only happens inside community. Alone, we will eventually fall.

> Though one may be overpowered,
> two can defend themselves.
> A cord of three strands is not quickly broken.
> (Ecclesiastes 4:12)

Christianity wasn't meant to be lived out alone.

We serve a God who models community by being three in one. The Father, Son, and Holy Spirit are unified in constant community. And yet Christians live like we are supposed to have a one-on-one relationship with God.

The very first man in all of creation had a one-on-one relationship with God. In Genesis we read how Adam walked with God, and talked with God, and had a one-on-one relationship we all would envy. And yet it's the first time that God looks at creation and says, "It's not good." It's not good for man to be alone.

Adam had a one-on-one relationship with God and God said that's not a good thing.

We were meant for community. In fact, to bring heaven to earth we have to have healthy community.

The greatest lie after we sin is the belief that we must go into hiding. We think we have to hide our sin because of the shame we feel. We weren't meant to carry the burdens of our secrets. Isolation will kill you.

In the prison system the penalty for inmates who misbehave is solitary confinement. That thought always fascinates me. The penalty for misbehaving criminals is alone time. There is something powerful about being separated from community. We all need a little alone time, but too much isolation will destroy you.

And we wonder why we are a country who can't overcome our anxiety. At some point we've believed the lie that our sin is ours to overcome.

When it comes to sin, it's Jesus' to forgive, yours to confess, and the church's to support.

We desperately need to create kingdom-minded churches that are safe places for people to struggle. At the same time, they should be places where broken people are inspired to find healing.

Not guilted into healing.

Not shamed into healing.

Not pretending to be healed.

True healing.

It happens.

But it doesn't happen outside of community.

Every support group in the world understands the power of this. Most of us are too prideful to admit we need a support group, but that is what the kingdom is. It's an invitation for the sick to come find healing. It's an invitation for the lost to come back home. It's an invitation to bring healing.

We desperately need each other.

If your friends are leading you to sin, then you have the wrong friends. True friends want what is truly best for you. They will love you no matter what, but they won't tempt you in the areas you are weak in. We need the support of others to become the best version of ourselves. God uses other people to help us change.

We need each other.

CROWDED ISOLATION

In America today, we have an epidemic of loneliness. We are wired for relationships and when we don't have stable, life-giving relationships, it wreaks havoc on our bodies. Loneliness leads to anxiety and depression, and the effects of loneliness impact your body in negative ways.

Vivek Murthy, former surgeon general of the United States, has said many times that the most prevalent health issue in the country is not cancer or heart disease or obesity. It is isolation.

Let that sink in. That's not a pastor or counselor speaking. It's the former surgeon general.

And a major problem with loneliness is that most of us don't think we are lonely. Loneliness seems like it is reserved for cat ladies or people who lack social skills. We think we aren't lonely because we have social media, or because we have a few friends.

But how often do you see people you would consider your best friend? One of my best friends lives in Georgia and I see him two or three times a year. Another one of my good friends recently said, "You and Monica are the best friends we never see." That's sad to me. We are all busy. We are so busy that we often don't realize how isolated we truly are.

We are surrounded by people, and yet we are very alone.

Our problems feel like something only we can fix.

Our sin leads us into hiding.

"The General Social Survey found that the number of Americans with no close friends has tripled since 1985. 'Zero' is the most common number of confidants, reported by almost a quarter of those surveyed. Likewise, the average number of people someone in need feels they can talk to about 'important matters' has fallen from three to two."[1]

We know loneliness makes you feel terrible. It's bad for your mental health: well-being goes down, depressive symptoms go up, your likelihood of developing mental and affective disorders increases. It's also bad for your physical health.

The results of the research on the impact of loneliness are staggering.

"In a meta-analysis of 3 million people, which controlled for confounding factors such as demographics and objective isolation, loneliness increased odds of an early death by 26%."[2]

---

1   Caroline Beaton, "Why Millennials Are Lonely," *Forbes*, February 9, 2017, https://www.forbes.com/sites/carolinebeaton/2017/02/09/why-millennials-are-lonely/#603390957c35.

2   Laura Entis, "Chronic Loneliness Is a Modern-Day Epidemic," *Fortune*, June 22, 2016, http://fortune.com/2016/06/22/loneliness-is-a-modern-day-epidemic/.

That's serious. Loneliness is a killer.

Problem: The problem is that most of us feel the symptoms of loneliness, but we resist the diagnosis.

Most Americans are busy and surrounded by people. When asked if lonely, most will reply with "Not me."

We are a country of artificial connections. Being surrounded by people but still feeling alone is called crowded isolation.

Crowded isolation—knowing lots of people but not having anyone truly know the real you.

Dr. Richard Schwartz is a Cambridge psychiatrist and he has noted…

"When people with children become over scheduled, they don't shortchange their children, they shortchange their friendships. And the public health dangers of that are incredibly clear."[3]

Translation?

We are so busy running our kids around that we don't make time for healthy relationships. Our busyness leads us to feel too exhausted to realize just how isolated we are.

So, what is the answer?

We need scheduled time to invest in and be invested in. If we don't schedule it, we will prioritize the immediate needs.

Great relationships happen intentionally, not accidentally.

We need relationships.

In order to form healthy relationships, we have to prioritize them.

---

3   Billy Baker, "The biggest threat facing middle-age men isn't smoking or obesity. It's loneliness," *Boston Globe*, March 9, 2017, https://www.bostonglobe.com/magazine/2017/03/09/the-biggest-threat-facing-middle-age-men-isn-smoking-obesity-loneliness/k6saC9FnnHQCUbf5mJ8okL/story.html.

We love the idea of things happening naturally. We hate the thought of forcing authentic relationships. We don't want to manipulate or force relationships, so we resist scheduling relationships. I get it. Forced time together sounds horrible.

The problem is, if we don't schedule relationships they won't happen.

It's one of the reasons why I prioritize small groups at church. My best intentions often don't make time for people. It's easy to live an undisciplined life and allow one's schedule to dictate life. We feel tired all the time. We let schedules dictate what we do and it leads to busyness, but not productivity.

We are like hamsters running in a wheel that spins nonstop.

If we do not prioritize and schedule time with others, it won't happen. If you are married and you do not prioritize a date night, your schedule will take over and months will go by without a date.

If you have someone you connect with, schedule time with them. Even if it's early morning, a monthly lunch, a weekly phone call, or after the kids go to bed once a week, you need meaningful time with life-giving people. If you are not a part of a small group or Sunday school class, then prioritize it. You may not feel the impact of missing a group immediately, but you will miss the impact of community if you are not intentional.

Isolation leads to issues.

In order to bring heaven to earth we cannot do it alone. On my good days I'm strong, but I'm only human. That means I have some not so good days.

When I'm motivated it's amazing. When I'm unmotivated it's equally amazing. It's amazing just how much stuff I can avoid doing when I'm not motivated.

The best accountability I have for going to the gym is meeting people there. On my own I'd let tiredness, bad weather, or the fact that I really don't like the gym stop me from going. Knowing I'm meeting someone there leads me to keep my commitment.

Spiritually it's the same way. I wish I was always passionate about God. I wish I was always motivated to read the Bible. I wish my go-to was to pray first. On my good days it is my go-to. On my not so good days I need the inspiration and motivation of others.

I love preaching. I love Sundays at church. Often, though, life change happens in conversations. That doesn't mean we don't need Sunday mornings or good preachers. I need it all. It just means that inspiration and motivation often come in the surprising form of influence through conversations.

I rarely think about changing when someone preaches at me, throws a judgment toward me, or yells on Facebook.

I have yet to meet anyone who changed their mind because they were yelled at.

I have made changes based off conversations I had.

Listening to a friend talk about the keto diet inspired me to give it a try.

Listening to an acquaintance talk about a life-changing book inspired me to buy the book.

Listening to an unchurched person talk about what he struggled with at church led me to make some changes at the church I lead.

Conversations propel life change because we feel we have a choice in it. No one likes being forced to do anything. When we make the choice, we feel more motivated to do it. That comes from listening to others. It comes from hearing other ideas. It comes from seeing what works with others. It comes in community.

You were made to live in community. We were made to live in community. Community is essential, but it has to be intentional. If you want to change the world, you need a crew, a group, a community. It's hard work changing the world. It's impossible to do it alone.

KINGDOM RELATIONSHIPS

People are not swipeable.

Love is not swipeable.

Spellcheck is telling me swipeable is not a word. It is now.

If you are single there is a great chance you have heard of or even experienced the dating website Tinder. Here is a description of the site from the site in 2015…

"Unlike real life, on Tinder you only get messages from the people you're interested in. Chats only get unlocked when both people swipe right on each other. That way you know the feeling is mutual. No more messages from people you don't want to talk to."

Tinder has introduced the ability to swipe right or swipe left. If we aren't interested in someone we simply swipe left. We swipe them out of our lives. This idea of dismissing people who don't fit our every need is not new to Tinder.

We've been choosing who to swipe for years.

I see this on Facebook often. In fact, I saw it this week.

A popular Christian author and speaker I follow was recently crucified online. She posted her opinion about letting refugees into America. Not everyone agreed. I don't think everyone has to agree. I don't know if I agree. I have mixed feelings.

But here is what happened in the comments. Over and over again people wrote, "Unfollow" or "Unfollowing."

It's as if all the good inspiration the author has provided, all the writing that has helped people fall more in love with God, all the funny things she has posted are all of a sudden void because a person doesn't agree with her opinion on refugees.

Huh?

She became swipeable.

Spellcheck is still not accepting swipeable. Spellcheck wants to change it to swappable. Unfortunately, we often swap out people to better meet our needs.

I see this with relationships.

I see this with church attendance.

I see this a lot online.

It's really easy to swipe people away.

If you don't like their stance.

If they get a little weird.

If they say some crazy thought.

If they vote different.

Just swipe them away.

And we all have every right to swipe people away. Sometimes it's just easier.

But I think a consequence of living in a swipeable culture is a lack of authenticity. We now have to learn to play the game in order to not get swiped away, or we have to embrace losing lots of people for simply sharing our thoughts.

Even in writing this book I've been bracing for the comments from those who want to make it known they are unfollowing me. I believe all truth is God's truth. Whether or not someone wants to acknowledge it as God's doesn't impact whether or not it belongs to God. That's why I use psychologists, secular publications, and non-Christian authors in my research. If something is truth I will redeem it for Jesus even if the original intent wasn't. I have found this helps a lot of people better understand themselves, the Bible, and God. And yet there have been times where I've been swiped right out of people's lives because they didn't want any outside sources as a part of a sermon.

I've even heard, "I was tracking with you until I saw _____'s name. I don't agree with them, so I stopped tracking with you."

Someone that we disagree with can still have something valuable to say. We don't have to agree with everything a person says. When I take in information I view it like eating hot wings. I'm going to eat the meat and leave the bones. When there is meat to be digested I will process that. The stuff that I don't agree with or believe is truth is the bones and I don't digest it.

I believe in Jesus. Over half of the Christian Bible is written by a Jewish perspective. To better understand God, I often look to the wisdom of Jewish rabbis. We do not agree on everything. In fact, the whole Jesus thing is a major disagreement. I don't go to them for insight on the New Testament. As far as the Old Testament goes, my faith has been strengthened by learning from rabbis. Eat the meat but leave the bones.

I've often heard Christians comment on not going to see a movie because of the beliefs of one of the actors. I don't go to the movies because of an actor's personal beliefs. I do not agree with a lot of Hollywood when it comes to religion, morality, and politics. That doesn't stop me from going to a great movie. If the content of the movie is life giving, entertaining, and enjoyable, I'm okay if on an actor's own free time he or she believes something different than me. I do not look to Hollywood for morality. We can disagree and still be friends.

Jesus didn't gather around him people that he agreed with 100 percent. In fact, many of Jesus' followers believed things that were contrary to his message.

THE FIRST SELFIE

I'm pretty sure the first group selfie was taken in AD 33.

This picture is incredibly famous.

I've been thinking a lot about the men around this table.

What would it have been like to be around Jesus?

And what was Jesus thinking being around a group of knuckleheads?

One of Jesus' disciples was Simon the Zealot. A Zealot was a person who radically opposed Roman rule and taxation.

Another one of Jesus' disciples was Mathew the tax collector. The tax collectors in Jesus' day were Jews who were working for the hated Romans. These individuals were seen as turncoats, traitors to their own countrymen. Rather than fighting the Roman oppressors, the tax collectors were helping them—and enriching themselves at the expense of their fellow Jews.

Can you imagine these two guys in the same room?

Simon the Zealot would have swiped Matthew out of his life by taking a swipe at Matthew. Literally punching him into the next life.

Two of Jesus' disciples were the Sons of Thunder. John and his brother James most likely looked like a professional rastling tag team duo. Wrestling is an Olympic sport. Rastling is what I used to watch as a kid on Saturday mornings with characters like Hulk Hogan, Macho Man Randy Savage, the Junkyard Dog, and Rowdy Roddy Piper. I see the Sons of Thunder looking like the tag team the Legion of Doom. I can't prove that, but that's how I see them.

At one point John and James asked Jesus if he would like for them to make it rain fire from heaven and destroy some people who didn't want Jesus staying in their town. Talk about swiping people away.

Jesus was headed to Jerusalem and there were prejudices against him in the village where he wanted to stay. When John and James saw this they wanted to make it rain fire and destroy them all.

Um...I've got to be honest and say I've had the same thoughts getting on Facebook every political season.

I personally think it's funny John and James suggested this to Jesus. Had they ever actually made it rain fire from heaven? Or was this a metaphor for opening a can of whoop butt?

Nevertheless, can you imagine these two sitting around Jesus? Add to that the very opinionated and often prideful Peter and the greedy Judas.

Jesus had twelve disciples and we have only covered a few of them. Jesus gathered a ragtag group of men who had different political, moral, and religious beliefs.

Imagine what their conversations were like around the campfire.

Jesus' posse was the equivalent of...

A Fox News personality

And...

An MSNBC personality

Then throw in...

A fundamentalist hellfire-and-brimstone preacher

And finally...

Throw in a controversial TV preacher who smiles nonstop and believes every day is Friday.

They all had ideas of who the Messiah was supposed to be. They all had their own crazy ideas. They all had their flaws.

And Jesus didn't swipe them away.

He invited them in.

Now, I am not Jesus. You are not either. We can only take what we can take. We have our limits, but we should be growing to become more like Jesus.

Maybe I'm the only one who feels this, but I'm scared to be myself because of the judgment that is out there.

I'm scared to share what's going on because I don't want to be swiped.

I've been swiped.

I'm not looking for sympathy. Everyone has their struggles. Everyone has their wounds. As a pastor I face being swiped often. I once heard that the greatest pain of a pastor is the slow death of a thousand little cuts. Every pastor has people he has invested in leave for a different church. Every pastor has been criticized. Every pastor has been swiped. It's very rarely one major wound that does a pastor in. It's the multitude of small cuts over the years.

One of the most difficult parts of being a pastor is the small little cuts that happen consistently. I'm convinced that burnout or just blatant moral failure is often a result of an attempt to find a quick release for thousands of small wounds. One major wound can be focused on. Multiple small wounds that have been given over time are often difficult to pinpoint. Before you know it, there are hundreds of wounds, and the easiest way to not think about them is a quick distraction. God help us pastors.

As a pastor it's difficult to share personal struggles or wounds. It's difficult to have community.

I've had personal things I've shared used against me. I've had friends end the friendship because they disagree with leadership decisions I made. Years ago, I found out about a group meeting to discuss how bad my leadership was. I wasn't invited.

My leadership probably was bad. I was in my early thirties. It was my first time being a lead pastor. I'm pretty open that I make mistakes. This group met regularly because they were upset I was leading our church to plant a church. I was asked to go to coffee with a church member I didn't really know. I enjoy getting to know people, so I accepted. This person led with she had been at some of these meetings and they were no longer going to go. They let me know it was toxic and they shared some of the things that were being said. I had no idea this was going on. What cut the deepest was that the people involved I considered close friends. When I asked the ringleader if there were any issues, I was assured everything was fine. It wasn't fine.

It's not just the criticism that happens to pastors on a regular basis. It's the unsafe feeling that anyone you consider a friend is one decision away from getting upset and walking away.

Another person rushed to a church member's house after a sermon to complain about how emotional I am when I preach. She was convinced I faked it. If I was going to fake something it would not be getting misty-eyed. It would be something manly like loving to fix cars, going bear hunting with my bare hands, or cage fighting on the weekends. Thankfully, this person was shut down when the person they were venting to wouldn't listen.

I'm already a recovering people pleaser. To have people that I love swipe me away created an incredibly unsafe world for me to live in. It was unsafe because I was afraid of offending, being judged, or upsetting someone else.

During one dramatic season, I was afraid to answer my phone when it rang. Either someone was upset or telling me they were leaving.

If you have ever been swiped out of someone's life because you offended them, you can relate. If you have ever had someone walk away, you can relate. If you have ever felt rejected, you can relate.

Love is not swipeable.

And so, what I want to do is create a safe place for my friends and family. I want to let people know it's okay to have some crazy thoughts. We can disagree and still be friends.

The church today is seen as unsafe. If you fail, you get crucified.

I want people to know I don't love them because we agree. I love them because they are in my life.

I don't do this perfectly. I still want to swipe. It's just easier. I think Jesus calls us to a higher standard. To love the unlovable is a God thing. To put up with those we disagree with is a God thing.

I think this must have been what it was like to be one of Jesus' followers. They had complete freedom to be themselves and know they weren't going to be kicked out.

At the same time, Jesus wasn't afraid to rebuke them in love. It was a safe place to have a relationship. It wasn't based on agreeing on every hot button item. It was based off being in relationship with each other.

At some point we turned everyone who we disagree with into a villain. It's not just that they have a contrasting idea. It's that they are evil. We try to call down fire from heaven on everyone who disagrees with us. But not everyone who thinks differently is a villain. And you don't want others making you into a villain because they disagree with you.

I long for a safe place to discuss theology without being crucified for some crazy thought. I long for a safe place to wrestle with a controversial topic that hears both sides of the argument and actually comes up with a plan that works. I long for a place where I can be 100 percent myself and not be afraid of being swiped away. I long for a place to be accepted in my failures in a way that inspires me to success. What about you?

Application: Who makes you better? Make intentional time to meet with them this week. Make plans to continue having intentional time with them.

Questions:
1. Do you have authentic community?
2. Who is a safe person for you?
3. Who are you a safe person for?

4. Is there someone in your life who has swiped you away? What will it take for you to forgive them?

5. We don't find community, we make it. What can you do this week to intentionally invest in others?

CHAPTER 13

I LIKE EGGS
BUT I DON'T LIKE YOKE

In order to have unswipeable relationships, we have to first receive the love of Jesus. When we realize what Jesus has done for us, it allows us to love others. We are loved in order to love. We are forgiven to forgive. We receive grace to give grace. Relationships outside of the love and grace of Jesus are exhausting. Jesus gives us what we need to have healthy relationships.

Jesus said…

"Come to me, all you who are weary and burdened, and I will give you rest. Take my yoke upon you and learn from me, for I am gentle and humble in heart, and you will find rest for your souls. For my yoke is easy and my burden is light." (Matthew 11:28–30)

Jesus said, "Come to me, all of you who are weary and burdened." There is a reason that so many people wait to come to God until they hit rock bottom. We were created in God's image and God made us pretty awesome. We are so self-sufficient that if we are not careful we will coast along without God. But live life long enough and eventually you will get worn slap out. We've all been broken somehow. Life is difficult. And when life gets hard what do we have a tendency to do?

We avoid it. We avoid problems because they are just too hard to deal with. We avoid talking to someone about our issues because it's too hard. Life is hard. We avoid hard work because I can't even. You can't even what? I literally can't even. We have become so great at avoiding problems that teenage girls have created a phrase to describe it…"I can't even."

I literally can't even.

When something happens and you just don't have the words to describe it, "I can't even." Growing up, my parents read me a book entitled *The Little Engine That Could*. Did you read that book as a kid? The book is about a train who struggled to get up a hill and he said a phrase over and over again. If you read the book say it with me, "I think I can, I think I can."

Well, today we read kids a new book.

The new book is the "Little Engine That Literally Can't Even."

It's for everyone who can't even deal with their problems. Adulting is hard. I can't even. Parenting is hard. I can't even. Dealing with the stress of life...I can't even.

And Jesus says to all of us who can't even to come to him. What an amazing invitation!

He then tells us to take his yoke upon us and learn from him because he is gentle and humble in heart. If we do this, we will find rest for our souls. That sounds absolutely amazing. I don't know about you, but I love the idea of rest for my soul. But let's explore this a little bit. According to this, following Jesus is an easy yoke and a light burden.

If this was the only verse in the Bible, one could think that following Jesus was about minimal effort and maximum benefits. We come to Jesus and the burden of following him is light. Right? Not so fast.

Jesus said a lot of things that are incredibly difficult to do. In fact, he said some things that are impossible to do.

For example, with money. It's no surprise to anyone that churches are funded by the financial donations of church members. Churches don't charge money to enter into the doors. Yet, churches have bills to pay. In order to pay the bills, we have to ask the people who go to church for financial support. That isn't an easy ask. Any time a pastor talks about money someone will immediately think, "That guy just wants my money." I get it. For most of us finances are tight, and truthfully there are other things I'd rather do with my money than give it to the church, and I work at one. I mean, after all, the money I give goes toward paying my own salary, and I don't make all that much to begin with. I give to the local church, and I try to give generously, but it's not always easy.

I started practicing giving 10 percent of my income to the local church when I was in high school. It was a lot easier to do then than it is now. I get the struggle. It's not easy. The truth is nothing worth having in life is easy. Following Jesus isn't easy, but it's worth it.

If Jesus was here today he would say, "If you want to follow after me sell all that you have and give it to the poor." You might say, "I am the poor." Well, the average person around the world lives off two dollars a day. We pay more for a Frappuccino than what most people spend in an entire day. So, giving all we have to the poor sounds like an impossible task and yet that is something Jesus said. Another time Jesus said, "If you want to be my disciple you must 'take up your cross,' 'die to yourself,' and 'follow me.'" I don't know about you, but that doesn't sound easy. That sounds impossible.

Another time, Jesus is preaching about murder, and he essentially said that the same judgment that is reserved for murder is reserved for those who hold on to anger. That doesn't sound easy. That sounds impossible. There are lots of idiots out there that make getting angry easy.

Jesus had a lot of practical teachings, but you want to know what was not one of them? His teaching on lust. When it came to lust, he said that it's on the same level as adultery, and then Jesus said if your eye causes you to lust, pluck it out. Thankfully, he wasn't being literal, but the point remains. If something causes you to sin, go to the extreme to avoid it.

None of that sounds easy. So, either Jesus is a big fat liar when he says his yoke is easy or there is something else going on here. I mean, is this the very first infomercial in the history of the world? All infomercials promise how easy it will be, but in reality, it's never as easy as it sounds, or it doesn't work. Just ask the Shake Weight. Remember the Shake Weight? It promised it was easy and guess what…it didn't work. It just made you look ridiculous. So, what is going on here?

In order to fully understand, we need to look at the cultural examples Jesus gives. Jesus was a master teacher and used illustrations his audience could relate to.

Jesus says,
"Take my yoke upon you…for my yoke is easy."

Now, if you grew up in church then you might be familiar with what the yoke is. If not, you might be thinking about eggs.

283

What really makes this teaching interesting is that in Jesus' day, there was a literal translation of what a yoke was and a figurative translation of a yoke. We will start with the literal. For those of you who don't have a fat clue what it is, let me show you…

This is a yoke.

It is a wooden bar that would allow two animals to pull something. Technically, what a yoke does is it relieves 50 percent of the weight. That's great because you don't have to carry the weight yourself. The yoke means there is help carrying the weight.

Jesus is saying get in the yoke with him. Now, one thing that is interesting is that when a weaker animal gets into the yoke of a stronger animal, the weight is not carried by the smaller animal at all. Literally the smaller, weaker animal gets to participate in the work but doesn't feel the weight of the yoke.

I think it is safe to say that Jesus does more than pull his weight.

It's easy to strive to do life in your own strength. We feel like we give 100 percent, and when that doesn't work, we try harder. When that doesn't work we give up. I literally can't even. It's just too difficult.

The Bible is so explicit on this.

"Not by might nor by power, but by my Spirit," says the Lord Almighty. (Zechariah 4:6)

It is the Spirit of God at work in and through us that helps us accomplish the plans and purposes of God. Jesus' invitation is to take on the weight of our souls.

If you are feeling not good enough, then this is for you. If you are feeling beat up by the world, then Jesus' invitation is for you. If you are feeling worn down by your own choices, then Jesus' invitation is for you. If you literally can't even, then Jesus' invitation is for you. It's for you, but that's only half of the invitation. That's the literal picture of the yoke.

The figurative picture of the yoke is interesting as well. A yoke was a Jewish rabbi's interpretation of Scripture. It was their unique teaching, their unique take on the religious law.

In Jesus' day they had taken a relationship with God and turned it into a bunch of rules to follow. Specifically, there were 613 laws that someone who followed God had to obey. In Jesus' day the religious leaders were the Pharisees. The Pharisees were the spiritual authority and they created a whole bunch of extra rules to control the people. That is, they added to the 613 rules.

For example, God told us to rest for one day a week. The Pharisees came up with over 600 different additional rules about what it meant to rest for this one day a week. If you had false teeth you could wear them for six days, but wearing them on the seventh day was seen as work and you were not allowed to put them in. You were not allowed to take internal medicine on the rest day. So, if you had an issue you could swish the medicine in your mouth, but you had to spit it out or you were accused of breaking the rest day. It was all very legalistic.

In Jesus' day one of the ways you would find out a rabbi's yoke is by asking the question, which commandment is most important? What was the yoke of the rabbi? When Jesus was asked that question he takes the 613 laws of the Old Testament and the commandments and he says love the Lord your God with all your heart and mind and soul and strength and love your neighbor as yourself. Does that sound familiar?

What's happening here is the equivalent of Jesus saying, "Let me take these 613 heavy laws and let's try loving God and loving people. Let's do that! That's my yoke."

Now why is this important for us today? Because Jesus gives you rest for your souls, but in order to understand what that means you have to know what you are taking on. Jesus said, "Take my yoke upon you." That's crucial.

The problem that we have is we read that as an individual invitation. We think that a relationship with God is a private matter. But Jesus wasn't from America. In Jesus' day it was about the community.

When you take the yoke of Jesus what are you getting? You are getting his assistance in carrying the burdens of your soul, and you are joining with the family of God, who is doing the work with you. Christianity isn't a solo mission between you and God.

If you feel beat up, alone, tired, worn out, or defeated, it's because you are trying to do it all on your own.

You cannot live life alone. You weren't meant to live life alone.

The problem is we apply "I can't even" to the wrong things. When it comes to the weight of your soul, you can't even. But you give Jesus your soul and you enter into the community that he has created and together, being led by Jesus, the problems of the world become lighter.

EASY LIVING

Following Jesus is challenging. Whenever God speaks it's scary. It's always for our best, but it is scary. God is good, but he's not easy to follow. A big God asks for big things from his followers. God inspires us to do more than we could ever do on our own. When Jesus says his yoke is easy, that doesn't mean it's easy work.

Jesus doesn't give us easy jobs. He gives an easy yoke.

Easy does not describe the problems I will face, easy describes the strength from beyond myself, with which I can carry my problems.

This leads us to our question for Jesus.

What does Jesus require of you? Is it easy or difficult to follow Jesus? Do I get to follow Jesus and then never do anything challenging? No!

The work is impossibly hard. We are called to be salt and light to the world; that's hard. We are called to fight against our selfish nature. That's hard. We are called to put others first. That's hard.

What does Jesus require of you? The work is impossibly hard. The burden is light.

An easy life doesn't come from what you carry,
but by who carries your soul.

Life is difficult. Jesus didn't say it was going to be easy. In fact, he said, "In this world you will have trouble." Life is difficult. And the things that Jesus requires of us are impossibly hard. They are impossibly hard unless we give him our souls.

Where you find stress, and anxiety, and pressure, and the burdens of life, you find your desire to carry the weight of the world on your own shoulders. There is something inside you that feels like you have to compare to the super moms you see on Pinterest. There is something inside of you that makes you feel like if anything is going to get done right you have to do it yourself. There is something inside of you that feels like the problem you are dealing with is unique to you and you have to carry it alone. There is something inside of you that says your sin is yours to carry. These strong feelings lead to isolation.

You were created in God's image, so you were made pretty awesome. But at some point, we all realize that we aren't strong enough to carry the weight of the world.

So, what do we do? We avoid it. We avoid problems because they are just too hard to deal with. I can't even.

Jesus didn't save you so you could avoid the problems of the world.

**Jesus lifts the burden of a soul,
so together we can handle the burdens of the world.**

Listen, I'm all about trying harder. I think we don't try enough. We give up way too easily. But if you find something is difficult in life, it's pointing to the fact that you are trying to carry that burden by yourself.

Your burden is yours, but you weren't meant to carry it alone.

We feel most alone when no one can share our burdens. When the pain we feel isn't relatable to those we know, it isolates us from community.

We believe the lie that no one can understand.

It's not just pain, it's any struggle.

The kingdom of God is here. It's bringing heaven on earth. It's knowing that Jesus helps you carry the burden. It's knowing that Jesus walks with you through trial and pain. It's knowing that you are connected to others who also struggle but are overcoming the struggle because of Jesus and the community he created.

Someone in the community can relate to your struggle.

You are addicted because you tried to handle it alone. You lie to yourself and believe that you can fix it yourself. If you could, it wouldn't be a struggle.

Your struggle is yours, but it wasn't meant to be carried alone. We come to Jesus and then are welcomed into his family, the church. To be a Christian is to love God and love other people.

Application: What weight are you carrying on your own? Let Jesus help you by specifically giving it to him throughout this week.

Questions:

1. What would it look like to allow Jesus to carry the weight of your life?
2. Who do you know that will be willing to help you in your struggles?
3. Who do you know that could use your support in their life?
4. What would it take to have a community that worked together to carry one another's problems?

CHAPTER 14

IS IT SAFE TO FALL?

I'm convinced so many Christians struggle alone because the church feels unsafe. I want the church I lead to be a place that is safe to fail. When we fail I hope we fall into the arms of grace and are inspired to live differently. I want the church I lead to be a place where Christians invite those who do not believe to come check out what we believe. I think Christians have the most compelling story ever told and it should be inviting people to hear it.

We have seen God honor this at the church I lead. We have stories of atheists, agnostics, and the de-churched coming to church...and then coming back. We have even experienced the unchurched become churched, follow Jesus, get baptized, and give back to the community by serving. It's amazing to experience.

The following is written to those who do not go to church. If you grew up in church, you can still read it. The following is from my heart. If, by chance, someone is reading this and you would not consider yourself a Christian, the following is for you.

To every non-Christian, former Christian, and wounded Christian I want to say, I'm sorry.

I'm sorry that so often the issues that Christians have with each other get in the way of Jesus' message. I'm sorry that collectively Christians are more known for what they are against than what they are for. I'm sorry that we are so entitled that we feel everyone has to agree with our understanding of God. I'm sorry that when people don't agree with us we offer very little grace. I'm sorry that we spend more time arguing online than we do out in the world making a difference. I'm sorry that we care more about being comfortable than we do about changing the world. I'm sorry that we haven't done a better job at making the church in America a safe place to struggle.

> **"The Christian army is the only army that kills its wounded."**
>
> **—Author unknown (but quote is famous)**

I'm sorry that we preach against sin while not being willing to deal with our own. I'm sorry that we preach against people while we don't practice what we preach. Sixty-four percent of Christian men and 15 percent of Christian women watch porn at least once a month. We have our own issues and yet we often ignore them in order to yell at you. I'm sorry that Christians were told by Jesus how to handle our offenses in Matthew 18 and yet we would rather talk bad about each other behind others' backs. I'm sorry.

Even though imperfect Christians have done a lot of harm, many people still give God a shot.

It makes me believe, despite the perceptions of Christians, the message of Jesus is still incredibly powerful.

If you are not a Christian, I hope you'll accept my apology. Even if we have never met.

If you are a Christian, then the following is aimed at you. And me. It's my goal to inspire all of us Christians to represent Jesus better.

A question I wrestle with is, "How does Jesus feel about all the fighting Christians do with each other online?"

The truth is we are all broken. Jesus is healing us but no one reading this has arrived. We are all broken, but we need to be walking toward healing.

As Christians I think we are called to bring heaven to earth. In order to do that we have to set the example.

Our culture today is easily offended by everything, so Christians need to set the example of what it means to be unoffendable.

This isn't easy, but I want to show you how. Look at something Jesus said…

"Do to others as you would have them do to you.
"If you love those who love you, what credit is that to you? Even sinners love those who love them. And if you do good to those who are good to you, what credit is that to you? Even sinners do that." (Luke 6:31–33)

Christians are great at loving those who love them back. The problem is that so is everyone else. Jesus raised the bar on love by dying on a cross for us, and now he is calling you to rise to the challenge.

"But to you who are listening I say: Love your enemies, do good to those who hate you, bless those who curse you, pray for those who mistreat you." (Luke 6:27–28)

What if Christians were known for how we treat those who disagree with us? Jesus says if you are listening…love your enemies. Now, how do you love an enemy? Jesus says you do good to those who hate you, bless those who curse you, and pray for those who mistreat you.

When was the last time you prayed for someone who mistreated you? Jesus doesn't say you have to keep letting them mistreat you. You may have to separate yourself when someone is a jerk to you. But you can pray for someone who has mistreated you even if they aren't around you.

We can't completely get away from other people mistreating us. We can't completely get away from other people being jerks to us. We can't completely get away from other people doing stupid stuff to us. We live in a fallen world.

And you need to stop being shocked when someone isn't nice to you. You need to stop being shocked when someone does something that hurts your feelings. Stop being shocked when people sin.

People are stupid. People are selfish. People are ignorant. You will never live in a world where someone won't do something offensive. And here's the truth of the matter…

"Few want to hear this, but it's true, and it can be enormously helpful in life: if you're constantly being hurt, offended, or angered, you should honestly evaluate your inflamed ego."[1]

—Brent Hansen

If you are constantly hurt, offended, or angered, then it points to how much time you spend thinking about yourself. There is too much work to be done to constantly be offended by other people.

Jesus says when you get mistreated then you get to praying.

"If someone slaps you on one cheek, turn to them the other also. If someone takes your coat, do not withhold your shirt from them. Give to everyone who asks you, and if anyone takes what belongs to you, do not demand it back." (Luke 6:29–30)

Now, this is radical, but it's even more radical when you understand the context. In Jesus' day the Jews were under the authority of the Roman Empire. Oftentimes Roman soldiers would demand things from them and they had to give it to them.

Specifically, if someone slapped you on the cheek it would have been the right cheek. And this would have been done with the right hand. In Jesus' day they didn't have the same kinds of sanitation that we have, so the left hand was not used. They used the left hand to clean themselves after a visit to the bathroom. It was dirty if you smell what the Rob is cooking.

---

1   Brent Hansen, *Unoffendable: How Just One Change Can Make All of Life Better* (Nashville: Thomas Nelson, 2015), 184.

Someone who viewed himself as superior would slap someone as an inferior. If a fight happened with someone who was an equal, they would have used their fists. So, a slap was a sign of someone being inferior. This would have been done with the right hand. The only way that I can slap the right cheek with my right hand is to backslap the cheek. The common response in Jesus' day was to either passively walk away after being slapped or to fight back. Jesus offers a third way. The third way is a way that would cause those who were in power to take notice. To offer the other cheek would mean that the soldier would have to hit the person again and in doing so the fight would mean he would be treating the person he hit like an equal. The one being struck was in effect saying, "I am your equal. I refuse to be humiliated anymore." That is not all. Jesus said if they take your coat give them your shirt. In Jesus' day most of the people were poor and their cloak was multipurpose. It was also used as a blanket. For the poor they would have only had an inner garment on under the cloak. Jesus was saying, "If the Roman government takes your cloak, give them your undergarment. Then you'll be naked, and they will have to see what their treatment of you is doing."

Jesus' teaching was truly radical in that when lived out it forced the world to notice. Now remember we don't have to will ourselves to live this out. We enter the yoke of Jesus and he leads us to love others like he first loved us.

As Christians, we demand people listen to us, but we aren't willing to listen to anyone else. Jesus' message was so radical that it forced the world to take notice.

For example, the Roman Emperor Julian, after many failed attempts to exterminate Christians from Rome due to their growing influence, wrote a letter to a friend expressing his frustration that Christians took better care of Rome's poor than Rome did.

Let that sink in.

Empires took notice at how Christians took care of others.

**Jesus tells us to live such a life
that we cause others to be frustrated with their own actions.**

Today, people often like Jesus but have a difficult time liking his followers. Often, we are judgmental, prideful, demanding others listen and not willing to listen to others.

I don't know about you, but I want to change that perception. I don't want to be a Christian that is not like Christ.

A couple of years ago we brought an author and speaker to our church. She has written some best-selling books, is a highly sought-after speaker, and is featured on a popular morning show on TV. There is no reason why we should have been able to have her speak at Next Level.

She normally speaks in large stadiums to thousands and yet she accepted our offer to come and speak to a few hundred people. I was greatly impacted by one of her books, so I took a shot and sent her an invitation to speak. Her management let me know that she was interested in coming. I was shocked.

On the day she was speaking she called the church office to let us know she was stuck because of a canceled flight. She ended up taking a different flight that landed her an hour away. She left her cell phone number so I could get in touch with her.

I'm kind of a fanboy to Christian celebrities. I enjoy being behind the scenes at events and seeing Christian celebrities in their element. As a churched kid the rock stars I looked up to were in

Christian bands. I write all of that to say I geeked out when I had her number in my phone.

My wife and I picked her up from the airport and had over an hour of amazing conversation. We talked about life, the church, and some hot button items.

That night she did an amazing job teaching on what a disciple of Jesus is. It was hot like fire.

A couple of years later she was crucified by many Christians. She was interviewed and some of her answers didn't fit what evangelical Christians believe. I agreed with some of her answers, but I didn't agree with all of them. It's not always easy to do, but I believe we can disagree and still be friends.

She was verbally crucified for her comments. She was shunned, she was talked about, she was dismissed, and she was treated as an enemy. On Easter she blogged and wrote the following...

"This year, I deeply experienced being on the wrong side of religion, and it was soul-crushing. I suffered the rejection, the fury, the distancing, the punishment, and sometimes worst of all, the silence. I experienced betrayal from people I thought loved us. I felt the cold winds of disapproval and the devastating sting of gossip. I received mocking group texts about me, accidentally sent to me; "Oh, we were just laughing WITH you!" they said upon discovery, an empty, fake, cowardly response. It was a tsunami of terror. One hundred things died. Some of them are still dead. Some are struggling for life but I don't know if they will make it.

"My mind knows the difference between the Christian Machine and Jesus, but this year it feels hard to separate. The whole system seems poisoned, and I struggle to drink any of it."

What's sad to me is the author knows Jesus. Just a few months before, she was praised, sought after, and loved by the Christian machine. What she said was controversial. I get the rub. We have to be careful with what we believe. But our faith is not so fragile that we have to freak out whenever someone believes something different.

We don't have to get angry whenever someone teaches something we disagree with. If anything, our hearts should break. Think about it: if we crucify those who we disagree with, will they ever want to come back if God corrects them? If we can't love those we disagree with, then haven't we made our faith more about our preferences? It's difficult to hear someone you respect say something you do not respect. I still hold to our response should be heartbreak and not fury.

If someone is truly wrong our hearts should break. We should want to do everything we can to bring them back. Instead we kick them out and post "open letters" on social media.

The way we treat others is seen by the world. And it impacts the way people see Jesus.

When we are treated poorly by Christians it impacts how we see Jesus.

Christians are the hands and feet of Jesus. When we cut our own it's not Jesus, but it can feel like it. The church wound is a unique wound that is complex to heal from. When someone is wounded by a Christian, it often messes with their ability to go to church and even can impact their relationship with God. That's what I was seeing when I read her blog post.

We can do better than this. When I read the author's post on Easter I wanted to text her.

I shouldn't really have her number. I didn't want to bother her. I also didn't want to come off as a psycho hose beast stalker. I tend to say stupid things around people I look up to and I don't want to make someone like her regret the fact that I have her number. So, I didn't text her. The following week I read an article about all the controversy around this author and I thought about texting her again after I read....

> **"Morality is doing right, no matter what you are told. Religion is doing what you are told, no matter what is right. Sadly, evangelicalism has become a movement of religionists who will execute anyone whose pursuit of morality leads them beyond the status quo. It is a movement marked by rigid tribalism, divided into warring fiefdoms, and managed by rigid rulers."[2]**

I wish those statements weren't true. Unfortunately, they are. After reading it I thought about texting her.

I believe when you think something nice you should say it. I thought about texting the author, but I just couldn't do it. After thinking about it for a third day in a row, I was convicted. I believe

---

2   Jonathan Merritt, "Why I'll take courageous Jen Hatmaker over her cowardly critics any day," *Religion News Service*, May 2, 2017, https://religionnews.com/2017/05/02/why-ill-take-courageous-jen-hatmaker-over-her-cowardly-critics-any-day/.

when I think something nice I should say it and here I was letting fear tell me not to.

I texted her.

I said a few encouraging things and made sure she knew there was no pressure to text back. My goal was to do for her what Jesus has done for me. Show love. To show that even when we disagree we can still be cordial.

That was on Wednesday.

On Thursday I got a reply.

This is so dear, Rob. Thank you for sending it. It ministered to me this morning. I loved your church and your people and I remember everything about our time together. Thank you for encouraging me. I am taking your words to heart. Please send all my love to your wife and family and people, and I mean it. We press on, brother! Too many people to love to get bogged down. Thank you for being such a light in your community. I am so glad to offer up a prayer for you this morning of thanks.

The truth is that every person you know will let you down at some point. Every person you know will offend you at some point. The truth is we are all way more fragile than we like to admit.

And when one of our own goes rogue, I see Jesus' example of chasing after them instead of rejecting them.

In order to have community we have to commit to not swipe people away. When someone is wrong we need to remember the words of Jesus…

"Do to others as you would have them do to you."
(Luke 6:31)

When someone offends you, this is the key. When you offend someone, how would you want them to treat you?

I love how the Message paraphrase words the familiar verse...

"Here is a simple rule of thumb for behavior: Ask yourself what you want people to do for you; then grab the initiative and do it for *them*! If you only love the lovable, do you expect a pat on the back? Run-of-the-mill sinners do that. If you only help those who help you, do you expect a medal? Garden-variety sinners do that. If you only give for what you hope to get out of it, do you think that's charity? The stingiest of pawnbrokers does that.

"I tell you, love your enemies. Help and give without expecting a return. You'll never—I promise—regret it. Live out this God-created identity the way our Father lives toward us, generously and graciously, even when we're at our worst. Our Father is kind; you be kind.
(Luke 6:32–36 The Message)

If our love is no different than a non-Christian's, then we must examine if we are truly following Jesus. Sadly, it is often the unchurched who show the most love and compassion to those who fall. One of my friends shared with me how rejected he felt by the church after his divorce. He said he often found more compassion from strangers at the bar than from Christians he had known his whole life. This shouldn't be the case.

To follow Jesus means to do what he did. Sure, we all make mistakes, but the very basis of following Jesus is to love God and love people like God has loved you.

YOU ARE NOT DEEP ENOUGH

In the church world pastors are often swiped away because their sermons are not deep enough.

Deeper.

I love the idea of going deep, but what exactly does it mean? If we are going scuba diving, it's easier to understand. It's not as easy when we are talking about a preacher's sermon.

A common phrase for church people to say is "I am not being fed at my church." Another common phrase is "I just don't feel like my pastor is going deep." Those are great spiritual-sounding phrases that are incredibly difficult to know the meaning of.

Maybe that's what is meant by deeper…if it's confusing, it's deep. If I don't understand something, is that deep? If that's the case, then Jesus' message was not deep.

I'm convinced that a lot of the time it means the listener is wanting some new information. When we go to church every week the stories don't change. Every time David fights Goliath he wins. Spoiler alert. Every time we get to a sermon on Easter Jesus rises from the dead. The outcome is the same. When we become familiar with something it often loses its impact.

It's like a great song. There are songs that move me the first twenty times I hear them. After the one hundredth listen I may still enjoy the song, but it no longer moves me.

The Scriptures were written thousands of years ago. I'm afraid way too often we disguise wanting to go deep with wanting to be entertained. We want to hear a new angle or take on the familiar texts.

Others may think that deep is taking a strong stance on a controversial subject. One of the first questions I get from people when they visit the church I pastor is "What do you believe about (insert hot topic here)?"

We are drawn to people we already agree with.

Maybe deeper is just a nice way of saying, "I'm moving on." A lot of people hate confrontation. We avoid it like the plague. Maybe "it's not deep" feels nicer than saying how we really feel.

The problem is, to be unclear is to be unkind.

Saying it's not deep is really unclear.

I'm all for digging in deep in the Bible. I love theology. I love discussing verses that people have argued about for thousands of years. *Love* it!

My concern is that most of us have way more knowledge about God than we are willing to apply.

We want something deeper, but we still struggle with the basics.

Jesus said the two greatest commandments are…

Love God with all your heart, soul, and mind.
Love your neighbor like you love yourself.
Love God and love others.

Historically we do not do a great job at loving God and others like God has loved us.

We can't get the basics right and yet we want to go deeper?

What would it look like if you loved God like he has loved you?

You wouldn't have any grudges.

You would offer grace where you have a right to give judgment.

You would seek to serve and put others first.

I'm all about going deeper, but it sounds like we are drowning in the shallow end of our faith.

What if we simply lived out the two greatest commandments? What if we truly put into practice loving God and loving others?

It's a guarantee that even if we got this right someone would still reject us. But how many more would be drawn to the message of Jesus because of the love of his people?

The last thing Jesus said to his followers is often the most ignored by Christians. Jesus said to "make disciples." The average Christian hasn't invited a lost person to church in the last year. Most Christians don't have meaningful relationships with the unchurched. Often when we do engage the unchurched it's to debate morality or throw stones.

How can we influence the world when we abandon it or constantly condemn the people we do not agree with?

Christians are called to a higher standard.

I love the following story I once heard Pastor Mark Batterson share…

In 1992, Larry Trapp hit the front page of newspapers across the country. He was the Grand Dragon of the Ku Klux Klan. For years, Larry Trapp terrorized a Jewish leader in his community, sent hate mail, threatening phone calls, bomb threats. Then he did an about-face. He burned his Nazi flags, destroyed his hate literature, and renounced the KKK. How does that kind of transformation happen?

The transformation happened in an amazing way.

Larry Trapp started dying from diabetes. He was eventually confined to a wheelchair and couldn't take care of himself any longer, and that's when this Jewish leader that he terrorized invited him to come into his home and live with him so that he could care for him. Larry Trapp was shown so much love that he couldn't help but love back.

That's the love of God I know.

Show more love. Show more kindness. Show more patience. Show more gentleness.

What if we changed the world through love? That sounds like Jesus.

Jesus loves individuals to himself to release them into community to change the world together. People are not swipeable. We are truly better together. We need each other. When I am weak, I need you to be strong. When you are weak, you need someone else to be strong for you. We are yoked together with Jesus. We don't have to carry the weight by ourselves. Together we can love one another. We can learn how to go deep in our love for God and love for each other. We can make the church a safe place to fail.

Application: Who makes you better? Make intentional time to meet with them this week. Make plans to continue having intentional time with them.

Questions:

1. Not everyone can handle everything about you. How can we distinguish between being authentic and oversharing?

2. Who is in your life that doesn't know Jesus? Does it change how you view them knowing you may be the only Jesus they know?

3. Do you tend to be more open or closed to people?

4. Based off this chapter, what is the one thing you are going to apply?

CHAPTER 15

THE DEVIL'S PLAYBOOK

To build God's kingdom we have to take our eyes off ourselves and keep them on Jesus. It seems we are constantly pulled to take our eyes off Jesus. Both success and laziness pull us away. We are often easily tempted to fall away. I'm unfortunately prone to wander.

Satan tempted Jesus with three things. It's my experience he tempts us with the same things today.

Self-Indulgence

Pride/Insecurity

Power

I'll break down the devil's playbook more a little later on. For now, let's wrestle with temptation.

**Why are we so tempted by things
that are not good for us?**

I wish that as an educated human being I would be tempted by vegetables. Or jogging. Or chores around the house. I wish I had the thought "I was just watching TV and all I could think about was doing the laundry. The laundry was just so tempting I finally gave in to it. I had a laundry binge!"

But no...we are tempted by things that aren't good for us. We all face temptations.

We are tempted all the time. The fact that we are tempted by things that are not good for us shows just how broken we are.

The tricky thing about temptation is it's simply an idea.

Temptation is not a sin. We can be tempted and still not sin. The thought of doing something we shouldn't points to why we need Jesus, but the thought alone isn't sinful.

Jesus was tempted and yet he did not sin. Sometimes when I see someone struggling to stay awake during my sermon, I become tempted. I'm tempted to sneak down and give them a wet willy, but I don't. You've been tempted and resisted. I have too.

A temptation is simply...

Temptation—the desire
to do something wrong or unwise

Temptation comes with little compromises. No one wakes up and says today is the day I'm going to ruin my life. We ruin our lives one compromise at a time.

In the first book of the New Testament we learn about the temptation of Jesus. This is before he starts his public ministry. Let's dive in to see what we can learn.

Then Jesus was led by the Spirit into the wilderness to be tempted by the devil. After fasting forty days and forty nights, he was hungry. (Matthew 4:1–2)

There are some days where I'm at my best and I feel like I can take on the devil. The Scripture teaches that the devil doesn't mess with us until we are at our weakest. And because he is deceptive we don't see him coming. Did you catch what the text said? It said that after Jesus fasted for forty days and forty nights he was hungry. He was at his weakest. He was tired. He needed a Snickers. And this is where the devil strikes.

You see, most of the temptations we face aren't blatantly wrong. They are little compromises.

I wonder if the greatest temptation of the devil is to keep us all so busy and tired we just don't have time to make the right choices. We are running around, doing so many things that our brains are exhausted. We are so exhausted that even when we are here we are not really here. We are stressed because we have made the choice to be busy. And if the devil can keep us busy then he knows we will be distracted. We won't have time for what's most important because we are just so busy. When you are stressed you are not at your best.

Sociologists have found we are working less than they were fifty years ago, but we feel like we are working more.

The reason is because we are so busy. We are addicted to multitasking. We are addicted to busyness.

We are so busy we are missing the presence of God. And as long as we are stressed and busy, we are prone to fall to temptation.

Let's keep reading our text.

> The tempter came to him and said, "If you are the
> Son of God, tell these stones to become bread."
> (Matthew 4:3)

Now, at this point, in order to get the full weight of this verse you must look at it through the lens of the Jewish audience. The Jewish audience would have leaned in on this part. They would have said, "I've heard this one before. I know where this is going."

The very first book of the Bible tells the story of the creation of the world. God created the first man and first woman, Adam and Eve, and placed them to work the garden. There was a tree that had fruit that looked good to eat, but God said not to eat from it. Some of you are very familiar with the Genesis account, but don't miss this. The first man, Adam, was tempted by food and he fell to the temptation. Let's read this story and see how it goes down.

> Now the serpent was more crafty than any of the wild
> animals the Lord God had made. He said to the woman,
> "Did God really say, 'You must not eat from any tree in
> the garden'?" (Genesis 3:1)

Now, the Scripture doesn't say that the serpent was the devil. Many Christians read that into the text. This text has become symbolic of the temptation coming from the devil, and what did he do? He simply asked a question: "Did God really say?"

You see, if the devil can get you to doubt God then your foundation will fall. During a difficult season in your life, the temptation might come in the form of a question. It may sound like this, "If God is good then why would he allow this to happen?"

Or maybe it sounds like this, "What's the point in this whole God thing anyway?" That's real. All of us go through doubts and that's why it's so important to know who God is. I don't let my circumstances tell me about God. I let God tell me about my circumstances.

Don't let your circumstances tell you about God.
Let God tell you about your circumstances.

The truth is all of us will go through difficult seasons, and God says you may be crushed, but you are not broken. God says no weapon formed against you shall prosper. God says nothing can separate you from the love of God. Nothing! No circumstance, no problem, no issue. Nothing! Let's keep reading.

> The woman said to the serpent, "We may eat the fruit from the trees in the garden, but God did say, 'You must not eat fruit from the tree that is in the middle of the garden, and you must not touch it, or you will die.'" (Genesis 3:2–3)

Did you catch how Eve responded? She quotes God. And then quickly the tempter comes right back at her.

> "You will not certainly die," the serpent said to the woman. "For God knows that when you eat from it your eyes will be opened, and you will be like God, knowing good and evil."
> When the woman saw that the fruit of the tree was good for food and pleasing to the eye, and also desirable

for gaining wisdom, she took some and ate it. She also
gave some to her husband, who was with her, and he
ate it. Then the eyes of both of them were opened,
and they realized they were naked; so they sewed fig
leaves together and made coverings for themselves.
(Genesis 3:4–7)

This is a bad scene. This is Scripture's answer to why we are
all broken. We all have sin. We all are selfish. We all have issues.
If you grew up in church then you know the end of the story, but the
original audience did not. They hear about Jesus being tempted by
food and immediately they think…here we go again.

Let's see how Jesus responds to the temptation.

Jesus answered, "It is written: 'Man shall not live on
bread alone, but on every word that comes from the
mouth of God.'" (Matthew 4:4)

Wait! What? Jesus responded by quoting Scripture. He didn't
fall for it. At this point the audience is drawing in. Because every
time they hear the story of temptation the man falls. But this man,
Jesus, is different. Let's keep reading.

Then the devil took him to the holy city and had him
stand on the highest point of the temple. "If you are
the Son of God," he said, "throw yourself down. For it
is written:
"'He will command his angels concerning you,
and they will lift you up in their hands,
so that you will not strike your foot against a stone.'"

Jesus answered him, "It is also written: 'Do not put the Lord your God to the test.'" (Matthew 4:5–7)

So now we see the temptation ramp up. The devil tempts Jesus again and once again Jesus hits him back by quoting Scripture.

Again, the devil took him to a very high mountain and showed him all the kingdoms of the world and their splendor. "All this I will give you," he said, "if you will bow down and worship me."
Jesus said to him, "Away from me, Satan! For it is written: 'Worship the Lord your God, and serve him only.'" (Matthew 4:8–10)

So this is the devil's playbook. The devil tempts three ways...

The Devil's Playbook
1. **Self-Indulgence**
2. **Pride/Insecurity**
3. **Power**

This is the devil's playbook and he has been running the same plays for thousands of years. If he can't get you with one, he'll get you with another.

And all of us have at one point or another fallen for one of these plays. Even when we know they are coming we fall for them. And that's the point of the temptation of Jesus.

I've often heard it said that Jesus' temptation is a blueprint for us to resist temptation. I'm not sure that's true.

The point of the temptation of Jesus is not a blueprint for us to fight the devil. It's proof that Jesus did what we cannot do.

On my best day I may be able to fight back against the devil, but when I'm at my worst that's when the devil comes. Same for you. It's why Jesus is so important. You don't get an off-season with Jesus.

Jesus does what we cannot do. Jesus defeats sin. Jesus resists the devil's playbook. What this teaches us is that Jesus is more powerful than sin. Jesus is more powerful than temptation. And here's the amazing thing...we can have a relationship with Jesus. I know that I'm weak and will fall to temptation, but when I am weak, Jesus is strong!

A problem for many Christians is we try to go at temptation alone. Jesus battled the devil's temptations and he was able to do what no other man can. When you follow Jesus he always leads you back to the two greatest commandments, love God and love people. When we try to battle sin on our own we fall. We go to Jesus and Jesus leads us to lean on others. It doesn't have to be one or the other. With Jesus it's both/and. We go to him and we lean on others. It takes the entire community to defeat temptation.

DEFYING GRAVITY

We know the devil's playbook but it's still difficult for us to resist. It often seems as if we take one step forward only to take two steps back.

Is it possible to truly change? I believe it is.

Life change isn't easy. What is easy is staying the same. One of the biggest losses we face as humans is not from the bad choices we make, but from the things we ignore. It's easier to ignore the things we need to work on than it is to actually work on them.

Life change happens when you get sick and tired of being sick and tired.

One of the main reasons life change is so difficult is because we do not replace the bad habit with an equally appealing good habit. Oftentimes when we stop doing one bad habit we end up picking up a different bad habit. So even though we stopped doing the bad thing we didn't really change. We just swapped out bad habits.

So, a smoker who wants to quit often replaces smoking with overeating. Because for every action in nature there is an equal or opposite reaction.

When I am stressed my natural go-to is food. When I am disciplined and eating healthy I find that other temptations become greater. True life change happens when we stop swapping out bad habits and replace them with something better. We have to get to the core issue of why it's a temptation for us.

I want to show you this from a weird teaching from Jesus. Jesus had some famous run-ins with the religious leaders of his day. Messy people didn't scare Jesus. People with a past didn't scare Jesus. People with major social taboos didn't scare Jesus. Jesus spent time with people who weren't great at hiding their sin. It was the religious people who frustrated Jesus. It was those who were pious and self-righteous that Jesus got into conflicts with. In one of those conflicts the religious leaders accused Jesus of being demon-possessed. His response is going to bring life to us.

I want to show you the text and then break it down.

"When an impure spirit comes out of a person, it goes through arid places seeking rest and does not find it. Then it says, 'I will return to the house I left.' When it arrives, it finds the house unoccupied, swept clean and put in order." (Matthew 12:43–44)

On a chapter called "The Devil's Playbook" this Scripture fits right in. If you grew up going to church this doesn't seem like a weird verse. If you didn't grow up in church maybe you are skeptical if there even is a spiritual world out there. Or maybe you believe there is a spiritual world out there, but you've only seen it portrayed in horror movies. The spiritual force that is out there is a lot less scary than we are led to believe.

When Jesus was tempted by the devil himself, it wasn't in some scary demon-possessed, drag you across the room confrontation. When Jesus was tempted it was in the form of a conversation.

The devil simply tries to get us to question, doubt, and redefine what God says. God makes something good and the devil has a way of turning it into temptation. Food is good but in the hands of the devil it becomes a temptation. Sex was created by God, but the devil has a way of taking what is good and turning it into a temptation. The temptations that you get aren't the scary things we see in the movies. The temptations you get are from conversations.

And it is so subtle. If the voice of the devil was scary we'd all run away. The voice of the devil starts with a conversation. When the devil speaks he asks questions that lead you to doubt who God is and who you want to be. And just know the devil will leave you alone when you are fired up, motivated, and passionate. He waits until you are tired, stressed, lonely, or bored. And that's when temptation is the highest. And listen, if you have doubt that there is a spiritual world that's fine. You can define temptation any way you want. But isn't it true that when you are at your weakest, temptation becomes the strongest? And it comes in the form of conversations that go on in your head. It sounds like: "You can work out tomorrow. Go ahead and skip today." "Do you really have to count calories?" "You can't change. Haven't you always failed in this area?" "They will never find out." "You failed. They won't understand. Hide your failure." "You have already messed up. Might as well keep diving into this sin."

In Jesus' day the religious leaders were addicted to power. Because they had some power they were threatened by Jesus' popularity. Jesus comes on the scene and heals someone and look at what the Pharisees say...

But when the Pharisees heard this, they said, "It is only by Beelzebul, the prince of demons, that this fellow drives out demons." (Matthew 12:24)

Based off this I would say we need to be careful whenever someone starts accusing another person of being demon-possessed. To me that is the upset stomach of accusations. As a kid if you tried to fake being sick and your parent pulled out a thermometer it was really hard to fake a temperature. But a stomach issue is easy to fake. A person can't prove that you don't have a stomach issue. Or so I've heard. That's not something I've done. Stop judging me. You don't know me.

To say someone is demon-possessed is really hard to prove. And at the heart of this accusation was jealousy. Whenever we feel the need to complain about someone, criticize someone, or talk about someone, we need to check our own hearts. Maybe there is an issue with them, or maybe the issue is with us. The Pharisees were jealous of Jesus, so they try to discredit him by saying he is possessed by the devil. Look at how Jesus responds.

> Jesus knew their thoughts and said to them, "Every kingdom divided against itself will be ruined, and every city or household divided against itself will not stand. If Satan drives out Satan, he is divided against himself. How then can his kingdom stand? And if I drive out demons by Beelzebul, by whom do your people drive them out? So then, they will be your judges. But if it is by the Spirit of God that I drive out demons, then the kingdom of God has come upon you." (Matthew 12:25–28)

First off, Beelzebul was a common name the people in Jesus' day called the devil.

Jesus was making the point that if he is possessed by the devil then why would he cast out demons? He says a household divided against itself will not stand. Now, Jesus was saying this to make the point that he is not possessed by the devil, but there is so much truth in this.

You can't defeat the demons you enjoy hanging out with.

A house divided against itself will not stand. Jesus' teachings seem so radical at times, but it just makes sense. You cannot love both Duke and UNC basketball. You cannot be faithful to your spouse and faithful to your affair at the same time. I mean you can, but it doesn't get you anywhere good. You will not see any improvement as long as you try to do both/and.

The one word to describe the devil is united. You never see an example of the devil or demons fighting amongst themselves. They are committed to their cause. They are united in disuniting Christians.

We often look for quick fixes and easy answers. Like that time I tried to do a low-carb diet while still eating pizza. I was so disciplined all day until I saw that pizza. Lots of low-carb fats plus pizza at night leads to purgatory.

In fact, I wonder if that's why so many people live in frustration. We go halfway in expecting full results.

When you don't fully commit it leads to mediocrity and ultimately frustration.

Results come when you get sick and tired of being sick and tired. When you have had enough and say, "I'm done playing this both/and game. I'm done being a house divided against itself. I'm going to choose God's way because it's best!"

I wish someone would have told me the following when I was a teenager. The demons you enjoy as a teenager will be the demons that haunt you as an adult.

Teenagers typically have more freedom than children. They also have raging hormones. When we experience pain in the teenage years we often look to quick fixes. The quick fixes often become lifelong problems.

If you are a teenager reading this I implore you to sell out to God today. Don't wait until you are old and gray. You will not have any regrets walking passionately with God as a teenager. God changed my life as a teenager. I went all in to this thing called

Christianity. I didn't get drunk in high school. I never smoked pot. I didn't experiment physically. I went all in. That doesn't mean I'm better than anyone. Each person takes their own path. My path was void of what many call the high school experience. I didn't experience that, but I loved high school.

After college I applied for a position as a youth pastor at a big church. One of the people in the interview asked me how I was going to relate to teenagers because most teenagers didn't live a life like I did in high school. My response was "The same way that Jesus did." Jesus was perfect and yet sinners were drawn to him. I'm not Jesus. I have my own issues. And even though I may have never had a season of wild living, I still felt the effects of gravity. As a teenager my outlet was food. I was my heaviest as a senior in high school. I lost a lot of weight in college. To this day, though, when I get stressed, hurt, or bored my temptation is to go to food.

One of the biggest issues we have is compartmentalization. You have your work life. You have your social life. You have your online life. And then you have your church life. Compartmentalization leads to different lives. Compartmentalization leads to a house divided against itself. You can't change when you are only partially in it.

Jesus goes on to explain to the Pharisees why their thought process is whackadoodle. Let's look at what he says...

"When an impure spirit comes out of a person, it goes through arid places seeking rest and does not find it. Then it says, 'I will return to the house I left.' When it arrives, it finds the house unoccupied, swept clean and put in order. Then it goes and takes with it seven other spirits more wicked than itself, and they go in and live

there. And the final condition of that person is worse than the first. That is how it will be with this wicked generation." (Matthew 12:43–45)

Now, Jesus used a lot of teaching techniques. Sometimes he used allegory, sometimes he used parables, sometimes he used hyperbole. Hyperbole is shocking statements that are used to get people's attention. For example, Jesus said if your eye causes you to lust pluck it out. We don't think Jesus was being literal with that one. In the verse we just read, we don't know if Jesus was being literal or using hyperbole. And at the end of the day it doesn't matter. What matters is the point he was making.

When we say no to a bad habit, but we do not replace it, we will end up worse than before.

Whenever we try to change we cannot focus on what we are giving up. It's too difficult. When we focus on what we are giving up we end up missing it. When we end up missing it we end up running back to it when life gets hard.

Discipline only takes us so far. Once our discipline fades we go diving head first back into the very thing we were trying to avoid.

The key is to…

Replace instant gratification with lifelong purpose.

Discipline is great, but until you get to the heart of the issue you are facing, discipline will only take you so far.

The real heart of the issue is giving into unhealthy patterns whenever we feel stressed, hurt, lonely, or bored. Discipline works for a little while, but then life hits us hard, and we end up trying to self-medicate to make ourselves feel better.

When it comes to overcoming something bad, we can't just replace it with the opposite. For example, if you are like me and trying to lose some weight, you can't just focus on eating healthy. For me there is no joy in eating healthy. Sure, I'd like a six-pack of abs, but when I'm stressed abs don't comfort me like Krispy Kreme. What pulls us away from instant gratification is a dedication to a better story of following Jesus.

What do you want your story to be? When you die what do you want people to say about you? I know no one likes to think about death, but we all are going to die at some point. When people talk about your life story what will they say?

Bill Gates famously said, "Most people overestimate what they can do in one year and underestimate what they can do in ten years."

With a little bit of effort, we can experience massive changes.

Fill in the blank with whatever instant gratification temptation you have. If you want to stop doing _____ you must replace it with a better story.

There is no better story than building the kingdom of God on earth as it is in heaven. Our purpose is to serve Jesus like we've been served. Our purpose is to be the hands and feet of Jesus.

Think about where you want to be in the next five years.

If you are like me, you won't do this exercise. In the past, whenever I read a book and the author asked me to do something, I'd roll my eyes. Reading is discipline enough for me. That is...until I wrote a book. Now, I try to do whatever the author asks. It's a small way to get the most out of a book and support my fellow authors. I digress.

I know it's a little annoying that I'm asking you to do something else besides simply reading this book.

I get it.

Whenever you are ready, take some time to think about where you want to be in the next five years.

Where do you want to be spiritually?

Where do you want to be financially?

Where do you want to be in five years? Now, how are you going to get there?

We can't just hope to change. Hope is an amazing feeling but a horrible strategy.

Take a baby step toward change by replacing something unhealthy with something healthy.

A few years ago, I found myself running out of time to read the Bible before I got ready for work. What changed was the invention of the smartphone. I was spending fifteen to thirty minutes on my phone before my alarm would go off. My alarm would go off and then I'd rush through a devotion because I no longer had time. I was convicted one morning about not "having time" for God. I made a small change. I would read my Bible before I checked other apps. It was a small change that led to great things.

We know the devil's playbook. Let Jesus do what only he can do, and you do your part. The question is, how do we find our lifelong purpose?

A LIFELONG PURPOSE

How do you discover your purpose? If purpose really is the thing that drives us away from temptation and into our future, the question is, how do we discover our purpose?

I'm not sure God has a specific calling for each of us, but more of a specific way to find our calling. God uses our passions, desires, and giftedness to help us find our purpose. At times it changes. If our purpose is just based around our giftedness, then we lose hope if something happens to our giftedness. For example, I'm gifted at communicating. What happens if I'm no longer able to preach? If my giftedness is my purpose, then it leads to discouragement when my giftedness changes.

Instead God uses every season to help us discover our purpose. When life changes we change with it to see how God wants to use the change.

You were created to do more than your current job. You were created to do more than just exist. You were created to thrive in every season of life.

That's why I love what is said about Jesus. Ultimately, our purpose is not found in a what, but a who.

In the beginning was the Word, and the Word was with God, and the Word was God. He was with God in the beginning. Through him all things were made; without him nothing was made that has been made. In him was life, and that life was the light of all mankind. The light shines in the darkness, and the darkness has not overcome it. (John 1:1–5)

Those verses were written by one of Jesus' best friends. He's one of the Sons of Thunder and known as the disciple whom Jesus loved.

When John wrote these words, he was living amidst incredible darkness. When John was alive the Roman Empire was in charge. During his lifetime the Romans built a ditch and wall around the city of Jerusalem, where John lived, and for seven months they wouldn't let any Jews leave the city of Jerusalem. Thousands starved to death or died by plague during these seven months. The temple was a major part of the Jewish religion and John was around when the Romans destroyed the temple and killed millions of Jews. Not only that but they took thousands as slaves and spread them all throughout the Roman Empire. By the time John wrote his account of Jesus, his friend Peter had been crucified by the Romans. Another guy that he would have known really well was named Paul, and Paul was killed by the Romans. At one point the focal point of the Roman Empire was to snuff out Christianity. To be a Christian in John's day meant you opened yourself up to being captured by the Romans, tortured, or worse, becoming a slave and becoming a part of their gladiator sports. John is exiled to an island to die. One of the first historical writers of Christianity is Tertullian, and he gives an account of John being dipped in boiling oil by the Romans in the Colosseum. According to Tertullian, John didn't die from the boiling, and the entire Colosseum came to faith in Jesus because of it. The Romans, not knowing what to do with John but wanting to snuff out Christianity, banished him to an island to die. So, with that understanding let's dig into what John wrote about why Jesus came to earth.

In him was life... (John 1:4)

Let's stop there. John is saying that in Jesus is life. Now, despite all that John has gone through, despite everyone he knows dying or even being killed for following Jesus, John makes the bold claim that in Jesus was life. Now, he is not talking about physical life. That is, you can suffer in this life and still experience something so supernatural it gives you hope. He is talking about a spiritual life.

His purpose. You can go through difficulty but still have purpose. Now, notice what John writes next.

and that life was the light of all mankind. (John 1:4)

Why is this so significant?

Because in the early times after Jesus rose from the dead, they viewed the good news of Jesus as something that was good only for a certain group of people. That this good news was good for the Jewish people, who had been waiting for a Messiah. But John says...oh no! Jesus is the light of all mankind. If the biblical authors used # they would have said, "#Jesusislit." Not, Jesus is a light. The claim that sets Jesus apart from every other person who has lived is that he is the light. Jesus isn't an answer, he is the answer. So often we get so accustomed to living in darkness that we don't go to the one thing that can help, Jesus.

When my son was two years old he was having a hard time sleeping because he was scared of a purple monster. One night I had done everything to console him and nothing was working. I turned on lights, I rubbed his back, I told him that monsters weren't real and if they were I'd beat them up. Nothing worked. Finally I said to Hayden, "When you get scared say 'Jesus' and God will protect you." Hayden looked up at me immediately and said, "No! I need a gun."

We are born in spiritual darkness and it is not natural to run to God. So often it takes us hitting rock bottom to admit we need some help.

Now, this is not just a bold claim, this is a fulfillment of a prophecy that was written seven hundred years before Jesus. And John connects the prophecy of what was said about Jesus with who Jesus was.

During a very dark time in Israel's history, the Assyrian army was sweeping through and threatening to destroy the Israelites. And in the midst of amazingly dark and awful times the prophet Isaiah gives some hope to those who are struggling. Look at what he said seven hundred years before Jesus.

> The people walking in darkness
> have seen a great light;
> on those living in the land of deep darkness
> a light has dawned. (Isaiah 9:2)

Now, Isaiah is talking about a future light. He is sharing a prophecy that he says God gave him. This is a prophecy that brought hope to a group of people who were suffering all types of darkness. The people walking in darkness have seen a great light. He goes on to tell us who this light of the world will be.

> For to us a child is born,
> to us a son is given,
> and the government will be on his shoulders.
> And he will be called
> Wonderful Counselor, Mighty God,
> Everlasting Father, Prince of Peace. (Isaiah 9:6)

If you grew up in church, you may have heard this verse before. It's a pretty popular one at Christmastime. And the author is saying that one day a child will be born, and that child is the light of the world. Now, the claim that the world is in darkness is not a radical claim. We see that everywhere. We experience the darkness. With every death. With every heartbreak we experience the darkness. At times this world is so dark it feels like God is absent. Have you ever wondered, God where are you? The authors of the Bible were living such dark times we can't even imagine it. The world has always been broken and we have all experienced that. But there is a light. In every season of darkness there is a light. And look at what John says next. This is so powerful for us today.

> The light shines in the darkness, and the darkness has
> not overcome it. (John 1:5)

Despite all that John has seen. Despite everyone he knows dying. Despite the fact that at the time of writing there is a government that is trying to snuff out Christianity. Darkness throughout time has tried its best to overcome the light but this light, Jesus, just keeps shining.

Why does that give us hope? Well, no matter what amount of darkness you have experienced or will experience, you can have hope in that it cannot snuff out the light of Jesus. This gives us hope. This gives us purpose.

In your life, there are problems you can't solve. There are issues that won't be resolved. There are people that you cannot control. There are people who will drive you crazy. There is darkness all around. And in the midst of all this darkness there is still a light. A light that gives us hope. The darkness has not overcome it. Not then and not now and not ever.

I think we should try to better ourselves any way we can. I think education is needed. I think psychology is needed. I think learning about ourselves and others is needed. None of that is bad, but all of it falls short. The thing that makes John's claim so radical is that he says Jesus is the answer for the darkness. Translation: Jesus is the answer for us.

Now, some people need more of a scientific backing. Some people reading this grew up in church and if Jesus said it that settles it you'll believe it. But others need something else. Science has proven that we live in darkness, but science hasn't come up with an answer for why.

The human brain is wired to focus on darkness, negativity, and things that are not good.

The human brain is actually wired to hold on to negative stimuli. According to scientific research, our brains use almost two-thirds of their neurons to detect negative experiences. That is, more brain power goes to looking for negative experiences than positive ones. And once the human brain starts looking for bad news, it is quickly stored in our long-term memory.

On the other hand, research has found that in order to remember a positive experience you have to hold on to it more than twelve seconds. That is, you have to take it in and intentionally think about it for twelve seconds in order to transfer positive emotions from short-term memories to long-term memories.

> **"The brain is like Velcro for negative experiences but Teflon for positive ones."**
>
> **—Dr. Rick Hanson**

This is why bad news makes the opening story on the news. Bad news sticks with us. It sells.

There are more negative emotional words (62 percent) than positive words (32 percent) in the English dictionary.

If you are not intentional, your brain will naturally look for the negative and forget the positive.

> **"Unless we are occupied with other thoughts, worrying is the brain's default position."[1]**
>
> **—Dr. Mihaly Csikszentmihalyi**

---

1 Ray Williams, "Are We Hardwired to Be Negative or Positive?" *ICF*, June 30, 2014, https://coachfederation.org/blog/are-we-hardwired-to-be-negative-or-positive.

Our brains naturally go negative. We are not only surrounded by darkness but have to fight against the darkness in our own lives.

So here is a challenge to you. Whether you've believed that Jesus is the light of the world for your whole life or you once believed but have walked away, or even if you would say you just don't believe...would you consider taking a step toward the light? What if you didn't view everything in life as right and wrong, black and white, but what if you viewed life as moving away from or toward the light? What if our ultimate purpose was found in the light? What if any form of darkness we face is a reminder of just how desperately we need God?

There have been times where people have told me they wished I would go more negative. That is, they wished I would just call out such-and-such sinners. I get it, but I believe in the gospel. The gospel is good news. Christians often yell at the darkness for being dark, but that won't change anything. It's my job to preach the gospel, it is God's job to convict.

Jesus is the light of the world. That is, no matter what darkness you've been in, he is the way out. No matter what tempts you or how many times you've fallen for Satan's playbook, the light of Jesus is welcoming you. For those of us who call ourselves Christians, this is incredibly challenging because Jesus flips the script on being the light of the world. Look at what Jesus says to those who follow him.

> "You are the light of the world. A town built on a hill cannot be hidden. Neither do people light a lamp and put it under a bowl. Instead they put it on its stand, and it gives light to everyone in the house. In the same way,

let your light shine before others, that they may see your good deeds and glorify your Father in heaven." (Matthew 5:14–16)

The reason that following Jesus brings light to your life is because he leads you out of darkness. You find your purpose in following Jesus because no matter what situation you face, your purpose is to love God and love others. Most of the darkness that we have comes from selfishness and an addiction to thinking about ourselves. When we follow Jesus, he leads us out of the darkness. And that light that we found we are to share with others.

You bring either light or darkness to every situation you face.

Tomorrow, you may face some darkness. You may be around people who drive you crazy. You might have to be around family who is living in darkness and doesn't even know it. And the temptation is to label them as bad, but don't. If you are a Christian your heart should break for anyone who is living in darkness. And as a Christian, instead of getting angry and bringing more darkness, decide right now how you can bring some light.

I love the quote from Dale Carnegie…

"Any fool can criticize, condemn and complain—and most fools do. But it takes character and self-control to be understanding and forgiving."[2]

---

2   Dale Carnegie, *How to Win Friends & Influence People* (New York: Pocket Books, 1998). Quote accessed online.

People will forget the nice things that you've done for them. But when you decide in your heart to bring light to every person you meet, people will never forget how you made them feel.

For every situation you face, don't just ask is it right or wrong. Ask is it light or darkness. And in every situation you face, think about how you can bring God's light. Right or wrong thinking leads to "If you treat me right I'll treat you right," but light versus dark thinking says, "If you bring darkness I am going to counter that with the light of God."

Our purpose is found in receiving God's light and then in turn sharing that light with others.

When we focus on bringing God's light it gives us purpose to overcome temptation. When we focus on being God's light it gives every situation meaning. It's not just about experiences. It's about bringing light to every experience.

The world doesn't need more opinions. It needs more love. Whenever we bring the light of God people will experience his love. That's our purpose.

COMMUNITY AGAIN???

This is something that every support group in the world understands. When a person goes through AA they do it with a group. If you do Weight Watchers they encourage you to do it with a support group. As I've mentioned, you cannot do life alone. We are better together.

And yet when it comes to Christianity the mindset is often to fight struggles alone. As Christians there is pressure to act like we do not sin. The funny thing is we know we do, and yet too often judge other people who sin differently than we do.

Very rarely will two Christians sit down and talk about sin specifics. If two Christians do talk about sin it is often in generalizations. I sinned...once. I used to struggle with that. The church community doesn't feel safe to share struggles with.

The problem is we will never get victory as long as we live in sin denial.

You sin. Your sin is ugly. Your sin is selfish. And I know it's easier to see other people's sins than it is your own, but your sin is just as stanky as the next person's. So is my sin. In a sermon I once mentioned how I am a sinner. In shocked disbelief someone in the front row shook her head. Her thought was "Surely the pastor doesn't sin." I do. You do.

I want to continue exploring this idea of light by looking at another text written by John, one of Jesus' best friends. For Jesus' birthday, December 25, they exchanged friendship bracelets. I'm joking. When talking about John, it is said he was the disciple whom Jesus loved. When you read his letters to the early church, they are dripping with the love of Jesus. Let's look at what John wrote and break it down.

> **This is the message we have heard from him and declare to you: God is light; in him there is no darkness at all. If we claim to have fellowship with him and yet walk in the darkness, we lie and do not live out the truth. (1 John 1:5–6)**

Now, this verse, out of context, can cause us a lot of harm. It seems incredibly black and white, but this verse is a part of the entire letter. God is light and in him there is no darkness at all. I think we can all get on board with that. God is light and therefore his followers are called to be the light of the world. He says if we walk in darkness we lie and do not live in the truth.

Without context that could mean that if you sin on a regular basis, it must mean you aren't saved.

Okay, in order to understand what it means to walk in the light, we have to read some more. We are going to skip a verse and come back to it. I want to show you what John says about sin.

If we claim to be without sin, we deceive ourselves and the truth is not in us. If we confess our sins, he is faithful and just and will forgive us our sins and purify us from all unrighteousness. If we claim we have not sinned, we make him out to be a liar and his word is not in us. (1 John 1:8–10)

Okay, on the one hand if you walk in darkness as a Christian you are a liar. On the other hand, if you claim to be without sin you are lying to yourself…and the truth is not even in you.

So, what is going on here? Well, all throughout John's letter he talks about the importance of relationships. Specifically, he says if you hate a fellow Christian you need to examine your life because that is not of God. But I now want to look at the middle verse between these two verses.

But if we walk in the light, as he is in the light, we have fellowship with one another, and the blood of Jesus, his Son, purifies us from all sin. (1 John 1:7)

Walking in the light, according to this verse, has to do with having fellowship with one another. John wrote this letter in Greek.

The word he used for fellowship is the Greek word *koinonia*. Now, why in the world are we talking about Greek? Great question. In the Greek language oftentimes one word meant multiple things. When we translate it in English we miss some of the other meanings of the word.

For me, I grew up going to church and fellowship was something we talked about all the time. I often heard after a social event at church, "It was a great time of fellowship." Fellowship became the church word for anything fun in the church. In the Baptist Church this typically involved food. But even when we would do something active someone would say that it was a great time of fellowship. When John writes about fellowship he is not talking about a church potluck in the fellowship hall. *Koinonia* is the idea of sharing all things in common.

The idea is that in Jesus you will have this bond with others who follow Jesus. And John's point over and over again in his letter is if you have issues with other humans, you are not walking in the light. You are deceived if you think you truly love Jesus when you have bitterness in your heart. Now, true fellowship starts with walking with Jesus.

Now, why is this important? Well, when you walk with Jesus and have true fellowship with one another, John says you will be so comfortable with the community of believers that you will confess your sin.

Christians, we have some work to do. One of the reasons we so struggle with sin is because we don't understand fellowship.

Fellowship is being so bonded that you share everything. It's a common bond. And in fellowship a person feels so much security and freedom that they willingly confess their sin.

Let me ask you some questions.

Who do you confess your sin to?

Who knows what you struggle with?

Who is checking in on you?

Who do you check in on?

For Christians, sin leads to isolation. Sin tells you that no one can relate to your struggle. Sin tells you that you need to go into hiding. Sin tells you that you can handle the struggle on your own.

Don't believe the lie. Sin wants to separate us as humans. God wants us connected. And a sign of walking closely with Jesus is fellowship with other believers.

If you are not sharing your life with others you are living in darkness. There is darkness that has led you to believe you can't trust people. There is darkness that led you to believe no one can relate to your struggle.

As a Christian you and I need other Christians. Because humans are broken you will be hurt by another human. And it only takes one bad relationship to mess up all others.

But fellowship with Jesus brings forgiveness. Fellowship with Jesus allows you to practice receiving grace and therefore share grace with others.

One of the core values of the church I lead is "You can't do life alone." That's not just a pithy statement written on the wall down the hall. You try to do Lone Ranger Christianity, you will not make it.

You may have really close friends, but there is a chance that even good friendships miss this level of fellowship. For you the challenge is to test the waters and see which one of your friends can be your person to confess sin to.

You may not have a close group of friends. You may even struggle in the friend department. You may be nice, but you may not currently have a close friend. The reason you haven't found a close friend is that somewhere in your thinking is some darkness. Maybe you've thought you just aren't friend material. Or maybe you have unrealistic expectations when it comes to friends. In order to die to one thing you have to live for something else. So to die to sin you must live for Jesus. And when you live for Jesus you will have fellowship with other Christians. A part of fellowship is confession.

Application: Who is your person to confess sin to, be accountable to, and support you when you struggle? If you don't have someone, ask God for wisdom to know who you should ask.

Questions:

1. Before reading this chapter, how did you view temptation?

2. What temptations did you struggle with as a teenager? How do those temptations impact you today?

3. If you had to define your purpose, what would you say?

4. Based off where you are currently, what is God's purpose for you in this season?

5. How can you bring light into the current darkness you face?

CHAPTER 16

MY PERFECTLY
BROKEN FAMILY

The word *church* doesn't actually appear in the New Testament. The word we have translated to church is the Greek word *ekklesia*.

Ekklesia—always refers to a gathering of people united by a common identity and purpose.

Somehow over the years, what Jesus meant when he said *ekklesia* has been translated as a building where Christians meet. The church is not a building but a group of people united by a common identity and purpose.

This chapter is called "My Perfectly Broken Family" because that is what the local church is. It's easy to forget that the church is a family and not a building. If you grew up in church you might have learned a little saying that has hand motions: "This is the church, this is the steeple, open the doors and here are all the people."

Whoever invented that had good intentions, but they are wrong. A building is not the church. The church is a group of people who have gathered together under one common purpose.

We are a family. We are broken. We are imperfect. We have our issues, but we are a family. A family that should be united over the most exciting mission known to man. And yet, so often the church is nothing more than another meeting we have to go to.

I grew up going to church, and one of the songs we used to sing was called "The Family of God." It's a really old song that was inspired by true events. Bill and Gloria Gaither are gospel singers, and one Sunday their pastor didn't show at the beginning of the service. One of the church members was critically injured in a fire at work, and the pastor was doing his best to meet his family's needs. The doctors said he wasn't going to make it. It was Easter Sunday and the church was so affected by this tragedy that no one was singing happy Easter songs. Eventually, the pastor walked into the church to update everyone on this injured church member's condition. He let them know that he was alive. He wasn't expected to make it through the night, but because of their prayers this man was alive and the doctors were now going to start treatment. He then let the church know that they were going to see this through. He told the church that they would have to step up to help this family with the kids, and to bring meals, and to provide financial support. The church erupted with applause and excitement that their fellow church member was alive and they were getting to be a part of meeting his needs.

After the service Bill Gaither went home and wrote the lyrics to "The Family of God."

Now, that story is inspiring to me. But growing up in the church, I heard this song sung by people who had one foot in the grave, if you know what I mean. This peppy song was sung by people who looked angry.

For so many people this is what church has become. It's a something we have to endure instead of something we get to do. For many, church represents the frozen chosen. That is, the church has become frozen in time and the people go through motions.

I'm not saying that churches need to be emotional pep rallies. But our story is the most exciting story in the history of the world. There should be some life for those who gather together as the church.

I want to show you a very important text that should inspire you to become the church. The text is written by Paul. He wrote over half of the New Testament. He wrote a letter to the churches in Ephesus to give them some instructions on how to be the church. Look at what Paul writes to them.

> **Consequently, you are no longer foreigners and strangers, but fellow citizens with God's people and also members of his household, built on the foundation of the apostles and prophets, with Christ Jesus himself as the chief cornerstone. In him the whole building is joined together and rises to become a holy temple in the Lord. And in him you too are being built together to become a dwelling in which God lives by his Spirit. (Ephesians 2:19–22)**

Consequently, you are no longer foreigners but fellow citizens. This is so important to us today. Christianity started as a little sect out of Judaism. Some people even referred to it as a cult of Judaism. In Judaism the temple was a really big deal.

The temple was a place of worship, and because Judaism was a Jewish religion, there was a part of the temple where Gentiles could not go. I mentioned this in an earlier chapter. Most of us reading this would be considered Gentiles. Judaism made it clear who was allowed in and who was not allowed in. There was a literal barrier preventing the Gentiles from coming into the temple. So, if you wanted to worship the Jewish God but you weren't Jewish, you had to do so at a distance. And if you weren't Jewish you were considered a stranger or an alien. How welcoming is that? But look at what Paul does...

> Consequently, you are no longer foreigners and strangers, but fellow citizens with God's people and also members of his household, built on the foundation of the apostles and prophets, with Christ Jesus himself as the chief cornerstone. In him the whole building is joined together and rises to become a holy temple in the Lord. And in him you too are being built together to become a dwelling in which God lives by his Spirit. (Ephesians 2:19–22)

Through Jesus you are no longer strangers or aliens. Through Jesus the dividing wall has been torn down. Through Jesus you are now members of his household. Now in ancient times to be a part of someone's household was the equivalent of what we today would call an extended family. What once separated us no longer separates us. We are no longer locked out of the building. We are now a part of the family of God.

Now the temple had oftentimes become a corrupt place. It was corrupt because the people who were in charge were powerful people. But now, a relationship with God is not built around a temple, but a people. This is a game changer!

But something happened. The church for the first three hundred years in existence was persecuted. The Roman Empire made it illegal for people to be Christians. Many were tortured and killed for their faith. And yet, no matter how hard the Roman government tried to snuff out this little religion, it couldn't. Christianity thrived during intense persecution.

In 313 AD, Constantine, the soon-to-be emperor of Rome, did something radical. He legalized Christianity. But wait, there's more. As Constantine's power grew so did his influence. And then, one day Constantine declared that he was a Christian. This is scandalous. This is preposterous. With this one major change, Christianity would be forever impacted.

Before this Christians met in homes in what they called love feasts. If that doesn't sound like a cult, nothing does. A love feast sounds super shady. A love feast was basically a potluck dinner. They would eat, have communion, pray, sing songs, and talk about God.

It was at this point in history that the church shifted from a people to a building. The church took on some of the practices of other religions. It became about the nice building, and a place to gather. Christianity spread rapidly at this point, but it also started to lose its impact. It went from being radical to recreational.

Jesus' original plan was not a building, but a group of people. A family. And in every generation there are those who want to turn the church into a corporation and make it centered around a building. At the same time, God continues to raise up leaders to fight against institutionalizing the church. There are those who are rebels. There are those who are passionate about making the church what Jesus originally intended it to be. A family.

Now, our verse talks about Jesus being the cornerstone of this family. Before the invention of concrete, builders used stones to lay a foundation for a new building. They would select one particular stone and call it the "cornerstone." The cornerstone would determine the placement of every other stone. So, the church, or Ekklesia, is a gathering of people like a family, and its cornerstone is Jesus. Why is this important?

Today, what do we make the focus of the church? Our preferences. We gather at churches based off what we like. We have churches to fit every preference out there. And if you don't like the brand of one church, no worries, you can just dump them and go to another one. Without even knowing it, you have made church about a building, or about a denomination, or about a style of music. We've made it about where we feel the most needed. We've made it about where we can have the most influence. We've made it a social club that comes with all the fixings.

You want to know what the focus of the church is? It's not you. It's not me. It's not a pastor. It's not a denomination. It's Jesus. It's all about Jesus. Whenever I meet someone who has walked away from the church, my heart breaks.

Listen, if you base your relationship with God on me, you will be disappointed. I am not perfect. I'm not the center of the church. If you base your relationship with God on preferences, then you will eventually grow disenchanted. The church is not a building, but a people.

And as for us, as a part of this family of believers, we have to fight against making the church about anything but Jesus. We are a family. A family that has different opinions, preferences, and even views of God. We are a broken, sometimes dysfunctional family, but we have to fight to make this thing about Jesus and only Jesus. The church may have let you down in the past, but Jesus will not. The church may have hurt you, but Jesus will not.

Anytime there is disunity or fighting in the church, it is a result of people making the church about something other than Jesus.

Stop it.

Are we moving or simply meeting?

Are we making a measurable difference in the world or simply conducting services?

Are we an ekklesia?

UNITY

A family doesn't need to be perfect, it just needs to be united. I love that idea. No family is perfect, but a united family can do some serious good in the world.

Now, a church being unified has to be one of the most difficult things in the entire world. The church is made up of all sorts of opinions, different backgrounds, preferences, and ideas. As kids in the eighties, whenever we would get to fill our own drink at a restaurant we would take the cup and then fill it with every soda that was at the drink fountain. A little root beer, some Coke, Sprite, orange soda, Dr Pepper, a little fruit punch, and then some sweet tea. I don't know what you called that, but we called it a suicide. I'm convinced taste buds don't take form until our teen years. That drink is gag nasty. Some things just should not be mixed together. And yet that is what the church is. A mixture of a whole bunch of different flavors. It's like when I was in kindergarten I went over to a friend's house and her mom made us peanut butter and mayonnaise sandwiches. To this day I can't eat mayonnaise. I am convinced they take all the fat liposuctioned from the movie stars in Hollywood and sell it as mayo. Gag nasty! I can't stand mayonnaise. Why in the world would you ruin a perfectly good peanut butter sandwich by putting mayo on it? If a parent tried to pull that today, they would have child services called on them. Some things just don't go together and yet here we are. Different. Unique. Together.

Each one of us brings our own life lessons, preferences, ideologies, and brokenness to church. So how in the world can such a diverse group of people become united?

This is a very important question. Whether you are a deacon, Sunday school teacher, small group facilitator, volunteer, staff member, pastor, or an occasional church attender, this is an important question to answer. How do we become a united people?

Our answer to how to become unified comes from the apostle Paul's letter to the church in Ephesus.

As a prisoner for the Lord, then, I urge you to live a life worthy of the calling you have received. (Ephesians 4:1)

Let's stop there for just a second. Do you know why Paul is a prisoner? If you grew up in church, you may know this answer. If you are newer to the church scene, you may not know. He was in prison because his message about Jesus caused a riot. Once he was in prison they didn't know what to do with him. He hadn't committed a crime, but those in charge wanted to keep him around to learn about this radical message that was sweeping the world.

Paul says, "Live a life worthy of the calling you have received." Now, if you are not a Christian, then feel free to tune this out. This is not for you. If you are a Christian, this is an important challenge. You are urged to live a life worthy of God's calling. Well, what did God call us to? To be the church. To be unified. To be the family of God. To represent Jesus everywhere you go. Let's keep reading and see what Paul writes next...

Be completely humble and gentle; be patient, bearing with one another in love. (Ephesians 4:2)

Be completely humble and gentle; be patient, bearing with one another in love. Why is this verse so important? Because we are a dysfunctional, broken, messy group of people. And sometimes you have to bear with one another in love. Sometimes you have to ignore a political post by someone you go to church with. Sometimes you have to bear with people who don't look like you but go to church with you. Sometimes you have to bear with people who are messy. With social media we have a greater opportunity to see personal areas of people's lives that used to be relegated to their family. Before social media I don't remember knowing people's political views, opinions about everything, and what they ate for dinner. With social media we often get an inside scoop into people's lives. That means that often you can see opinions from other Christians that are different than yours. You don't have to unfollow them. You don't have to call them out. You can just keep scrolling, just keep scrolling (said in the voice of Dory from Finding Nemo). Not everything needs to be called out. Not everything needs to become an issue. Sometimes you have to just keep scrolling past someone's post. You don't have to agree with them to be church family with them. The exception to this is if someone is participating in harmful behavior. If you see bullying, then you should do something about that. But most of our issues aren't because a real foul has been committed. We get upset because we want everyone to agree with how we think.

Now, here is something interesting about the local church. You want to know who has free rein to complain? You do. If you don't like something about church, you can complain to everyone. You want to know who doesn't have free rein? The pastor. If I wrote about you the way that some people have talked about church leadership, you would need to see a counselor. This is a major problem with the local church.

A church wasn't meant to be a lone pastor who ministers to a group of people. It was meant to be a group of people ministering to the world.

You won't like everything about the church you are a part of. And the pastor won't like everything about you. I can't speak for all pastors, but you want to know what I'm committed to? Bearing with others in love. That's what Christians do. Can you smell what the Rob is cooking?!

Dietrich Bonhoeffer was a German pastor who resisted Adolph Hitler. He was imprisoned and eventually killed for his stance against Hitler. His writings have been incredibly influential to the modern church. Well, Bonhoeffer wrote that all people who enter a church tend to carry a "wish dream."

The wish dream is an illusion about the ideal kind of church a person feels entitled to be a part of. The wish dream is different for everyone. For some it's a place where everyone who wants to sing gets to sing. Even if they can't sing. Some of you grew up in churches that never said no to anyone.

Some people have a wish dream where everyone gets to preach. That's not realistic. Not everyone is gifted to speak. Some people have a wish dream where the music is a certain style. If it doesn't fit their style, it frustrates them. Some people have a wish dream about how decisions are made. Some have a wish dream that the pastor is perfect. Some have a wish dream that the pastor will be at their beck and call.

Look at what Bonhoeffer said about the wish dream in his book Life Together.

> "Every human wish dream that is injected into the Christian community is a hindrance to genuine community and must be banished if genuine community is to survive. He who loves his dream of a community more than the Christian community itself becomes a destroyer of the latter, even though his personal intentions may be ever so honest and earnest and sacrificial."
>
> —Dietrich Bonhoeffer

The wish dream destroys the family of God because it's not based off reality. It's a dream. It's an impossible dream for any church to live up to.

Bonhoeffer goes on to say...

> "When a person becomes alienated from a Christian community in which he has been placed and begins to raise complaints about it, he had better examine himself first to see whether the trouble is not due to his wish dream that should be shattered by God; and if this be the case, let him thank God for leading him in to this predicament. But if not, let him nevertheless guard

against ever becoming an accuser of the congregation before God."

—Dietrich Bonhoeffer

You may have left a church because your wish dream was crushed. Now, if a pastor sexually abused you, or verbally abused you, then that is so wrong. That is not a wish dream. That is sinful behavior. But a lot of the time it's not that a pastor or church has sinned, it's that they didn't meet our wish dream.

The church is made up of imperfect leaders. It's made up of imperfect people. Not every decision is going to be the right decision. Sometimes we are going to try things and fail. Sometimes you're going to have an idea, and as great as that idea is, it's not going to be something your church can do. Sometimes you may not like the sermon series your church does. Sometimes you may not like the guest preacher when the pastor is out of town. Sometimes you may not like your small group. And guess what...that is a part of the journey. We are a family, and not a corporation. Some of the best groups I've been a part of started out looking like an episode of Jerry Springer. It was dysfunctional, and we didn't have a lot in common at first. We ended up coming together even though we were so different.

One group I was in came together over funerals. I wouldn't wish this on anyone. Within a few months of gathering together, multiple group members had family die. The running joke became "Who is going to die next?" It wasn't funny, but we had to find some humor in it because it was truly a difficult season. My wife had two grandparents die, other members had parents die. Our group was newly formed, but small groups exist to help church feel small. They exist so needs can be met. Our group came together because we were making meals or dropping off food, crying with those who lost a loved one, or supporting each other at the funeral home.

After my wife's second grandparent died, our group provided a glorious amount of food. We showed up to be with our family and they instantly replied, "You guys brought too much food! We can't believe you bought all of that." I'm a pastor on a pastor's salary, and my wife is a teacher. They thought we would have had to take out a small loan to buy all of that food. We quickly let them know that we didn't buy any of it. They gasped and asked who provided that food. When we told them it was our small group, one of my wife's family members said, "Why would they do that? They didn't even know Grandma." Through tears I replied, "I think they did it because they love us. That's just what groups do." My wife's family was blown away by the support they felt from people who didn't know them.

Let's keep reading what Paul says next.

Make every effort to keep the unity of the Spirit through the bond of peace. (Ephesians 4:3)

Make every effort to keep the unity. Make every effort to keep the unity. Make every effort to keep the unity. Make every effort to keep the unity.

No matter what church you go to, it is your job to make every effort to keep the unity.

I've been on a church staff since I was eighteen years old. Before that I had two other jobs. I worked at a Christian bookstore and then I worked at Subway. Eat Fresh. I was a lousy sandwich artist. At the age of seventeen, God called me to ministry, and by the age of eighteen I was working at a church. I've worked at multiple churches. Small churches, mega churches, traditional churches, and contemporary churches. I'm friends with a lot of pastors in my area. I meet and talk with them a lot. You want to know one thing that every church in the world has in common? Complaining. Disunity. Disgruntled people who make a stink about not getting their way.

Now, I want to show you how we can be different than every other church. Look at what Paul writes next...

> There is one body and one Spirit, just as you were called to one hope when you were called; one Lord, one faith, one baptism; one God and Father of all, who is over all and through all and in all. (Ephesians 4:4–6)

This is so important. What are we unified about? God knows it's not politics. We are not unified on opinions of church governance. We are not unified on style of music. We are not unified on what our theological preferences are. What are we unified about? Jesus. There is one faith, one Spirit, one Lord, one God, and it is God that unites us.

We are not unified about an idea, but by a Savior.

And we have to let Jesus crucify our wish dreams. We have to allow Jesus to unify us. We have to allow Jesus to crucify our selfish ambitions and actions.

A group of people unified over Jesus can radically change the world.

Erwin McManus is a pastor in southern California. He wrote about a trip to the zoo with his family. On his trip he noted how the tour guide pointed out what the various groups of animals were called.

"With insects, most of us know that bees are called swarms and ants are called colonies... Cattle are herds, birds are flocks, and if you watch Lion King you know a tribe of lions is a pride...

352

"[A] group of buzzards waiting around together to feast on leftover carnage is called a committee." And that, my friends, is why we don't have committees at Next Level where I pastor.

A group of baboons is called a congress. I'll just let that one sit there.

McManus then noted that a group of rhinos is called a crash.

"You see, rhinos can run at thirty miles an hour, which is pretty fast when you consider how much weight they're pulling…just one problem with this phenomenon. Rhinos can see only thirty feet in front of them. Can you imagine something that large moving in concert as a group, plowing ahead at thirty miles an hour with no idea what's at thirty-one feet? You would think that they would be far too timid to pick up full steam, that their inability to see far enough ahead would paralyze them to immobility. But with that horn pointing the way, rhinos run forward full steam ahead without apprehension, which leads us to their name.

"Rhinos moving together at full speed are known as a crash. Even when they're just hanging around enjoying the watershed, they're called a crash because of their potential. You've got to love that. I think that's what we're supposed to be. That's what happens when we become united. The church becomes a crash. We become an unstoppable force. We don't have to pretend we know the future. Who cares that we can see only thirty feet ahead? Whatever's at thirty-one feet needs to care that we're coming and better get out of the way…

"We need to stop wasting our time and stop being afraid of what we cannot see and do not know. We need to move forward full force because of what we do know."[1]

---

1   Erwin McManus, *The Barbarian Way: Unleash the Untamed Faith Within* (Nashville: Thomas Nelson, 2005).

What do we know? Jesus! Jesus loves us and died for us and that is the only thing we need to be united. And listen, when a church is united, it's powerful. Marriages get restored. Families get put back together. The hurt become healed. Lives become changed.

Back in 2012 I was a nervous wreck about starting a church. I didn't have the finances or the people. I met with a guy named Ben Arment. He told me that if I could get fifty people I could start a church and make a difference. Well, we got fifty people. We actually got sixty to jump out and start a church. And what we did should have been impossible. We started a church in seven weeks. Why? Because we were unified over the idea that all we had was Jesus.

Listen, if you are miserable at your church, then please find a place where you can be a crash. Just be careful. The wish dream is difficult to kill. We often bring into church our unrealistic expectations.

Every church has problems. Find a church where you care about being a part of the solution.

ONE FAMILY WITH MANY MEMBERS

A couple of summers ago I went on a trip to Israel with thirty-two other pastors. One thing that all of the pastors had in common was wounds and hurts and scars from leading as a pastor of a church. None of us were perfect. We've all caused our own issues. But it was sad how the conversation would so often center around people who were disgruntled at church.

It's not just pastors though. If you stick around the church long enough, you'll get some nicks and wounds from being let down by a local church. The church isn't perfect. It's filled with flawed people who are led by flawed people.

Together, though, we are a family. And together we pursue a God who is known as the Great Physician. The Father God wraps his infinite arms around us and heals our broken wounds. He redeems our mess. He loves broken people so that we can then go and reach more broken people.

The church is a family, and since the church is a family you must find your place in the family. Everybody has a place.

But there is one major issue that continually impacts a person's ability to plug into the family of God.

The church is not a product to consume, but a family to participate in.

In the early days of the church, each person had to pull their own weight. You couldn't just come and consume church. That is, people didn't say things like "I'm church shopping." There was no church shopping. There was a group of believers that were dedicated to each other. If you didn't like that group, you were out of luck. There weren't different denominations or preferences. Today, many view the church as a product to consume. We look for churches to meet our every need and rarely ask how we can give back.

As Americans we love to be catered to.

I cannot prove this, but I believe consumerism started in the eighties. Back in the seventies and early eighties companies didn't do as much catering to customers. For example, when a person ordered fast food, it wasn't made to order. You got what they gave you. If you were alive back then you'll remember this commercial...

"Two all beef patties, special sauce, lettuce, cheese, pickle, onion, on a sesame seed bun."

—Big Mac jingle

You knew that if you walked into McDonald's, that's what you would get. You couldn't even fathom making a special order. But then something happened that would forever change the world.

Burger King introduced an idea that radically impacted every single one of us.

"Have it your way."

The mindset radically changed the world. Today, the customer is always right. Companies attempt to make things special ordered so that the consumer will be happy.

That mindset has crept into the church. I want the church my way.

You are important. You matter. But just like every family, every member of the family matters. In my family we don't always agree on everything.

"Have it your way." Before Burger King, you couldn't special order a sandwich. But they came along and said, "Hold the pickle, hold the lettuce, special orders don't upset us."

Today the consumer mindset has dominated Christian thinking. We want the church to do it our way or we go find another church.

The church is not a product to consume, but a family to participate in.

It's easy to have the consumer mindset. It happens to all of us. Today, if you want to maximize your church experience, you have to move from a consumer to a family member. I want to show you this in a very important Scripture. It's written to some of the earliest Christians. The verses are an explanation of what the church should look like.

> So Christ himself gave the apostles, the prophets, the evangelists, the pastors and teachers, to equip his people for works of service, so that the body of Christ may be built up until we all reach unity in the faith and in the knowledge of the Son of God and become mature, attaining to the whole measure of the fullness of Christ. (Ephesians 4:11–13)

This is a fascinating verse. Many times, people see pastors as some sort of spiritual cook. The thought is the pastor's job is to feed the people. And so, pastors work really hard cooking up spiritual recipes to make sure all the people leave the service on Sunday feeling fat and happy. That mindset is incredibly consumeristic. Paul is the author of the verse we just read. Paul doesn't say the role of the pastor is to cook up the food. The role of the pastor is to equip the people for works of service.

The pastor isn't a chef but a coach. The consumer mindset focuses on having things my way. Now, I've been in the church world a long time. I care about people greatly. Every church I've ever been to has had consumers. People who aren't looking to serve but are looking to consume. You can always tell when someone views the church through the lens of a consumer because they say the same phrases. Things like...

The sermons are just not feeding me.

My small group is just not meeting my needs.

The music just isn't inspiring me.

I don't know if you have ever watched Cookie Monster eat a cookie on Sesame Street, but when Cookie Monster eats he makes this amazing sound. Some of you make this same sound when you eat something amazing. Are you ready for it? Here it is…

Om Nom Nom Nom.

When I start hearing people talk about not being fed, that's the sound I hear. The church isn't meeting my needs. Om Nom Nom Nom. I can't believe they didn't let me sing in the band. Om Nom Nom Nom. I didn't like my small group. Om Nom Nom Nom. That sermon wasn't deep enough. Om Nom Nom Nom.

A consumer asks, "What's in it for me?"

A family member asks, "What's my role?"

As a pastor my role is to equip people to go do ministry. If you are a Christian, you are a shareholder in the local church. You don't simply sit back and consume, you have the honor of doing the ministry.

It is each Christian's responsibility to grow. As a parent my number one goal is to raise my kids to leave. I want to raise kids that are productive members of society. I don't want to produce leeches who don't make a difference. I love having my kids at home, but I want them to go out on their own and start families of their own. So as a parent I equip my kids. My wife and I spend time teaching our kids how to do chores. We give them responsibilities. We don't want them to just consume. We want them to grow and bloom.

A pastor's job is to equip you to leave to go do ministry. Now if you don't grow, it leads to all sorts of problems. Look at what Paul writes next.

Then we will no longer be infants, tossed back and forth by the waves, and blown here and there by every

wind of teaching and by the cunning and craftiness of people in their deceitful scheming. (Ephesians 4:14)

Notice the terminology Paul uses. The goal of all Christians is to become mature. It's to grow. Until spiritual maturity happens the church is filled with spiritual infants. Infants say feed me, change me, watch me, do everything for me. And spiritual infancy is a scary place to be. A spiritual infant can easily have their faith torn away from them and believe all sorts of deceitful things.

In order to become mature, you must apply what you know and teach it to spiritual infants.

FOUR TYPES OF CHURCH FAMILY

The church is a family and each family has different members. In order to be a healthy family, a church must have the following four types of people.

4 Types of Church Family
Non-Churched
New Christian
Growing Christian
Mature Christian

In order to be a church family, you need all four types. A church with all non-church members is unhealthy. A church with all mature Christians is unhealthy. A well-balanced, healthy church has all four types of people.

So what type of family member are you? Are you heading toward being a mature Christian? Mature Christians multiply. We don't stop growing in our faith. As seasoned veterans of faith we should be mature in what we believe. One of the signs of maturity is reproducing. We have to invest in others or we will stop growing. This is why an older Christian desperately needs a new Christian in their life.

Look how Paul ends this section.

Instead, speaking the truth in love, we will grow to become in every respect the mature body of him who is the head, that is, Christ. From him the whole body, joined and held together by every supporting ligament, grows and builds itself up in love, as each part does its work. (Ephesians 4:15–16)

Each person in the family must pull their own weight. If you don't pull your weight, we all suffer. Now, the most important part about all of this is that we are to build each other up in love.

Paul wrote that we are to build each other up in love and we do that by each part of the body doing its work.

We are better together. Mature Christians need new Christians to disciple or they become insider focused. Non-Christians should benefit from having Christians intentionally invest in their lives. We need growing Christians to ask the tough questions that we have taken for granted because we've been in church for so many years.

Work hard to view church as a family and not a product to consume. You won't always get your way. You won't always like every decision. Things won't always cater so you can have it your way. And that's okay. By having a family mindset you'll find more joy. As a parent I find a lot of joy in making my kids happy. It's the same with the church. When we serve one another, we find joy.

But you don't have to plug into the church. A person can stay casually attending, but they miss out. We don't have to be the church, we get to. Being a part of something bigger than yourself is an honor. Seeing people you have invested in come to Jesus is exciting.

Today, less than 5 percent of people who attend church have actually invited someone or shared their faith in the last twelve months. Match that stat with the percentage of unchurched that would be likely to attend if invited and you have a major disconnect. According to Dr. Thom Rainer, "Eighty-two percent of the unchurched are at least somewhat likely to attend church if invited." What is even more convicting is that seven out of ten unchurched people have never been invited to attend a church.

There is no greater honor than using your unique gifts and talents to build the church.

Here's how this works out. When I am weak, you are strong. When you are weak, someone else gets to be strong for you.

We are better together. But we need each other. When you do not use your gifts in the local church, you suffer and so do they. You suffer because you weren't created to use all of your gifts and talents on yourself. The church suffers because when you are not plugged in, a part of the church is missing.

The church will never be perfect because you are in it. It will never be perfect because I am in it. It will never be perfect because humans are imperfect. But we are better together. Together we are a family that has the potential to change the world.

Application: Define what part of the church family you are and take a step toward growth.

Questions:

1. Before reading this chapter, how would you have defined "the church"?

2. How does knowing the church is a family to belong to instead of a product to consume help you understand how to respond to difficult situations in the church?

3. What was your biggest takeaway from this chapter?

4. Based off what you read, what is one thing you will do?

CHAPTER 17

DON'T GIVE UP ON
THE CHURCH

Every church has issues. It's difficult to be a part of a church. At times it may feel easier to give up on the church. I get that. As humans we are wired for comfort. It is natural to quit things that bring us more pain than comfort. If you have ever given up on church then I understand. The hurt that comes from a church is a unique hurt.

DON'T SHUT OUT THE CHURCH

A general rule of thumb is when people in church feel burned out or upset or become disconnected, there are other factors impacting their emotions.

In fact, the vast majority of the time when someone says a pastor "is not deep enough," there is a wound/frustration/offense that has happened between the church member and the pastor. That same pastor at one time was deep enough. What changed was the perception of the pastor. Once an offense takes place it becomes difficult to hear from God during a sermon the pastor has preached.

This isn't 100 percent the case. It's a general rule of thumb.

The human body is meant to avoid pain. Some pain we cannot avoid and therefore we cannot escape it. When we cannot escape it we look for something to escape from.

When there is a death, marital trouble, family drama, or extra pressure from work, we look to find an escape. Often there isn't one. It's difficult to quit your family, a job, etc. What becomes expendable is the church.

Again, this isn't 100 percent true. I know there are lots of examples of people feeling burned out, abused, hurt by church leaders. I'll write to you in the next section. This section is for those who are hurting in life and do not have the energy to go to church.

This is a section for those who are feeling disenfranchised and do not know why. This is for those who are hurting and are wanting to retreat because of the pain of life. This is for those who are thinking about shutting the church out.

It takes time to heal. It takes time to find a new normal after a loss. The pain of life often leads us to focus inward. One of the benefits of church is giving back. When we focus on others we often find healing. When we help others we often find help. You may be so exhausted with life you have nothing to give. That's real. I get that. You may have to step back, but I encourage you to not step away from church.

Because the body hates pain, the natural survival instinct is to shut down. Often when we go through difficult situations we turn inward. We shut down. We close people out because the pain is so difficult to get through.

As tough as it may be, when you are feeling like shutting down you need to push forward.

God loves you. You may be wounded but you are not done. You may be pressed, but you are not done.

The next time the pressure of life leads inward and away from community in church, count to five.

1

2

3

4

5

And then move.

Go to a small group. Meet a friend from church for coffee. Go to a service. Go toward community even though your natural pull is away.

Slowly but surely life will come back. Let God and the community be a part of the healing. It's easy to quit, but stick with it. The miracle you are looking for just might be around the corner.

THE CHURCH WOUND

There are a lot of people who have been hurt or disillusioned by pastors in the local church. This is different than feeling burned out. This is carrying a wound from a pastor or staff member or church.

Every church is imperfect. When you become involved in a church you get to see behind the curtain. What you'll find are imperfect people who do not have all the answers. We often want to turn church leaders into superheroes, but we are mere mortals. We have bad days. We get grumpy. We sin.

There is real hurt out there caused by the local church. The church wound is difficult to overcome. It not only impacts what a person thinks about church, it ultimately can impact what a person thinks about God.

To anyone who reads this who has been hurt I want to say, "I'm sorry."

If you gave your all only to be dismissed quickly as if you no longer matter, I'm sorry.

If you were lied to by pastors, I'm sorry.

If you are still struggling with wounds caused by church staff, I'm sorry.

If you didn't have your needs met, I'm sorry.

If you felt you were only a number, I'm sorry.

If you felt your needs didn't matter, I'm sorry.

If you felt you only mattered because you had money, I'm sorry.

If you felt no one was there for you in your greatest time of need, I'm sorry.

If you are hurt because you feel the pastor and staff moved on quickly after you left, I'm sorry.

If you gave, and gave, and gave, and never received a thank-you, I'm sorry.

If your pastor wasn't who you thought he was, I'm sorry.

If your pastor took advantage of you, I'm sorry.

If you grew up in a fundamental church and were told if you believe differently you are going to hell, I'm sorry.

If you had guilt or pressure "in the name of Jesus" put on you to stay in a church, I'm sorry.

If you feel like you had to pretend to be better than you were in order to belong in the church, I'm sorry.

If you only get texts from a pastor because he needs something, I'm sorry.

If you felt you had to pretend to be okay in order to help others, I'm sorry.

If you have been sexually abused by someone in spiritual authority, I'm so sorry.

If you feel you were shut out by a church, I'm sorry.

If you were misunderstood in the church, I'm sorry.

If you love Jesus but just can't take any more hurt from church leaders, I'm sorry.

If you walked away from the faith because of judgmental pastors or staff, I'm sorry.

If your hurt was met by trite answers and a quick Bible verse, but no empathy, I'm sorry.

If you are carrying around the wounds from a pastor or church staff, I'm sorry.

If I'm the pastor who hurt you, I'm sorry.

If your pastor never says, "I'm sorry," I'm sorry.

Maybe my "sorry" won't help you. I hope it will at least be a start.

If anything, please know, you are not alone. Every relationship opens up the door for love and hurt. When hurt happens in the church it can lead to feeling disillusioned with God.

God's plan is for his bride, the local church, to be the light of the world. That's a giant risk because each church is made up of imperfect leaders.

Sometimes the leaders don't mean to cause any pain. Sometimes it's because they are simply a bad leader.

Sometimes the hurt is caused because the pastor hasn't dealt with his own demons, insecurity, or pain.

Sometimes the hurt is caused because we allow pain to get in the way of relationships.

It can be difficult to talk to someone in spiritual leadership about your feelings of hurt.

If you are hurt, I'm sorry.

If you are healing, but still feel fragile, I'm sorry.

Please know, the pain caused by someone is never bigger than the love of God.

Whether the pain you feel was caused intentionally or unintentionally there is healing in the name of Jesus.

And maybe your healing can start with "I'm sorry."

ANOTHER PASTOR BITES THE DUST

It's not just church members who have been hurt by the church. Pastors often are hurt by imperfect members.

There is a former pastor who started an amazing church in Tennessee. He has written multiple books and has seen God do amazing work. He built a church where "no perfect people are allowed."

In 2016 he stepped down from the church he started because in his own words, "I'm tired. I'm broken."

When I read about it I felt heartbroken.

I don't want to see any pastor step down. I hate that he is hurting. I don't have a lot of answers. I don't know his full story. I'm sure there are things we will never know about what led to his decision.

The pastor did say, "Most of you in this church only experience what I do on Sundays, especially those of you who watch online. You just see me when I kind of come up here on Sundays, but the reality is as leader and the pastor of a church, what happens in between those Sundays is just as important and it requires a lot of leadership and it requires a lot of leadership energy. And leaders in any realm of life, leaders who lead on empty don't lead well and for some time now I've been leading on empty."

This came on the heels of another pastor I know who is going through intense personal struggles. It feels like everywhere I turn pastors who are helping broken people are becoming more broken themselves.

Just like it's not the pastor's fault if a church member sins, it is not a church member's fault if a pastor struggles. With that in mind, I don't think church people are responsible for a pastor's struggle.

At the same time, I do believe there are things church members can do to support their pastor. It won't mean a pastor won't struggle. Pastors are imperfect humans. Just like if a pastor does everything he can it does not mean church members won't struggle. But together I think pastors and church members can help each other.

The main emotion I felt when I read about pastors falling is fear. I want to retire a pastor. I want to have a ministry where I finish strong. I'm far from perfect. I make mistakes. I want to be able to learn from mistakes, continue to set up accountability, and get to the end of my life finishing strong.

Every job has difficulties. This isn't meant to compare struggles of other jobs. The pastor has some unique challenges that I don't think anyone can fully relate to until they have walked in the shoes of a pastor.

Here are some challenges pastors go through.

- After spending hours prepping a sermon, memorizing a sermon, studying, and praying, being told that you are not deep enough.

- Having people scrutinize your pay. Because it's "church work" many believe being a pastor means living as an indentured servant to the church. There are some pastors who live extravagantly or have abused church finances. There are also church boards who make it their job to pinch every penny. If a pastor drives a new car someone will complain, judge, and assume he is in it just for the money. I've heard so many complaints against pastors making money it has permanently left a mark. I don't even mean to, but I feel I have to explain how we can afford to take a vacation, go to the movies, or buy something new. I'll often start a story with "Our friend gave us their house in Nags Head for the week. That's the only way we could afford it."

- Having close relationships end because of a decision you've made. This happens all the time in the church world. I just met with a pastor who ended up leaving his church because some elders were mad he didn't want to hire one of their granddaughters as the worship leader. She was still in high school and had zero experience in it. The church almost split because he kindly disagreed. This happens all the time. All. The. Time. Best friends become sworn enemies overnight in the church world. I have seen more grace being shown toward Pastor Perry Noble after he admitted to struggling with alcohol than I have seen toward a pastor who disagreed with a church member, staff member, or church board. No one can keep all people happy. The pressure is unreal once a pastor realizes every relationship is one decision away from ending. When relationships end it's never pretty. Many times the pastor learns the relationship is over from a third-party source. Other times when the pastor is told a person is leaving a church, the message seems to come out of nowhere.

- Loneliness. Loneliness comes from multiple places. Because relationships can be fragile, a pastor has to be incredibly careful who he trusts. When a pastor struggles there aren't many who he can confide in. Often what is confessed ends up being ammunition against the pastor once church members become upset. According to LifeWay Research, 55 percent of pastors feel lonely. Loneliness often comes because when things go bad pastors tend to try to take the high road. If a pastor posted the things he has seen behind the scenes it wouldn't do anyone any good. During difficult seasons many pastors take the heat and never share their perspective. This isn't saying every pastor is perfect. Pastors are imperfect people who can hurt others. But in a lot of instances when someone gets mad they blast the pastor to many people and the pastor is left trying to pick up the pieces with just his family. No one but my wife and counselor knows the full details of what led me to see a counselor. I attempted to blog about some of the struggles without being specific. That post led to at least one person leaving the church. The feeling of loneliness during that season still weighs on me.

- Having to deliver a sermon when you are spiritually empty. Every human I know goes through seasons in the proverbial desert. Sunday comes every week. No matter what is going on, the church needs the pastor to deliver. Have you ever cried through an entire worship set and then had to get up to preach? Pastors must take care of themselves, but even the healthiest pastors go through seasons. Pete Wilson talked about trying to lead on empty. I don't know a single pastor who cannot relate to that.

- Temptation. No one asks the pastor about how he is dealing with temptation. It just doesn't happen. But pastors are human. They struggle just like everyone else. With a lack of accountability, it is easy to let things slide. Other times the pressure of the church world is so weighty a pastor literally feels the only way to escape is to sabotage his ministry by giving in to temptation.

Please know, this is not directed at anyone. I am in no way trying to be passive-aggressive. I'm writing what I believe is a common struggle in hopes that no matter what church you call home, you'll have a unique insight into the struggles your pastor may face.

At the end of the day I think there is one major thing all of us can do to help pastors.

Don't turn a pastor into a saint and don't turn him into the devil.

Here's what I mean. Often people make pastors into saints. It's as if when they poot it does not stink. Every pastor is imperfect. Do not wait for them to let you down to discover this. No pastor should be put on a pedestal. Sure, pastors should have honor showed to them. That's biblical. But honor doesn't mean creating them into something they are not...perfect.

At the same time, whenever we get upset with a pastor let's not turn them into the devil. A disagreement doesn't mean everything about them is pure evil. Disagree. You might even have to leave a church over a disagreement. But unless the disagreement is over sin, resist the temptation to turn the pastor into the antichrist.

If you know a pastor, spend time praying for them right now. It is not up to the church to keep a pastor emotionally healthy, but they can help. Show me a pastor who retires at an old age without a scandal and I'll show you some amazing Christians who have supported him throughout the years. It takes a village to run a church.

THE BRIDE OF JESUS

There are a lot of major issues in the church in America. *Lots!* Pastors have been hurt. Church members have been hurt. The unchurched have been neglected. There is hurt on all sides.

With so much hurt it's no wonder we haven't fixed the many issues in the church today. It's still one of the most segregated places in America. We have way too many dying churches. There are scandals and hurts. Church attendance is on the decline in America. Many college-aged kids are leaving the church as soon as they graduate, not looking to return. The church has some issues, y'all.

I get the issues in the church.

There are roughly 350,000 churches in America. I pass 300K of them on my way to Next Level. I kid, I kid. There are an estimated 140,000 orphans in America today. I don't know how to fix it, but if half of the churches were serious about true religion that takes care of orphans and widows, every kid born in America would have a family.

I get the issues.

It's my world.

I get that there are lots of hypocrites. I get that it often seems that the church cares more about your money than you. At times it feels you give and give and then when your needs are not met, no one is there for you.

I get the issues.

I'm not dismissing them or diminishing them. There are real issues.

Just like how every family has issues, the church has issues. For the Christians, giving up on the church is simply not an option.

Ephesians 5:25–27 paints a picture of the church as the bride of Jesus. This is a very important analogy.

As the bride we should take our position seriously. As the bride it makes sense why Jesus' brother would say that friendship with the world is adultery. How can you love Jesus and not be committed to him?

No wife is perfect, but we should be fiercely loyal.

And yet there is a growing trend of people who just don't like the church. Maybe they don't like the new style of music, maybe they were burned, maybe they were hurt, maybe they just got busy.

When I say *they* I'm not writing about anyone in particular. This isn't a passive-aggressive message directed at someone in hopes that they will change. I talk to a lot of pastors, and read a lot about the church, and the message is the same everywhere.

People are giving up the local church.

Here's the deal, if you want a relationship with me then you need to know my wife comes with me. You cannot have a meaningful relationship with me and hate my bride. You tell me that you love me and then say you don't like my wife and I will look at you like you have just drunk crack or smoked some beer. That's crazy talk.

It's the same with the local church. The Church (with a big *C* and not a particular church with a small *c*) is the bride of Jesus.

If you have been hurt by the church, I am truly sorry. I am. I hate it for you. But if you are following Jesus, he will always lead you back to his bride. Always. It may not be a traditional Sunday morning church, but falling in love with Jesus means you fall in love with his bride.

Jesus' intention is that you would be connected with other believers to sing, study the Bible, evangelize, baptize, and remember his sacrifice by taking communion.

If you currently go to church, you need to make sure you are following Jesus and not a pastor, a style of church service, or a ministry. You need to make sure you are prioritizing the church. You need to make sure you are helping fix the issues in the church. You need to make sure you are following Jesus, because the bride is imperfect. And when you get let down by the bride, the temptation will be to run away forever.

As much as it hurts to be let down by a church, if you follow Jesus, he will lead you back to the bride.

WHEN SHOULD YOU LEAVE A CHURCH?

Not everyone leaves the church for good. In America it is a blessing and a curse that we have so many options. For many, as soon as one church doesn't meet all their needs they bail. Almost everyone has switched churches at some point. This isn't a judgment.

With the church being the bride, I feel we should take seriously how leaving a church impacts those we leave.

Churches are imperfect. Imperfect people make up the church, so that equals every church having blemishes. Similar to beautiful people, churches that look really pretty and seem like they have it all together have blemishes.

I've been on a church staff since I was eighteen years old. I've been on staff at megachurches, seeker churches, traditional churches, church plants, and even a country church. All churches have one thing in common. No matter what style the church, it will come with some imperfections. Those imperfections can lead people to think about leaving. Minor imperfections shouldn't be the reason why someone leaves a church. It should be more.

Before you leave you should pray about it and seek God's leading. Before you leave take care of the issues you have. It may mean saying sorry. It may mean offering forgiveness. It may mean an awkward conversation. Before you leave take care of the issues. If you are just going to bring drama and unresolved issues from your last church with your transfer, you will quickly find new issues at the new church.

Please read: I'm not saying that you have to be healthy to go to a church. The church should be like a hospital birthing life and helping the spiritually sick. I'm talking about the drama of being dysfunctional at church and then bringing that dysfunction into a new church. Don't talk bad about your past church or pastor. Don't leave one place filled with drama only to go to another place and create even more drama. Give the church some grace.

My ministry coach, Chris Sonksen, often says, "Frustration is never content until it's expressed."

If you are frustrated about something, it will not change until you express it. Often, because we hate confrontation, we express our frustrations to the wrong people.

We often talk about people instead of to people.

We often talk about people in the disguise of sharing a prayer request or looking for advice.

A general rule of thumb is talk to someone who can do something about your frustration.

If you are frustrated with something at church, please don't talk to other church members about it. Talk to someone who can do something about it.

And if you have talked to them and nothing has changed, try it again. Show some grace. Offer to help fix the problem if it's something that can be fixed. If you don't have an answer, ask if there is a way for you to help make the change. Be willing to work hard at making things better.

If truly nothing has changed and it's not going to, then it may be time to leave. Just know, if you do not talk about your frustration to the person you are frustrated with, it will never be content. You'll carry that frustration on with you to the next church.

Seek God. Make a wise choice. Be a blessing to whatever church God leads you to.

WHEN YOU SHOULD STAY AT YOUR CHURCH

Since middle school I've left five churches. Three of them were because of moves and two of them were because of job changes that I felt God was leading me to take. I've been blessed to be a part of some incredible churches. None of them were perfect but God used all of them to shape me.

When it comes to church attenders there tends to be a few categories that most people fit into.

- The miserable faithful. Let's say that I only got to eat out once a week and even though I have a ton of options I choose to eat at Moe's every week. After I go I complain about the dirty rice that doesn't compare to Chipotle's. I complain about the quality of the food being subpar to Chipotle. When I talk to my friends I say things like Moe's is just like Chipotle if you took a Chipotle burrito and dropped it on a public bathroom floor and then smothered it with queso. You would look at me and tell me I'm stupid for staying there. And that, my friends, is the miserable faithful. They complain about everything at church and yet they won't leave. They won't change their attitude or admit that Moe's…er…their church isn't that bad. They just go every week and complain about everything.
- The all-in. These are the people who are all in with their church. If the doors are open they are there. They serve, give, and invite others to come along with them.
- The ChrEasters. ChrEasters are the ones who are incredibly faithful at attending church twice a year, on Christmas and Easter.
- The bandwagon fans. These are the churchgoers who always select a winning church. When a church has momentum they find a way to get plugged into that church. The second a church isn't the main attraction in town they split to the next big thing.

- The casual attenders. These are the people who attend church once or twice a month.

Now the church is made up of imperfect people and almost every church has the above people at their church. For some reading this, the real issue isn't the church, it's your heart. The church is the bride of Jesus and should be treated that way. You represent the body of Jesus and when you don't pull your weight, when you complain, when you don't attend, the body suffers.

Taking all of that into account, I present the 10 Reasons You Should Not Leave a Church...

1. There is a new better preacher in town. Remember the church as a whole is the bride of Jesus. Being at a church should equal a commitment. You shouldn't leave your spouse because a prettier girl moves to town. Same thing with preachers. If your pastor preaches the Bible and God hasn't called you somewhere else, then just listen to the new better preacher online and support your pastor 100 percent.

2. The church isn't meeting your needs. The problem with this is that it's all about you. The church is not a rec center. The church is the body. If your body wasn't meeting your needs what would you do? You'd try to fix it. If the church doesn't offer sports leagues then go out and start a sports team at a public league. I know people who love line by line studying of the Bible but go to a seeker topical-preaching church. To supplement what they like, they founded and now lead a Bible study called Bible Study Fellowship. They

still volunteer at their church, give to their church, and support their church. There was something missing, so instead of complaining about it they did something about it. All churches can't be all things to all people. Understand that. Be careful that you don't take this to mean that you plug into five different churches so that you get all that you need. If you do that no one will really get to know you because you are spread too thin. The point is don't leave your church because one of your many needs isn't being met.

3.   The pastor and/or staff made a mistake that wasn't a sin. Pastors are human and with that comes being imperfect. Don't get mad and leave a church because your pastor forgot to email you back one time. Show the pastor some grace. He's probably juggling a family, the many needs of the people who go to his church, and trying to have some type of a personal life himself. Also show grace if the pastor forgot your name. It's hard to remember everyone's name.

4.   The church is too big. I understand the selfishness behind this. We like it when the pastor knows our name, we are in the know with everything that's going on at the church, and we know almost everyone. I get it. What I don't get is how you don't see that leaving for those reasons is really selfish. It would be like a kid running away from home because the parents had more kids. Now if God is calling you to something smaller then that's fine, but don't just leave because there are more people attending your church.

5. You are not being fed. Now if the pastor is not preaching the Bible or is preaching heresy, then you have permission to leave. But if you are simply not being fed then once again this is selfish and on you. There comes a point where you have so much Bible knowledge that it's time for you to start sharing that with others. To simply sit and soak up the teaching of someone else without sharing it yourself is like eating at a buffet for years and not being able to go to the bathroom. The problem is that you are bloated spiritually. I know that you've heard the story of David and Goliath a million times, but what else do you want? It's not like the pastor can invent new parts of the Bible. As a Christian you should grow and learn to feed yourself. No preacher can continually feed everyone's needs for twenty years. Grow with the pastor and help them by teaching those who haven't heard David and Goliath a million times.

6. The pastor left to go to another church. I personally think that if you are a part of a church and the pastor leaves, you should do what you can to help out until they find a new pastor. Then at that time if you feel like it's time to move on, pray about it, and then do so. Now the exception to this is if the interim leadership does any of the things mentioned on this list.

7. The church has made a change that you don't like. With growth comes change. I know nobody likes change but it needs to happen. As long as it's not unbiblical try to look at it from the pastor and staff's position.

8. Rumors you've heard. I've heard some crazy rumors in the church world. Before you get worked up you should give your pastor the benefit of the doubt and then talk to the source. I once heard that my youth pastor posed for *Playgirl.* That rumor got people worked up but had 0 percent truth to it.

9. Your church doesn't do things the way your old church did. You left your old church for some reason. Trying to make your new church like that and then leaving because it's not just doesn't make sense.

10. Number ten will cover a multitude of other reasons. Don't leave if you are just being selfish. If it's all about you then you will make your next church all about you.

Now, that list is simply built from observations from real reasons people have left churches.

As long as we treat the church like it's something to consume we will be a part of the problem and not part of the solution.

The church has lots of issues, but together we can change things. There are enough churches and enough Christians out there to truly change the world. It is not easy. Change never is. We have to fight against the norm. We have to resist consuming. We have to give back. We have to be the light of the world Jesus asked us to be.

WE DON'T HAVE TO...WE GET TO

The church is messy, broken, imperfect, but so amazing. When the bride of Christ lives as the bride, communities change.

I know there is a lot of work to be done, but I don't see it as a bad thing. It's exciting.

We don't have to be the church, we get to.

We don't have to volunteer at church, we get to.

We don't have to, we get to.

It's an honor that God trusts us to represent him. It's an honor to serve him. It's an honor to be the bride.

I pray you have a renewed passion for the church. I pray God uses you to spark a fire. I pray God reignites your fire for him. I pray God does immeasurably more than you can ask or imagine through you. We are better together and together we can end homelessness in America, provide homes for orphans, bring races together, heal the broken, and so much more. We don't have to do this…we get to.

BE THE CHANGE

I'm not perfect. You are not perfect. That doesn't mean that we can't be better.

If the people we come in contact with are not moved by our lives or our churches, then we must be doing a horrible job of representing Jesus.

It took thousands of years for Christianity to end up like it is today. It may take a thousand more years to change the perception of Christians. Let's not let that stop us from trying.

We cannot change anyone. We cannot change how people respond online. We cannot change Christians who are angry at the world. We cannot change anyone. We can pray that God changes our hearts. You can pray that God will change your heart.

If enough of us attempt to be the light of Jesus in our little worlds, eventually massive change will happen.

People will always disagree with our opinions. People will always disagree with our theology. People will always disagree with our understanding of morality. Let them. That doesn't change our calling to show love.

> **Live such good lives among the pagans that, though they accuse you of doing wrong, they may see your good deeds and glorify God on the day he visits us. (1 Peter 2:12)**

I love the band Switchfoot. They were once protested by a group of Christians yelling Bible verses at them. The members of Switchfoot are Christians. The fans who were lined up to go into the stadium were also being yelled at by the protestors. When word got back to Jon Foreman (Switchfoot's lead singer) he personally brought water out to the protesters. Later that night he encouraged his fans to show the protestors love.

Which one seems more effective in relating the message of Jesus?

When I first planted Next Level Church, we didn't have offices. I would go to Chick-fil-A at 8:00 a.m. and stay until 5:00 p.m. They have free Wi-Fi and free refills. It was glorious. During this time an article came out about the founder's views on homosexuality. For about a week Chick-fil-A was bashed by bloggers everywhere. It created such noise it was decided to protest against Chick-fil-A.

On the day of the protest only one person showed up to protest the Chick-fil-A I was working from. As far as protestors go she was very nice. She didn't curse or throw things at anyone. She stood with a sign that encouraged people to not go to Chick-fil-A.

The owner of this Chick-fil-A is a Christian. When one of his employees told him about the protestor he walked out to meet her.

He walked out with free food and drink. She wouldn't accept it, but she was incredibly appreciative.

She came back the next day and this time the owner had water brought out to her.

She didn't come back a third day.

Now, her opinion of what Chick-fil-A believes didn't change. I am assuming that she still disagrees with them. As the verse says,

> "Though they accuse you of doing wrong, they may see your good deeds and glorify God."

People will never agree with everything we believe. That doesn't stop us from loving them well.

COMMIT TO A CHURCH

I'd like to revisit the challenge from chapter one. What would it take for you to commit to go all in at a church for one year? You cannot change other people. The change starts with you. It starts with me. Let's be the change we wish to see in the world.

Go all in for Jesus. Love Jesus, love people, and you will make a difference.

I know you have your own story. The church is imperfect, but it's worth sticking with. It's worth making better. It's worth it to experience God in community with others.

It starts with each person looking at what they can do. It's easy to look at a church and think the problems are from other people.

It's easy to think, "If I was in charge I'd do this differently."

It's like watching sports. It's easy to become a Monday morning quarterback. That is, it's easy to dissect what players and coaches should have done after the game. You want to know what's tough? Being a pro athlete. Very few people can do it.

It's easy to dissect what a leader should do. What's tough is actually leading.

It's easy to dissect a sermon. What's tough is writing a sermon and preaching it every week.

It's easy to dissect what others do. It becomes a lot more difficult to do it.

What would happen if instead of viewing church as someone else's problem to solve, you viewed it as something you can make better?

What would happen if instead of looking at problems as someone else's job to fix, you viewed them as a way for you to get more involved?

Have you ever been a part of a church small group that was not great? I have. You want to know what I did? I complained. Sometimes I simply endured it because I thought that's what great Christians do.

My perspective was changed when I was challenged to make each group the best it can be. Instead of waiting for the group to be amazing I was challenged to make it amazing.

If the group was boring I took responsibility to do my part to make it engaging. I can't fix all the problems in every group. I can work on what I'm going to bring to the table.

After I was challenged to do that, I started viewing groups differently. Every group is a chance for me to leave a mark. I can't control anyone. I can only work on controlling myself. I can only work on making the group the best it can be.

It's the same for every aspect of the church.

Have you ever had a worship leader who couldn't sing? I have. It is horrible. But I didn't have anyone else. I had someone who was willing to sing to middle school students every week. Great guitar player. Horrible singer. I don't lead worship. I didn't have anyone else. Worship was a priority for me. So I made a decision. I was going to help the worship leader be the best he could be. And…I was going to sing a little louder to drown out his voice. I would meet with him to talk about what songs his voice sounded best on. We developed some silly songs to start worship to help engage students and simply get them to sing. Have you ever sung "Amazing Grace" to the tune of *Gilligan's Island*? I have. It's not my pick for worship, but it worked for that environment. Once everyone was singing on the silly songs they were more likely to sing during the more worshipful songs. It worked. People stopped complaining. I stopped having a brain aneurism from the stress of listening to a worship leader butcher Kari Jobe songs.

Now, I'm sure you can criticize my decision. You can probably come up with a better idea. That's my point. Do it. If there are better ideas then be a part of the solution and not part of the problem.

Commit to be known for what you are for and not just what you are against. Commit to make everything you are a part of better.

I know it's hard because it feels like everyone is an idiot. Everyone is doing everything wrong. Want to change your perspective? Become the leader. Become the change. Be the difference. Become part of the solution.

Don't Monday morning quarterback your pastor. Find what is great and help make what's not as great better.

If you wait for something to become great it may never happen.

Commit for one year to go all in for Jesus at your church and see what happens. See what happens when you show up excited to serve at church. See what happens when you are excited to give. See what happens when you are excited to be the church.

Be the change in the name of Jesus. Commit to be positive. Commit to bring solutions and not problems. Commit to make things better.

And when something is out of your control, let it go.

What would happen if we prayed for our churches as much as we complained about them?

BENEDICTION

At the end of every service at Next Level I recap the sermon by challenging our church to live it out. I start every recap with the phrase "May we be a people." As this book comes to an end I'd like to speak the same words over everyone who reads it.

May we be a people that are known by our love for Jesus. May we love him the same way that he has loved us. May we forgive those who have wronged us. May we overcome temptation and may we fall into the arms of grace when we fail. May we know that we cannot do this alone. May we commit to live in community. May we be a light in a dark world. And may we do this for the glory of God. May we practice what we preach and may our lives change the world.

Application: Commit to one church for a year. Go all in. See what God does.

Questions:
1. What was your biggest takeaway from this chapter?
2. Based off what you read, what is one thing you will do differently?
3. How can we help people heal from a church wound?
4. How can you support your pastor or staff?

AFTERWORD

Thank you for reading this book. I pray that God used it to encourage and inspire you. I hope you laughed. As an author I know not everyone will love this writing, but I truly hope God used it to inspire you.

If you loved the book, would you take a moment to write a review on Amazon or other booksellers? Writing a positive review helps small-time authors like me spread the word about the book.

If you hated the book feel free to leave a review as well. Remember the name of this book is *Purpose Driven Life* and my name is Rick Warren. I kid, I kid. If you hated this book please remember to treat me like you would want to be treated. Feel free to share a constructive review, but let's keep it classy.

One hundred percent of the proceeds of this book go to needy children.

My needy children. One day when you see a pic of them in college you can know you helped pay for them to go. Thank you. I kid, I kid.

If you liked this book and want to connect you can find me on social media at...

Facebook—Rob Shepherd

Instagram—rob_shep

Twitter—robshep
Blog—robshep.com

Thanks for reading! Thank you for sharing positive words about this book. I look forward to connecting with you soon on the World Wide Web.